Economics

FOR

DUMMIES

**by Peter Antonioni and
Sean Masaki Flynn**

WILEY

A John Wiley and Sons, Ltd, Publication

Economics For Dummies® Portable Edition

Published by
John Wiley & Sons, Ltd
The Atrium
Southern Gate
Chichester
West Sussex
PO19 8SQ
England

E-mail (for orders and customer service enquires): cs-books@wiley.co.uk

Visit our Home Page on www.wiley.com

Copyright © 2011 John Wiley & Sons, Ltd, Chichester, West Sussex, England

All Rights Reserved. No part of this publication may be reproduced, stored in a retrieval system or transmitted in any form or by any means, electronic, mechanical, photocopying, recording, scanning or otherwise, except under the terms of the Copyright, Designs and Patents Act 1988 or under the terms of a licence issued by the Copyright Licensing Agency Ltd, 90 Tottenham Court Road, London, W1T 4LP, UK, without the permission in writing of the Publisher. Requests to the Publisher for permission should be addressed to the Permissions Department, John Wiley & Sons, Ltd, The Atrium, Southern Gate, Chichester, West Sussex, PO19 8SQ, England, or emailed to permreq@wiley.co.uk, or faxed to (44) 1243 770620.

Trademarks: Wiley, the Wiley Publishing logo, For Dummies, the Dummies Man logo, A Reference for the Rest of Us!, The Dummies Way, Dummies Daily, The Fun and Easy Way, Dummies.com and related trade dress are trademarks or registered trademarks of John Wiley & Sons, Inc. and/or its affiliates in the United States and other countries, and may not be used without written permission. All other trademarks are the property of their respective owners. Wiley Publishing, Inc., is not associated with any product or vendor mentioned in this book.

For general information on our other products and services, please contact our Customer Care Department within the US at 877-762-2974, outside the US at 317-572-3993, or fax 317-572-4002.

For technical support, please visit www.wiley.com/techsupport.

Wiley also publishes its books in a variety of electronic formats. Some content that appears in print may not be available in electronic books.

British Library Cataloguing in Publication Data: A catalogue record for this book is available from the British Library

ISBN: 978-1-119-97444-4 (paperback), 978-1-119-97496-3 (ebk), 978-1-119-97497-0 (ebk), 978-1-119-97498-7 (ebk)

Printed and bound in Great Britain by Bell & Bain Ltd, Glasgow

10 9 8 7 6 5 4 3 2 1

WILEY

About the Authors

Peter Antonioni was educated at Pembroke College, Oxford, and Birkbeck College, London, and has worked in both academic and private sectors as an economist before finally ending up as Lecturer in Management at University College London.

His research interests are diverse, and include the football transfer market, the process of enterprise in technology markets, and the techniques and practice of the arcane field of Long Range Scenario Planning.

His great passions include composing and recording electronic music, practicing the mystical martial arts of ancient China, and weeping with uncontrollable dismay at Spurs' latest setbacks. Amongst his talents are an uncanny ability to recall every plot point and line of dialogue from Battlestar Galactica, and the superpower of creating a mean penne arrabiata. He blogs some of the above at pja.typepad.com.

Sean Masaki Flynn earned his Ph.D. in Economics at the University of California, Berkeley, studying under Nobel Prize winners George Akerlof and Daniel McFadden.

He is a member of the American Economic Association, the American Finance Association, the Economic Science Association, and the Society for the Advancement of Behavioral Economics.

His research focuses on the often puzzling and seemingly irrational behavior of stock market investors, but he's also investigated topics as wide-ranging as the factors that affect customer tipping behavior at restaurants and why you see a lot of unionised workers only in certain industries. He's also a leading expert on closed-end mutual funds.

His great passion is the Japanese martial art of aikido, which he has taught for over a decade to thousands of students both in the United States and abroad. If you like the martial arts, you might enjoy reading his book, *Shodokan Aikido: Basics Through 6th Kyu,* which gives an insight into both the mental and physical aspects of aikido.

Finally, he's gone out of his way to post extensive supplementary material for this book at www.learn-economics.com. Check it out.

Dedication

To all the family, friends, and colleagues who did so much to set me on the true path, and especially to Andrew Scott, who showed an inordinate amount of faith in me, and Vinetta Archer-Dyer who tirelessly cleared up the mess I left in my wake.

– Peter Antonioni

To my dad, Thomas Ray Flynn, who always impressed upon me the importance of good economic policy both for improving our quality of life and as our last, best hope for lifting billions out of poverty and disease.

– Sean Masaki Flynn

Publisher's Acknowledgments

We're proud of this book; please send us your comments through our Dummies online registration form located at www.dummies.com/register/.

Some of the people who helped bring this book to market include the following:

Acquisitions, Editorial, and Media Development

Project Editor: Rachael Chilvers

Commissioning Editor: David Palmer

Assistant Editor: Ben Kemble

Proofreader: Kelly Cattermole

Production Manager: Daniel Mersey

Cover Photos: © K-PHOTOS / Alamy

Cartoons: Ed McLachlan

Composition Services

Project Coordinator: Kristie Rees

Layout and Graphics: Samantha K. Cherolis

Proofreader: Jessica Kramer

Contents at a Glance

Introduction 1

Part I: Economics: The Science of
How People Deal with Scarcity 7
Chapter 1: What Is Economics? 9
Chapter 2: Tracking Consumer Choices 17
Chapter 3: Producing the Right Stuff in the Right Way 29

Part II: Macroeconomics: The Science of
Economic Growth and Stability 49
Chapter 4: Measuring the Macroeconomy 51
Chapter 5: Inflation: More Money Isn't Always a Good Thing 71
Chapter 6: Understanding Why Recessions Happen 91
Chapter 7: Fighting Recessions with Monetary and Fiscal Policy 121

Part III: Microeconomics: The Science of
Consumer and Firm Behaviour 151
Chapter 8: Supply and Demand 153
Chapter 9: Getting to Know the Utility-Maximising Consumer 179
Chapter 10: The Core of Capitalism: The Profit-Maximising Firm... 199
Chapter 11: Why Economists Love Free Markets
and Competition 227
Chapter 12: Monopolies: How Badly Would You Behave
If You Had No Competition? 255

Part IV: The Part of Tens 279
Chapter 13: Ten Seductive Economic Fallacies 281
Chapter 14: Ten Economic Ideas to Hold Dear 289

Index 295

Table of Contents

Introduction.. *1*

About This Book 2
Conventions Used in This Book.............................. 3
Foolish Assumptions 3
How This Book Is Organised 4
    Part I: Economics: The Science of How
       People Deal with Scarcity 4
    Part II: Macroeconomics: The Science of
       Economic Growth and Stability 4
    Part III: Microeconomics: The Science of
       Consumer and Firm Behaviour 5
    Part IV: The Part of Tens....................................... 5
Icons Used in This Book... 5
Where to Go from Here 6

Part 1: Economics: The Science of
How People Deal with Scarcity *7*

Chapter 1: What Is Economics? **9**

Considering Economic History 9
    Pondering just how nasty, brutish
       and short life used to be 9
    Identifying the institutions that led
       to higher living standards.. 10
    Looking towards the future....................................... 11
Separating Macroeconomics and Microeconomics 12
Framing Economics as the Science of Scarcity.................... 13
Understanding How Economists Use Models and Graphs 13
    Abstracting from reality is a good thing..................... 14
    Introducing your first model: The demand curve 14

Chapter 2: Tracking Consumer Choices **17**

A Model of Human Behaviour 17
    Maximising happiness 18
    Examining your limitations... 20
    Making your final choice... 23

Limitations and Violations of the Economist's
    Choice Model 25
        Uninformed decision-making 25
        Irrationality 26

**Chapter 3: Producing the Right Stuff
in the Right Way 29**

Determining the Possibilities 30
    Classifying the resources 30
    Getting less of a good thing: Diminishing returns 31
    Allocating resources 33
    Graphing the possibilities 34
    Pushing the line with better technology 37
Determining What Should Be Produced 39
    Weighing pros and cons of government
        interventions 40
    Opting for a mixed economy 45
Encouraging Technology and Innovation 47

**Part II: Macroeconomics: The Science of
Economic Growth and Stability 49**

Chapter 4: Measuring the Macroeconomy 51

Using GDP to Track the Economy 52
    Tallying up what counts in GDP 52
    Considering flows of income and assets 54
    Tracing the flow of income 54
    Following the funds, around and around 55
    Counting stuff when it's made, not when it's sold 57
    All things increase GDP 58
Introducing the GDP Equation 58
    C is for consumption 60
    I is for investment in capital stock 61
    G whizz! Government, that is 63
    NX: Exports less imports 64
The Effect of International Trade 65
    Trade deficits can be good! 66
    Considering assets 67
    Wielding a comparative advantage 68

Chapter 5: Inflation: More Money Isn't Always a Good Thing 71

The Risks of Too Much Money.. 72
  Balancing money supply and demand 72
  Giving in to the inflation temptation 74
  Tallying up the effects of inflation 78
Measuring Inflation: Price Indexes... 81
  Creating your very own market basket...................... 82
  Calculating the inflation rate....................................... 83
  Setting up a price index 84
  Determining the real standard of living
    with the price index... 85
  Identifying price index problems............................... 86
Pricing the Future: Nominal and Real Interest Rates 87
  The Fisher equation 88
  Predictions aren't perfect.. 89

Chapter 6: Understanding Why Recessions Happen... 91

Examining the Business Cycle... 92
Striving for Full-Employment Output 94
Returning to Y^*: The Natural Result of Price Adjustments....95
Responding to Economic Shocks.. 96
  Defining some critical terms 96
  The Tao of P: Looking at price adjustments
    in the long run 98
  Adjusting to a shift in aggregate demand................. 99
  Dealing with fixed prices in the short run............... 101
  Putting together the long and short of it.................. 103
Heading Toward Recession: Getting Stuck
  with Sticky Prices... 105
  Cutting wages or workers... 106
  Adding up the costs of wages and profits 107
  Returning to Y^* with and without government
    intervention 107
Achieving Equilibrium with Sticky Prices:
  The Keynesian Model 108
  Adjusting inventories instead of prices.................... 110
  Boosting GDP in the Keynesian model...................... 119

Chapter 7: Fighting Recessions with Monetary and Fiscal Policy............................**121**

Stimulating Demand to End Recessions.............................. 122
    Aiming for full-employment output........................... 122
    Putting people back to work 124
Generating Inflation: The Risk of Too Much Stimulation.....124
    An exercise in futility: Trying to increase
        output beyond Y*... 125
    A temporary high: Tracing the movement
        of real wages.. 127
    Failing to stimulate: What happens when
        a stimulus is expected.. 130
Figuring Out Fiscal Policy 133
    Increasing government spending
        to help end recessions 133
    Dealing with deficits.. 135
Dissecting Monetary Policy 138
    Identifying the benefits of fiat money 138
    Realising that you can have too much money!........ 140
    Getting to know bonds.. 142
    Seeing the link between bond prices
        and interest rates... 143
    Changing the money supply to
        change interest rates... 145
    Lowering interest rates to stimulate the economy....146
    Understanding how rational expectations can limit
        monetary policy.. 147

Part III: Microeconomics: The Science of Consumer and Firm Behaviour..........................*151*

Chapter 8: Supply and Demand....................**153**

Making Sense of Markets.. 153
Deconstructing Demand 154
    Getting our terms straight.. 154
    Graphing the demand curve.. 156
    Determining the slope of the demand curve............ 159
    Defining demand elasticity 160
Sorting Out Supply... 162
    Graphing the supply curve.. 163
    Extreme supply cases 166

Interacting Supply and Demand to Find
  Market Equilibrium 168
    Finding market equilibrium 168
    Demonstrating the stability of
      the market equilibrium 170
Adjusting to New Market Equilibriums When Supply
  or Demand Changes.. 172
    Reacting to an increase in demand 173
    Reacting to a decrease in supply............................. 174
Constructing Impediments to Market Equilibrium........... 175
    Raising price ceilings.. 176
    Propping up price floors.. 177

Chapter 9: Getting to Know the Utility-Maximising Consumer 179

Measuring Happiness: Utility 180
Diminishing Marginal Utility.. 181
Choosing Among Many Options When
  Facing a Limited Budget..................................... 184
    Trying to buy as much (marginal)
      utility as you can....................................... 185
    Allocating money between two goods
      to maximise total utility 187
    Equalising the marginal utility per pound
      of all goods and services......................... 190
Deriving Demand Curves from Diminishing
  Marginal Utility... 192
    Seeing how price changes affect
      quantities demanded............................... 192
    Forming a demand curve 194

Chapter 10: The Core of Capitalism: The Profit-Maximising Firm 199

Maximising Profits Is a Firm's Goal...................................... 200
Facing Competition.. 200
    Listing the requirements for perfect competition... 201
    Acting as price takers but quantity makers 202
    Distinguishing between accounting profits and
      economic profits... 204
Analysing a Firm's Cost Structure 206
    Focusing on costs per unit of output 206
    Examining average variable costs 209

Watching average fixed costs fall 210
Tracking the movement of average total costs 211
Focusing on marginal costs 212
Noticing where the MC curve crosses the AVC and
    ATC curves 213
Marginal Revenues and Costs 215
The magic formula: Finding where MR = MC 216
Visualising profits 218
Visualising losses 221
Pulling the Plug: When Producing Nothing
Is Your Best Bet 222
The short-run shutdown condition: Variable
    costs exceed total revenues 223
The long-run shutdown condition: Total costs
    exceed total revenues 225
At the mercy of the market price 225

**Chapter 11: Why Economists Love
Free Markets and Competition 227**

The Beauty of Competitive Free Markets:
Ensuring That Benefits Exceed Costs 228
Examining prerequisites for properly
    functioning markets 228
Analysing the efficiency of free markets 230
Using total surplus to measure gains 233
When Free Markets Lose Their Freedom 240
Dissecting the deadweight loss from
    a price ceiling 240
Analysing the deadweight loss of a tax 241
Hallmarks of Perfect Competition: Zero Profits
and Lowest Possible Costs 245
Understanding the causes and consequences
    of perfect competition 246
Peering into the process of perfect competition 247
Graphing how profits guide firm entry and exit 248

**Chapter 12: Monopolies: How Badly Would You
Behave If You Had No Competition? 255**

Profit-Maximising Monopolies 256
The problems that monopolies cause 256
The source of the problem: Decreasing
    marginal revenues 257
Choosing an output level to maximise profits 262

Comparing Monopolies with Competitive Firms 267
    Looking at output and price levels........................... 267
    Deadweight losses: Quantifying the harm
        caused by monopolies 269
    Focusing on efficiency... 270
Considering Examples of Good Monopolies...................... 270
    Encouraging innovation and investment
        with patents... 271
    Reducing annoyingly redundant competitors 271
    Keeping costs low with natural monopolies............ 272
Regulating Monopolies... 273
    Subsidising a monopoly to increase output............. 273
    Imposing minimum output requirements................. 274
    Regulating monopoly pricing.................................... 274
    Breaking up a monopoly into several
        competing firms 277

Part IV: The Part of Tens *279*

Chapter 13: Ten Seductive Economic Fallacies 281

The Lump of Labour Fallacy... 281
The World Is Facing an Overpopulation Problem 282
The Fallacy of Confusing Sequence with Causation.......... 283
Protectionism Is the Best Solution to
    Foreign Competition 283
The Fallacy of Composition 284
If It's Worth Doing, Do It 100 Per Cent............................... 285
Free Markets Are Dangerously Unstable 286
Low Foreign Wages Mean that Rich Countries
    Can't Compete 286
Tax Rates Don't Affect Work Effort..................................... 287
Forgetting that Policies Have Unintended
    Consequences Too.. 288

Chapter 14: Ten Economic Ideas to Hold Dear.......289

Society Is Better Off When People Pursue
    Their Own Interests 289
Free Markets Require Regulation... 290
Economic Growth Depends on Innovation......................... 290
Freedom and Democracy Make Us Richer.......................... 290
Education Raises Living Standards....................................... 291

Protecting Intellectual Property Rights
Promotes Innovation 291
Weak Property Rights Cause Many
Environmental Problems.. 291
International Trade Is a Good Thing 292
Free Enterprise Has a Hard Time Providing
Public Goods.. 293
Preventing Inflation Is Easy(ish) 294

Index... *295*

Introduction

●●●

*E*conomics is all about humanity's struggle to achieve happiness in a world full of constraints. Too little time and money is available to do everything people want. And things like curing cancer are still impossible because the necessary technologies haven't yet been developed.

But people are clever. They tinker and invent, ponder and innovate. They look at what they have and what they can do with it and take steps to make sure that if they can't have everything, they at least have as much as possible.

Making trade-offs is key. Because you can't have everything, you have to make choices. For example, you have to choose whether to save or spend, whether to stay in school or get a job, and whether the government should spend more money on primary education or on cancer research.

Choice is a fundamental part of everyday life. The science that studies *how* people choose – economics – is indispensable if you really want to understand human beings both as individuals and as members of larger organisations.

Sadly, though, economics has typically been explained so badly that people dismiss it as impenetrable gobbledygook or stand falsely in awe of it – after all, if economics is hard to understand, it must be important, right?

We wrote this book so that you can quickly and easily understand economics for what it is – a serious science that studies a serious subject and has developed some seriously effective ways of explaining human behaviour out in the (very serious) real world. Read this book to understand more about people, government, international relations, business, and even environmental issues such as global warming and endangered species. Economics touches on nearly everything, so the returns on reading this book are huge.

About This Book

Reading this book enables you to discover the most important economic theories, hypotheses, and discoveries without a zillion obscure details, outdated examples, or complicated mathematical 'proofs'. Among the topics covered are the following:

- ✔ How the government fights recessions and unemployment using monetary and fiscal policy.
- ✔ How and why international trade is good for us.
- ✔ Why poorly designed property rights are responsible for environmental problems such as global warming, pollution, and species extinctions.
- ✔ How profits guide businesses to produce the goods and services we take for granted.
- ✔ Why competitive firms are almost always better for society than monopolies.
- ✔ Why government policies such as price controls and subsidies typically cause much more harm than good.
- ✔ How the simple supply and demand model can explain the prices of everything from comic books to open-heart surgeries.

We do our best to explain these things, and much more, clearly and directly.

Economists like competition, so don't be surprised that a lot of competing views and paradigms exist among economists. Indeed, only through vigorous debate and careful review of the evidence can the profession improve its understanding of how the world works.

In this book, we try to steer clear of fads or ideas that foster a lot of disagreement. This book contains core ideas and concepts that economists agree are useful and important.

However, economists have honest disagreements about how to present even the core concepts, so we had to make some decisions about organisation and structure. For example, we present macroeconomics using a Keynesian framework even when we explain some rather non-Keynesian concepts. (You don't need to worry if you don't know who this Keynes fellow is or what makes him so *Keynesian*, because we introduce him to you later in the book.) Some people may quibble with this approach, but we think it makes for a succinct presentation.

Conventions Used in This Book

Economics is full of two things you may not find very appealing: jargon and algebra. To minimise confusion, whenever we introduce a new term, we put it in *italics* and follow it closely with an easy-to-understand definition. Also, whenever we bring algebra into the discussion, we use those handy *italics* again to let you know that we're referring to an algebraic element.

We try to keep equations to a minimum, but sometimes they actually help to make things clearer. In such instances, we sometimes have to use several equations one after another. To avoid confusion about which equation we refer to at any given time, we give each equation a number, which we put in parentheses. For example,

Foolish Assumptions

We wrote this book assuming some things about you:

- ✔ You're sharp, thoughtful, and interested in how the world works.

- ✔ You want to know some economics, but you're also busy leading a very full life. Consequently, although you want the crucial facts, you don't want to have to read through a bunch of minutia to find them.

- ✔ You're not totally intimidated by numbers, facts, and figures. Indeed, you welcome them because you like to have things proven to you rather than taking them on faith because some pinhead with a PhD says so.

- ✔ You like discovering *why* as well as *what*. That is, you want to know why things happen and how they work rather than just memorising facts.

- ✔ Finally, you're better-looking than average and have a good sense of style. In particular, you really love this book's stylish yellow and black cover and feel almost hypnotically compelled to buy a copy.

How This Book Is Organised

This book is divided into four parts to make the material easier to understand and access. Part I covers the big concepts that motivate how economists look at the world. Parts II and III follow the traditional division of economics into two halves – *Macroeconomics* and *microeconomics*

Part I: Economics: The Science of How People Deal with Scarcity

Economics is all about how people deal with scarcity. Too little time is available, and only a finite supply of natural resources such as oil and iron. Consequently, people have to be clever about getting the most out of life – choosing wisely about what to do with the limited resources they're given. Part I explains how people go about dealing with scarcity and the trade-offs that it forces them to make. The rest of economics is just seeing how scarcity forces people to make trade-offs in more specific situations.

Part II: Macroeconomics: The Science of Economic Growth and Stability

Macroeconomics views the economy from on high, at the national or international level, and deals with the choices that countries face about economic growth and development and about how to best manage their economies to avoid recessions. Macroeconomics also deals with the misery caused by things such as unemployment and inflation. In this part, you find out about monetary and fiscal policy, the Bank of England, the effects of taxation on the economy, and international trade and trade policy.

Part III: Microeconomics: The Science of Consumer and Firm Behaviour

Microeconomics focuses on the behaviour of individual people and individual firms, studying what motivates them and how they act to achieve their goals given the constraints they face. In this part, you discover what motivates firms to produce output and how buyers and sellers interact in markets to allocate that output. You also find out about supply and demand, competition, monopolies, Adam Smith's invisible hand, and lots of nifty applications of economics.

Part IV: The Part of Tens

Every *For Dummies* book ends with top-ten lists that are both helpful and fun. In this part, we review economic ideas to hold dear, and false economic assertions that you probably hear repeated all the time in the media and by self-serving politicians.

Icons Used in This Book

To make this book easier to read and simpler to use, we include a few icons that can help you find and fathom key ideas and information.

Theories are always easier to understand with an example. So when you see this icon you know you're in for some help, usually using everyday items like pizza and beer. (We find pizza and beer help in all sorts of ways.)

This icon alerts you that we're explaining a really fundamental economic concept or fact. It saves you the time and effort of marking up the book with a highlighter.

Sometimes we find it helpful to kick theories out into the real world to see how they actually work. This icon alerts you that a helpful real-world application is nearby.

Where to Go from Here

This book is set up so that you can jump in anywhere and understand what you're reading. But, hey, if you don't know where to begin, just do the old-fashioned thing and start at the beginning. As that popular song from the film *The Sound of Music* says, 'Let's start at the very beginning! A very good place to start.'

Part I
Economics: The Science of How People Deal with Scarcity

'It used to be called "The Economic Miracle" in the boom days.'

In this part . . .

*E*conomics studies how people deal with scarcity and the inescapable fact that our wants typically exceed the means available to satisfy them. The fact that life has limits may not at first seem like a good basis for an entire social science, but every government decision, every business decision and a large chunk of your personal decisions all come down to deciding how to get the most out of limited resources. Consequently, as we explain in this part, economics is fundamental to almost all aspects of life.

Chapter 1

What Is Economics?

· ·

In This Chapter

▶ Observing how people cope with scarcity

▶ Separating macroeconomics and microeconomics

▶ Getting a grip on the graphs and models that economists love to use

· ·

*E*conomics is the science that studies how people and societies make decisions that allow them to get the most out
of their limited resources. Because every country, every business and every person deals with constraints and limitations,
economics is literally everywhere. Economics gets to the heart
of these issues, analysing individual and firm behaviour, as well
as social and political institutions, to see how well they perform
at converting humanity's limited resources into the goods and
services that best satisfy human wants and needs.

Considering Economic History

To better understand today's economic situation and what
sort of policy and institutional changes may promote the
greatest improvements, you have to look back on economic
history to see how humanity arrived at its current situation.

Pondering just how nasty, brutish and short life used to be

For most of human history, people didn't manage to squeeze
much out of their limited resources. Standards of living were
quite low, and people lived poor, short and rather painful
lives. Consider the following facts, which didn't change until
just a few centuries ago:

✔ Life expectancy was about 25 years.

✔ More than 30 per cent of newborns never reached their fifth birthdays.

✔ Women had a 10 per cent chance of dying during childbirth.

✔ The standard of living for one generation was no higher than that of previous generations. Except for the nobility, everybody lived at or near subsistence level, century after century.

In the last 250 years or so, however, everything changed. A process of rapid innovation led to the invention or exploitation of electricity, engines, complicated machines, computers, radio, television, biotechnology, scientific agriculture, antibiotics, aviation and a host of other technologies. Each of these items enabled humankind to more with the limited amounts of air, water, soil and sea available on planet earth.

The result was an explosion in living standards, with life expectancy at birth now well over 60 years worldwide and many people able to afford much better housing, clothing and food than was even imaginable a few hundred years ago.

Of course, not everything is perfect. Grinding poverty is still a fact of life in a large portion of the world, and even the richest nations have to cope with pressing economic problems like unemployment, poverty or lack of access to resources.

But the fact remains that the modern world is a much richer place than it has been in the past, and we now have sustained economic growth in most nations, which means that living standards have been rising consistently year after year.

Identifying the institutions that led to higher living standards

The obvious reason for higher living standards, which continue to rise, is that human beings have recently figured out lots of new technologies, and we keep inventing more. But if you dig a little deeper, you have to wonder why a technologically innovative society didn't happen earlier.

Despite the fact that every society has had its share of really smart people, it wasn't until the late 18th century, in England, that the Industrial Revolution got started and living standards in many nations rose substantially and kept on rising.

So what factors combined in the late 18th century to acceler-ate economic growth so radically? The short answer is that the following institutions were in place:

- ✔ **Democracy:** You're more likely to invest if your invest-ment is protected by the rule of law instead of depending on the whim of a tyrant. Also, the governments of the democratic era have been better at incorporating the views of the merchants and manufacturers who created the wealth that we now enjoy.

- ✔ **The limited liability corporation:** Under this business structure, investors would lose only the amount of their investment and not be liable for any debts that the corporation was unable to pay. Limited liability greatly reduced the risks of investing in businesses and, conse-quently, led to much more investing.

- ✔ **Patent rights to protect inventors:** By giving inventors the exclusive right to market and sell their inventions, patents gave a financial incentive to produce lots of inventions.

- ✔ **Widespread literacy and education:** Without highly educated inventors, new technologies don't get invented. And without an educated workforce, the invented prod-ucts can't be mass-produced. Consequently, the deci-sion that many nations made to make primary and then secondary education mandatory paved the way for rapid and sustained economic growth.

Looking towards the future

The world faces many challenges now, some of which are the results of our successes and some are about extending them to all the world's citizens. Among the former are the potential changes in climate and our reaction to them, and among the latter the question of how we improve the condition of poorer citizens without creating environmental damage.

Some problems, like grinding poverty, can be alleviated by extending to poorer nations the institutions that have already been proven in richer nations to lead to rising living standards. But other problems, like the pollution and resource depletion that come with the institutional structures used in richer nations, require new inventions and new institutions.

Consequently, we offer two related and very good reasons for you to read this book and find out about economics:

- ✔ You'll discover how modern economies function, providing you with an understanding not only of how they've so greatly raised living standards, but also of where they need some improvement.

- ✔ You'll get a thorough grasp of fundamental economic principles, allowing you to judge for yourself the economic policy proposals that politicians and others promote.

Separating Macroeconomics and Microeconomics

The main organising principle we use in this book is to divide economics into two broad pieces:

- ✔ *Macroeconomics* looks at the economy as an organic whole, concentrating on economy-wide factors such as interest rates, inflation and unemployment. Macroeconomics also encompasses the study of economic growth and how governments use monetary and fiscal policy to try to moderate the harm caused by recessions.

  Studying macroeconomics is useful because certain factors, such as interest rates and tax policy, have economy-wide effects, and also because when the economy goes into a recession or a boom, every person and every business is affected. Macroeconomics is the stuff of the big picture that gets reported on the news.

- ✔ *Microeconomics* focuses on individual people and businesses. Microeconomics explains how individuals behave when faced with decisions about where to spend their money or how to invest their savings, and how profit-maximising firms behave both individually and when they're competing against each other in markets.

Underlying both macroeconomics and microeconomics are some basic principles such as scarcity and diminishing returns. Consequently, we spend the rest of Part I explaining these fundamentals before diving into macroeconomics in Part II and microeconomics in Part III.

Framing Economics as the Science of Scarcity

Scarcity is the fundamental and unavoidable phenomenon that creates a need for the science of economics. Without scarcity of time, scarcity of resources, scarcity of information, scarcity of consumable goods and scarcity of peace and goodwill on earth, human beings would lack for nothing.

Scarcity is why you can't have everything, even if you're the richest person in the world. Even if money's not scarce, time and/or physical resources will be. At some level, you're going to make choices about what you spend all that lovely lolly on.

Sadly, scarcity is a fact. Chapter 2 gets deep into scarcity. Chapter 3 builds on Chapter 2 by showing you how economists analyse the decisions that people make about how to best maximise human happiness in a world of scarcity. That process turns out to be intimately connected with a phenomenon known as *diminishing returns*, which describes the sad fact that each additional amount of a resource that's thrown at a production process brings forth successively smaller amounts of output. Like scarcity, diminishing returns is unavoidable.

Understanding How Economists Use Models and Graphs

Economists like to be logical and precise, which is why they use a lot of algebra and maths. But they also like to present their ideas in easy-to-understand and highly intuitive ways, which is why they use so many graphs. We want to spend a few pages helping you get acquainted with what you're going to encounter in other chapters.

Abstracting from reality is a good thing

Economists use graphs that are almost always visual representations of economic models. An *economic model* is a mathematical simplification of reality that allows you to ignore all the irrelevant details in order to focus on what's really important.

For example, the economist's model of consumer demand focuses on how prices affect the amounts of goods and services that people want to buy. Obviously, other things, such as changing styles and tastes, affect consumer demand as well, but price is key. Consider orange juice, for example. The price of orange juice is the major thing that affects how much orange juice people are going to buy. (We don't care what dietary trend is in vogue – if orange juice costs £50 a litre, you're probably going to find another diet.) Therefore, abstracting from those other things is helpful and allows you to concentrate solely on how the price of orange juice affects the quantity of orange juice that people want to buy.

Introducing your first model: The demand curve

Suppose that economists go out and survey consumers, asking them how many litres of orange juice they would buy each month at three hypothetical prices: £10 per litre, £5 per litre and £1 per litre. The results are summarised in Table 1-1.

Table 1-1	Litres of Orange Juice that Consumers Want to Buy
Price	**Litres**
£10	1
£5	6
£1	10

Economists refer to the quantities that people are willing to purchase at various prices as the *quantity demanded*, at those prices. When you look at the data in Table 1-1, you find that the price of orange juice and the quantity demanded of orange juice have an *inverse relationship* with each other – meaning that when one goes up, the other goes down.

Because this inverse relationship between price and quantity demanded is so universal and holds true for nearly all goods and services, economists refer to it as the *Law of Demand*. The Law of Demand becomes much more immediate and interesting if you can *see* it rather than just think about it.

Creating the demand curve by plotting out data

The best way to *see* the data in Table 1-1 is to plot it out on a chart. In Figure 1-1, we mark three points and label them *A*, *B* and *C*. The horizontal axis of Figure 1-1 measures the number of litres of orange juice that people demand each month at various prices per litre. The vertical axis measures the prices.

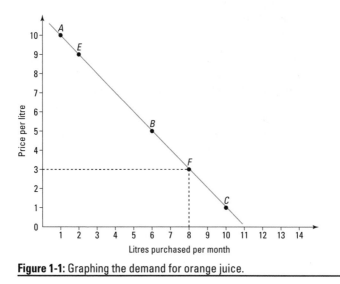

Figure 1-1: Graphing the demand for orange juice.

The straight line connecting the points in Figure 1-1 is called a *demand curve*. We know it doesn't curve at all, but for simplicity, economists use the term *demand curve* to refer to all plotted relationships between price and quantity demanded, regardless of whether they're straight lines or curvy lines.

You can now *visualise* the fact that price and quantity demanded have an inverse relationship. The inverse relationship implies that demand curves slope downward: when price goes up, quantity demanded goes down.

Using the demand curve to make predictions

Graphing out the demand curve also allows for a much greater ability to make quick predictions. For example, the straight line in Figure 1-1 can be used to estimate that at a price of £9 per litre, people are going to want to buy about 2 litres per month of orange juice. We label this point *E* on the graph.

Suppose that you can only see the data in Table 1-1 and can't look at Figure 1-1. Would you be able to estimate quickly how many litres per month people are likely to demand if the price of orange juice is £3 per litre? Looking at the second and third rows of Table 1-1, you have to conclude that people are going to demand somewhere between 6 and 10 litres per month. But working out exactly how many litres are going to be demanded would take some time and require some annoying algebra.

If you look at Figure 1-1, working out how many litres per month people are going to demand is easy. You just start at the price £3 on the vertical axis, move sideways to the right until you hit the demand curve at point *F*, and drop down vertically until you get to the horizontal axis, where you discover that you're at 8 litres per month. The dotted line in Figure 1-1 follows this path.

Chapter 2

Tracking Consumer Choices

In This Chapter

▶ Deciding what brings the most happiness

▶ Modelling choice behaviour like an economist

▶ Evaluating the limitations of the choice model

*E*conomics is all about *how* groups and individuals make choices and *why* they choose the things that they do. Because group choice behaviour usually turns out to be very similar to individual choice behaviour, our focus in this chapter is on individuals. Our explanation of individual choice behaviour focuses on *consumer behaviour*, because most of the daily choices people make involve which goods and services to consume. People must also make choices about long-term things like whether to get a job or continue in education, as well as things of the greatest possible seriousness like whether to continue negotiating or declare war.

Human beings are constantly forced to choose because our wants almost always exceed our means. Limited resources, or *scarcity*, is at the heart not only of economics, but also of ecology and biology. Economics is about human beings choosing among limited options to maximise happiness.

A Model of Human Behaviour

Human beings may be complicated but we can understand their choices in a fairly universal way. As a result, a lot can be gained by studying choice behaviour because if we can understand the *how and why* of the choices people made in the past, we stand a very good chance of understanding the choices they're going to make in the future.

In order to predict how self-interested individuals make their choices, economists have created a model of human behaviour that assumes rationality and the ability to calculate subtle trade-offs between possible choices. This model is a three-stage process:

1. **Evaluate how happy each option can make you.**

2. **Look at the constraints and trade-offs limiting your options.**

3. **Choose the option that maximises your overall happiness.**

Although not a fully complete description of human choice behaviour, this model generally makes accurate predictions. However, many people question this explanation of human behaviour. Here are three common objections:

- ✔ Are people really so self-interested? Aren't people often motivated by what's best for others?

- ✔ Are people really aware at all times of all their options? How are they supposed to choose rationally among new things that they have never tried before?

- ✔ Are people really free to make decisions? Aren't they constrained by legal, moral and social standards?

We spend the next few sections expanding on the three-step economic choice model and addressing the objections.

Maximising happiness

To economists, people are fully rational and capable of deciding things on their own. But that begs the question of what motivates people and, in turn, of what sorts of things people choose to do given their free wills.

In a nutshell, economists assume that the basic motivation driving most people most of the time is a *desire to be happy*.

This assumption implies that people make choices on the basis of whether or not those choices are going to make them as happy as they can be given their circumstances.

Utility: A measure of happiness

If people make choices on the basis of what's going to bring them the most happiness, they need a way of comparing how much happiness each option brings. Along these lines, economists assume that people get a sense of satisfaction or pleasure from the things life offers. Sunsets are nice. Eating ice cream is nice. Friendship is nice.

Economists suppose that you can compare all possible things that you may experience with a common measure of happiness which they call *utility*. Things you like a lot have high utility, whereas things that you like only a little have low utility.

The concept of utility is inclusive. For a hedonist, utility may be the physical pleasure enjoyed from experiencing various things. But for a morally conscientious person, utility may be the sense of moral satisfaction that comes with doing the right thing. The important thing for economists is that people can ascertain and compare the utilities of various possible activities. Utility acts as a common denominator that allows people to compare even radically different things sensibly.

Taking altruism and generosity into account

Economists take it as a given that people make choices in order to maximise their personal happiness. This viewpoint immediately raises objections because people are often willing to endure great personal suffering in order to help others.

Yet, to an economist, you can view the desire to help others as being a personal preference. Donating to charities, which most people consider to be 'selfless', can also be seen as being consistent with assuming that people do things to make themselves happy. If people donate to charities because doing so makes them feel good, their selfless action is motivated by 'selfish' intention. Because economists see human motivation as selfish, economics is often accused of being immoral.

Economics is concerned with how people achieve their goals instead of questioning the morality of those goals. For example, some people like honey, but others don't. Economists make no distinction between these two groups regarding the rightness or wrongness of their preferences. Instead, what interests economists is how each group behaves given its preferences. Consequently, economics is amoral rather than immoral.

Economists, however, are also people, and they're concerned with things like social justice and poverty. They just model the desire to pursue morality and equity as an individual goal that maximises individual happiness rather than as a group goal to be pursued to achieve some sort of collective good.

Realising that self-interest can promote the common good

Adam Smith, one of the fathers of modern economics and the face on the £20 note, believed that if society is set up correctly, people chasing after their individual happiness provide for other people's happiness as well. As he pointed out in *An Inquiry into the Nature and Causes of the Wealth of Nations*, published in 1776, 'It is not from the benevolence of the butcher, the brewer, or the baker, that we can expect our dinner, but from their regard to their own interest.'

To put it bluntly, the butcher, the brewer and the baker don't make stuff for you because they like you, but because they want your money. Yet because they want your money, they end up producing for you everything that you need to have a nice meal. When you trade them your money for their goods, everyone is happier. You think that not having to prepare all that food is worth more to you than keeping your money. And they think that getting your money is worth more to them than the toil involved in preparing all that food.

Examining your limitations

Life is full of limitations. Time, for example, is always in limited supply, as are natural resources. The second stage of the economic choice model looks at the constraints that force you to choose among your happy options. This section outlines the various constraints, as well as the unavoidable cost – the *opportunity cost* – of getting what you want. For more about how markets use supply and demand to allocate resources in the face of constraints, turn to Chapter 8.

Resource constraints

The most obvious constraints on human happiness are the physical limitations of nature. Supplies of oil, water and fish are limited, as are the number of radio frequencies on which to send signals and the hours of sunshine to drive solar-powered cars.

The limited supply of natural resources is allocated in many different ways. In certain cases – for example, some endangered species – laws guarantee that nobody can have any of the resource. With the electromagnetic spectrum, national governments apportion the spectrum to broadcasters or mobile phone operators. But, for the most part, private property and prices control the allocation of natural resources.

Under such a system, the use of the resource goes to the highest bidder. Although this system can discriminate against the poor because they don't have much to bid with, it does ensure that the limited supply of the resource at least goes to people who value it highly – in other words, to those who have chosen this resource to maximise their happiness.

Technology constraints

No more oil, sunlight or timber exists today than 1,000 years ago, but you have a much higher standard of living than your ancestors. You have a cushier life because of improvements in the technology of converting raw resources into things we use.

In just the last 200 years, people have figured out how to immunise children against deadly diseases, how to use electricity to provide light and mechanical power, how to build a rocket capable of putting people on the moon and how to increase farm yields dramatically so that we can feed many more people. In just the last 20 years, the Internet and cheap mobile phones have revolutionised everything from how stock markets price and trade shares to how people receive their electronic entertainment.

As technology improves over time, people are able to produce more from the limited supply of resources on our planet. Or, put differently, as technology improves, we have more and better choices from which to choose. Yet, because technology improves slowly, how advanced the technology is at any given moment limits our choices. So, thinking of technology as being a constraint that limits choices is natural. Fortunately, though, technology does improve over time – meaning that if we just wait, more and better choices become available.

Time constraints

Time is a precious resource. Worse yet, time is a resource in fixed supply. So, the best that technology can do is to allow people to produce more in the limited amount of time that they have, or to grant a few more years of life through better medical technology.

But even with a longer life span, you can't be in two places at the same time. Otherwise, time wouldn't be a limit and you'd do double the work in the same amount of time. But because you can only be in one place at one time, you're constantly forced to choose, at each and every moment, to do the thing that makes the best possible use of that instant in time.

Opportunity cost: The unavoidable constraint

The economic idea of *opportunity cost* is closely related to the idea of time constraints. You can do only one thing at a time, which means that, inevitably, you're always giving up a bunch of other things.

The opportunity cost of any activity is the value of the next-best alternative thing you may have done instead. For example, imagine you have three options: chatting on the phone with a friend, watching TV or concentrating on reading this chapter. If you choose to chat with your friend because that makes you happiest, we're not going to hold that against you. We just assume that of the two things that you don't choose, you consider reading this chapter to be better than watching TV. So the opportunity cost of chatting on the phone was sacrificing the chance to read this chapter.

Opportunity cost depends only on the value of the next-best alternative. It doesn't matter whether you have 3 alternatives or 3,000. The opportunity cost is simply the value of the next-best alternative because you can always reduce a complicated choice with many options down to a simple choice between two things: option X versus the best alternative out of all the other alternatives.

Opportunity costs can tell you when *not* to do something as well as when to do something. For example, you may love ice cream, but you love chocolate cake even more. If someone offers you only ice cream, you're going to take it. But if you're offered ice cream or chocolate cake, you're going to take the cake. The opportunity cost of eating ice cream is sacrificing the chance to eat chocolate cake. Because the cost of not eating the cake is higher than the benefits of eating the ice cream, it makes no sense to choose ice cream.

Of course, if you choose chocolate cake, you're still faced with the opportunity cost of giving up having ice cream. But you're willing to do that because the ice cream's opportunity cost is lower than the benefits of the chocolate cake. Opportunity costs are unavoidable constraints on behaviour because you always have to decide what's best and give up the next-best alternative.

Making your final choice

At its most basic, the third stage of the economic choice model is nothing more than cost-benefit analysis. In the first stage, you evaluate how happy each of your options is going to make you. In the second stage, you determine the constraints and opportunity costs of each option. In the third stage, you simply choose the option for which the benefits outweigh the costs by the largest margin.

The cost-benefit model of how people make decisions is very powerful in that it seems to describe correctly how most decisions are made. But this version of cost-benefit analysis can tell you only whether people choose a given option. In other words, this model is only good at describing all-or-nothing decisions like whether or not to eat ice cream.

A much more powerful version of cost-benefit analysis uses a concept called *marginal utility* to tell you not just whether you're going to eat ice cream, but also *how much* ice cream you're going to decide to eat.

To see how marginal utility works, you need to recognise that the amount of utility that a given thing brings usually depends on how much of that given thing a person has already had. For example, if you've been really hungry, the first slice of pizza that you eat brings you a lot of utility. The second slice is also pleasant, but not quite as good as the first because you're no longer starving. The third, in turn, brings less utility than the second. And if you keep forcing yourself to eat, you may find that the 12th or 13th slice of pizza actually makes you sick and brings you negative utility.

Economists refer to this phenomenon as *diminishing marginal utility*. Each additional, or *marginal*, piece of pizza brings less utility than the previous piece so that the extra utility, or *marginal utility*, brought by each successive slice diminishes as you eat more and more slices.

To see how diminishing marginal utility predicts how people make decisions about how much of something to consume, consider having £10 to spend on slices of pizza or bags of chips. Suppose that slices of pizza cost £2 each, and chips also cost £2 a bag.

Economists presume that the goal of people faced with a limited budget is to adjust the quantities of each possible thing they can consume to maximise their *total utility*. In this example, because you know that the marginal utility of pizza diminishes quickly with each additional slice, you don't spend all £10 on pizza, because the fifth slice of pizza just isn't going to bring you very much marginal utility. You're better off allocating some of your spending to the chips.

If you buy only four slices of pizza, you free up £2 to spend on a bag of chips. And because the bag of chips is your first bag, eating it probably brings you lots of marginal utility. Indeed, if the marginal utility gained from that first bag of chips exceeds the marginal utility lost by giving up that fifth slice of pizza, you're certain to make the switch. You keep adjusting the quantities of each food until you find the combination that maximises how much total utility you can purchase using your £10.

Because different people have different preferences, the quantities of each good that maximises each person's total utility are usually different. Someone who detests chips spends all his £10 on pizza. A person who can't stand pizza spends all her money on chips. And for people who choose to have some of each, the optimal quantities of each depend on their individual feelings about the two goods and how fast their marginal utilities decrease. Check out Chapter 9 for more detail on diminishing marginal utility and how it causes demand curves to slope downward.

Allowing for diminishing marginal utility makes this choice behaviour model very powerful: not only does it tell you what people are going to choose, but also how much of each thing they're going to choose.

Limitations and Violations of the Economist's Choice Model

Economists assume that people are fully informed and totally rational when they make decisions. That's a pretty strong assumption – you'd be justified in asking if it's remotely realistic. The answer to your question is that it varies over the range of decisions we make and the type of behaviour we're looking at. For example, being able to understand risk and probability and take them into account in making our decisions isn't a typical human ability. Other cases might not be remotely representative of a given individual, but after you average them out across everybody in the world the result stands up more robustly. In still others people make decisions that are influenced by the amount of information they have or the behaviour of other people (for instance deciding in which pub to meet up). The model of human behaviour favoured by economists works well as a starting point, but isn't able to tell you with 100 per cent accuracy that Mrs Miggins of East Cheam will choose cream buns over arctic roll on a Tuesday.

Uninformed decision-making

When economists apply the choice model, they assume a situation in which a person knows all the possible options, how much utility each option is going to bring and the opportunity costs of each option. But how do you evaluate whether sitting on top of Mount Everest for five minutes is better than hang-gliding over the Amazon for ten minutes? If you've never had either experience, you aren't well-informed about the constraints and costs of the choice and probably don't even know the utilities of the two options.

Politicians with novel new programmes often ask people to make similarly uninformed choices. They make their proposals sound as good as possible, but in many cases nobody really knows what they may be getting into.

Things are similarly murky when making choices about random events. People buying lottery tickets in the national lottery have no idea about the eventual possible gain or the eventual likelihood of winning, because both the size of the prize and the likelihood of winning depend on how many tickets may or may not be sold before the draw is made.

Economists account for this reality by assuming that when faced with uninformed decisions, people make their best guesses about not only random outcomes, but also about how much they may like or dislike things with which they have no previous experience. Although this may seem like a fudge, because people in the real world are obviously making decisions in such situations (they do, in fact, buy a whole lot of lottery tickets), the people in those situations must be fudging a bit as well.

Whether people make good choices when they are uninformed is hard to say. Obviously, people prefer to be better informed before choosing. And some people do shy away from less certain options. But, overall, the economist's model of choice behaviour seems quite capable of dealing with situations of incomplete information and uncertainty about random outcomes.

Irrationality

Even when people are fully informed about their options, they often make logical errors in evaluating the costs and benefits of each. We go through three of the most common choice errors in the following sections, but as you read them, don't be too alarmed. After these logical errors are explained to them, people typically stop making the errors and start behaving in a manner consistent with rationally weighing marginal benefits against marginal costs.

Sunk costs are sunk!

Suppose that you just spent £15 to get into an all-you-can-eat sushi restaurant. How much should you eat? More specifically, when deciding how much to eat, should you care about how much you paid to get into the restaurant?

To an economist, the answer to the first question is: eat exactly the amount of food that makes you most happy. And the answer to the second question is: how much it costs you to get in doesn't matter because whether you eat one piece of sushi or 80 pieces of sushi, the cost is the same. Put differently, because the cost of getting into the restaurant is now in the past, it should be completely unrelated to your current decision of how much to eat.

Economists refer to costs that have already been incurred and which should therefore not affect your current and future decision-making as *sunk costs.* Rationally speaking, you should consider only the future, potential marginal costs and benefits of your current options.

After all, if you were suddenly offered $1,000 to leave the sushi restaurant and eat next door at a competitor, would you refuse simply because you felt you had to eat a lot at the sushi restaurant in order to get your money's worth out of the $15 you spent? Of course not.

Unfortunately, most people tend to let sunk costs affect their decision-making until an economist points out to them that sunk costs are irrelevant, or, as economists never tire of saying, 'Sunk costs are sunk!' (On the other hand, non-economists quickly tire of hearing this phrase.) Fortunately, we have other ways of saying the same thing: for example, we talk about the Concorde fallacy, in honour of the supersonic jet that never broke even, no matter how many pounds or francs were thrown at the project.

Mistaking a big percentage for a big pound amount

Suppose you decide to save 10 per cent on a TV by making a one-hour round trip to a store in another town to buy the TV for only $90 instead of buying the TV at your local store for $100. Next, ask yourself whether you'd also be willing to drive one hour in order to buy a home theatre system for $1,990 in the next town rather than for $2,000 at your local store. You do the maths, and because you're going to save only 0.5 per cent, you decide to buy the system for $2,000 at the local store.

You may think you're being smart, but you've just behaved in a colossally inconsistent and irrational way. In the first case, you were willing to drive one hour to save $10. In the second, you were not. Costs and benefits are absolute, but people make the mistake of thinking of the costs and benefits of driving to the next town in terms of percentages or proportions. Instead, compare the total costs against the total benefits because the benefit of driving to the next town is the absolute amount in pounds you save, not the proportion you save.

Confusing marginal and average

Suppose that your local government recently built three bridges at a total cost of £30 million: that's an average cost of £10 million per bridge. A local economist does a study and estimates that the total benefit of the three bridges to the local economy adds up to £36 million, or an average of £12 million per bridge.

A politician then starts trying to build a fourth bridge, arguing that because bridges on average cost £10 million but on average bring £12 million in benefits, it would be foolish not to build another bridge. Should you believe him? After all, if each bridge brings society a net gain of £2 million, you'd want to keep building bridges forever.

However, what really matters to this decision are *marginal* costs and *marginal* benefits, not *average* ones (see the section 'Making Your Final Choice' for more on marginal utility). Who cares what costs and benefits all the previous bridges brought with them? You have to compare the costs of that extra, marginal bridge with the benefits of that extra, marginal bridge. If the marginal benefits exceed the marginal costs, you should build the bridge. And if the marginal costs exceed the marginal benefits, you shouldn't.

For example, suppose that an independent watchdog group hires an engineer to estimate the cost of building one more bridge and an economist to estimate the benefits of building one more bridge. The engineer finds that because the first three bridges have already taken the three shortest river crossings, the fourth bridge needs to be much longer. In fact, the extra length raises the building cost to £15 million.

At the same time, the economist does a survey and finds that a fourth bridge isn't really all that necessary. At best, the bridge is going to bring only £8 million per year in benefits. Consequently, this fourth bridge shouldn't be built because its marginal cost of £15 million exceeds its marginal benefit of £8 million. By telling voters only about the *average* costs and benefits of past bridges, the politician supporting the project is grossly misleading them. So watch out whenever somebody tries to sell you a bridge.

Chapter 3

Producing the Right Stuff in the Right Way

In This Chapter

▶ Determining your production possibilities

▶ Allocating resources in the face of diminishing returns

▶ Choosing outputs that maximise people's happiness

▶ Understanding the role of government and markets

*A*lthough human beings face scarcity and can't have everything they want, they do have a lot of options. Productive technology is now so advanced that people can convert the planet's limited supply of resources into an amazing variety of goods and services, including cars, computers, aeroplanes, cancer treatments, video games and even great books like this one.

This chapter explains how economists analyse the process by which societies choose exactly what to produce in order to maximise human happiness. For every society, the process can be divided into two simple steps:

1. **The society must figure out all the possible combinations of goods and services that it can produce given its limited resources and the currently available technology.**

2. **The society must choose one of these possible output combinations – presumably, the combination that maximises happiness.**

Economists view success in each of the two steps in terms of two particular types of efficiency:

✔ *Productive efficiency* means producing any given good or service using the fewest possible resources.

✔ *Allocative efficiency* means producing the kinds of goods and services that make people most happy, and producing them in the correct amounts.

This chapter shows you how a society achieves both productive and allocative efficiency – that is, how a society determines what's possible to produce, as well as what's best to produce.

Determining the Possibilities

In determining what's possible to produce in an economy, economists list two major factors that affect both the maximum amounts and the types of output to be produced:

✔ Limited resources

✔ Diminishing returns

The first factor is obvious: if resources were unlimited, goods and services would be as well. The second factor, despite affecting nearly every production process known, isn't understood by most people. Basically, *diminishing returns* means that the more you make of something, the less return you get on each successive unit. Eventually, the costs exceed the benefits, which limits how much of it you want to produce, even if the product is your favourite thing. Your resources should be devoted to producing units of other things for which the benefits still outweigh the costs. Diminishing returns implies that, in general, we're better off not putting all our eggs in one basket.

Classifying the resources

You can't get output without inputs of resources. Economists traditionally divide inputs, or *factors of production*, into three classes:

✔ **Land:** All naturally occurring resources that can be used to produce things people want to consume.

✔ **Labour:** The work that people must do in order to produce things.

✔ **Capital:** Man-made machines, tools and structures that aren't directly consumed but are used to produce other things that people do directly consume. Capital includes factories, roads, electrical grids, and so on.

In addition to these three traditional inputs, economists now often speak of *human capital*, which is the knowledge and skills that people use to help them produce output.

If you put a person to work at a job for which he or she has high human capital, he or she produces much better or much more output than a person with low human capital, even though they both supply the same amount of labour in terms of hours worked. An important consequence is that skilled workers (high human capital) get paid more than unskilled workers (low human capital). Therefore, a good way for societies to become richer is to improve the skills of their workers through education and training. If societies can raise workers' human capital levels, not only can they produce more with the same inputs of limited land, labour and capital, but also their workers are going to be paid more and enjoy higher standards of living.

But building up human capital is costly, and at any given instant, you need to think of the level of human capital in a society as being fixed. Combined with limitations on the amount of land, labour and capital, the limitation on human capital means that the society can only produce a limited amount of output. And along these same lines, the decisions about where to best allocate these limited resources become crucial because the resources must be used for production of the goods and services that are going to bring with them the greatest amount of happiness.

Getting less of a good thing: Diminishing returns

Diminishing returns is probably the most important economic factor in determining what to produce out of all the things that can possibly be produced given the limited supply of resources. Diminishing returns refers to the fact that for virtually everything people make, the amount of additional output you get from each additional unit of input decreases as you use more and more of the input.

In our discussion of diminishing returns, do bear in mind that we are discussing returns to one changing factor whilst holding others constant. This is key. It makes sense to talk about diminishing returns to labour holding capital fixed. If capital can change too, we'd have to adapt the model by making a new calculation for returns to labour every time we changed the amount of capital used. We get around that by holding capital constant, that is, working out return to labour for a *given amount of capital used*.

Diminishing returns is sometimes referred to as the *low-hanging fruit principle*. Imagine being sent into an apple orchard to pick apples. During the first hour, you pick a lot of apples because you go for the low-hanging ones that are the easiest to reach. In the second hour, however, you can't pick as many because you have to start reaching awkwardly for fruit that is higher up. During the third hour you pick even fewer apples; you now have to jump off the ground because the only ones left are even farther away. Table 3-1 demonstrates how your productivity – your output for a given amount of input – diminishes with each additional hour you work.

Table 3-1 Diminishing Returns to Apple Picking

Hour Worked	Apples Picked	Labour Cost per Apple
1	300	2p
2	200	3p
3	120	5p

Another way to see the effect of diminishing returns is to note the increasing costs for producing output. If you pay workers £6 per hour to pick apples, your cost to have 300 apples picked in the first hour is 2 pence per apple, as shown in Table 3-1. The second hour yields only 200 apples, costing you 3 pence per apple (because you still have to pay the worker £6 for that hour's work). Only 120 apples get picked in the third hour, so the labour cost per apple rises to 5 pence. Eventually, the effects of diminishing returns drive prices so high that you stop devoting further labour resources to picking additional apples.

Virtually all production processes show diminishing returns, and not just for labour. Additional amounts of any particular input usually result in smaller and smaller increments of output, holding all other inputs constant.

Allocating resources

Because the diminishing returns factor assures that a production process eventually becomes too costly, a society normally allocates its limited resources widely, to many different production processes.

To understand why this happens, imagine that you can allocate workers to picking apples or picking oranges and crucially you have a fixed number of ladders. You can sell both apples and oranges for £1 each, but the production of both fruits involves diminishing returns so that additional workers acting as fruit pickers yield successively smaller increases in output no matter which fruit they're picking.

Allocating all your workers to picking oranges, for example, is unproductive because the output you get from the last worker picking oranges is much less than the output you get from the first worker picking oranges.

The smart thing to do is to take a worker away from picking oranges and reassign him to picking apples. As the last worker picking oranges, he didn't produce much. But as the first worker picking apples, he's going to pick a lot of them. Because you pay him the same wage regardless of which fruit he picks, you use your labour more intelligently by having him pick apples, because one apple sells for as much money as one orange.

You may also want to reassign a second worker, and perhaps a third or a fourth. But because diminishing returns applies just as much to picking apples as it does to picking oranges, you don't want to reassign all the workers. Each additional worker assigned to picking apples produces less than the previous worker picking apples. At some point, moving additional workers from picking oranges to picking apples no longer benefits you, and you've reached what economists refer to as an *optimal allocation* of your labour resource. As soon as you've found this sweet spot, you have no further incentive to move workers from picking one fruit to picking the other because no additional moving of workers increases total fruit picking. At this point, you've maximised your fruit-picking potential.

Graphing the possibilities

Economists have a handy graph called the *Production Possibilities Frontier* (PPF) that lets you visualise the effect of diminishing returns and view the trade-offs you make when you reallocate inputs from producing one thing to producing another. The Production Possibilities Frontier, which is sometimes referred to as the *Production Possibilities Curve*, also shows how limited resources limit your ability to produce output. Figure 3-1 shows a PPF graph that corresponds to the data in Table 3-2.

Table 3-2 shows how the total output of apples and oranges changes as you make different allocations of five available workers to picking apples or oranges. For example, if you put all five people to work picking only apples for one whole day, you get 700 apples picked and zero oranges picked. If you move one worker to oranges (so four workers are picking apples and one worker is picking oranges), you get 680 apples picked and 300 oranges picked. Because of diminishing returns, taking one worker away from apples reduces apple output by only 20. But moving that worker to oranges increases orange production by 300 because that worker is the first one picking oranges and can get the low-hanging fruit.

Table 3-2	Outputs of Apples and Oranges as the Allocation of Labour Changes					
	Combo 1	*Combo 2*	*Combo 3*	*Combo 4*	*Combo 5*	*Combo 6*
Workers picking oranges	0	1	2	3	4	5
Workers picking apples	5	4	3	2	1	0
Output of oranges	0	300	500	620	680	700
Output of apples	700	680	620	500	300	0

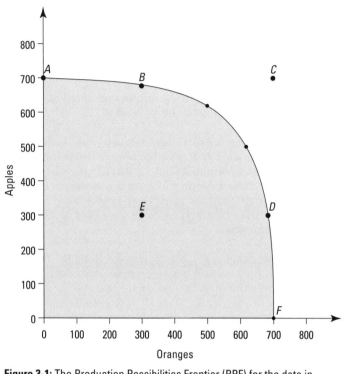

Figure 3-1: The Production Possibilities Frontier (PPF) for the data in Table 3-2.

Figure 3-1 plots out the six output combinations that result from varying the allocation of workers in Table 3-2, thereby graphing all your production possibilities. Point *A* corresponds to putting all your workers to work picking apples. Point *B* corresponds to the output you get from four workers picking apples and one worker picking oranges.

Note that each of the six points is *attainable* in the sense that you can actually produce the corresponding quantities of each fruit through some allocation of the five workers' labour. On the other hand, a point like *C* is not attainable. You can't allocate your five workers in any way to produce that many apples and oranges.

Imagine that instead of allocating labour by worker, you allocate it by time. The five workers each work for one day, so you have five *worker-days* of labour to allocate. You can now allocate, for example, 3.2 worker-days to apple picking and 1.8 worker-days to orange picking. This arrangement allows you to fill in the graph and draw a line connecting the six points that correspond to the output combinations that you get when allocating labour by worker.

This curve is called the *Production Possibilities Frontier*, or PPF, because it divides the area of the graph into two parts: the combinations of output that are possible to produce given your limited supply of labour are under, or on, the line, and those that are not possible to produce are above it. In this way, the PPF graph captures the effect of scarce resources on production.

The changing slope as you move along the frontier shows that the trade-off between apple production and orange production depends on where you start. If you're at point *A,* where you're allocating all your resources to the production of apples, you can, by reallocating resources, produce a lot more oranges at the cost of giving up only a few apples. But if you start at point *D,* where you're already producing a lot of oranges, you have to give up a lot of apples to get just a few more oranges.

The changing slope of the PPF in the face of diminishing returns is due to the fact that the *opportunity costs* of production vary depending on your current allocation of resources. If you're already producing a lot of apples, the opportunity costs of devoting even more labour to more apple production are very high because you're giving up a lot of potential orange production. On the other hand, the opportunity costs of devoting that labour to orange production are very low because you have to give up producing only a few apples. Clearly, you should devote the labour to picking the fruit that has the lower opportunity costs because, in this example, both fruits bring the same benefit: £1 per fruit sold.

The PPF is also very handy because any points that lie on the PPF itself (on the frontier) clearly show the output combinations you get when you're *productively efficient*, or wasting none of your resources. You can't increase the production of apples without reducing the production of oranges, and vice versa. For example, if you start at point *B*, the only way to increase apple production is to slide up along the frontier, which implies reducing orange production. You have to make this trade-off because you don't have any wasted labour lying around with which you can get more apples without reducing the amount of labour already devoted to orange picking.

All the points below the line are productively inefficient. Consider point *E* in Figure 3-1, which corresponds to producing 300 apples and 300 oranges. You produce at a point like *E* only if you're being productively inefficient. In fact, you can see from Table 3-2 that you can produce these numbers by sending only one worker to pick apples and another worker to pick oranges. You're using just two of your five workers; the labour of the other three workers is being wasted or not used at all.

Any manager who has five workers to allocate but produces only output combination *E* would be fired! If we were to aggregate across all the firms in an economy, we'd say that efficient economies should always be producing at some point on their frontiers because if they are inside that frontier line, they are wasting their limited resources and not maximising the happiness that can be had from them.

Pushing the line with better technology

This PPF is a simplification of the real world, derived by allocating one input between just two outputs. The real world is, of course, more complicated, with many different resources allocated among many different outputs. But the principles of limited resources and diminishing returns that show up so clearly on the PPF graph also apply to the much greater variety of both inputs and outputs in the real world.

Another simplification of the diminishing returns model is that, other than the particular input you are allocating, you are implicitly holding constant all other productive inputs, including technology. But humanity's level of technological sophistication is constantly increasing, allowing people to produce much more from a given set of resources than before.

Economists represent this increase in productivity by shifting the PPF outward. In Figure 3-2, the shaded area represents new combinations of output that, thanks to better technology, can now be produced using the same amount of resources as before. The PPF is still curved because better technologies don't get rid of diminishing returns. Even with a better technology, if you start increasing the amount of a particular input, you get successively smaller additional increases in output.

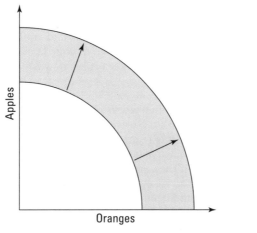

Figure 3-2: A technologically balanced outward shift of the PPF.

In Figure 3-2, the new technology shift is *balanced* in the sense that it increases your ability to produce more of both goods. An example of a balanced technological change is improvements in fertilisers or pesticides that increase crop yields of both apples and oranges.

But most technological innovations are *biased*. For example, suppose that you're considering a PPF where the two output goods are wheat and steel. An improvement in steel-making technology obviously allows you to make more steel from your limited resources but has no effect at all on your ability to make wheat. Consequently, as Figure 3-3 shows, the PPF doesn't shift out evenly. Rather, it shifts out at the end where all your particular input (say, labour) is devoted to steel, but remains fixed at the end where all your particular input is devoted to wheat production.

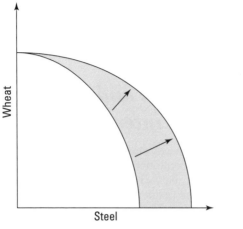

Figure 3-3: A technologically biased outward shift of the PPF.

Determining What Should Be Produced

After a society locates the frontier of efficient output combinations, the next step is choosing the point along the frontier that produces the combination of goods and services that makes people most happy. Choosing only from among frontier combinations guarantees *productive efficiency*. Choosing the single frontier combination that maximises happiness assures *allocative efficiency*.

Because determining where the frontier lies is mostly a matter of engineering and applying current technology to available resources, it engenders little controversy. But deciding which particular combination of outputs a society as a whole should choose is much more complicated.

Because citizens have competing preferences and priorities, some sort of decision-making process must be established to determine what actually gets produced and to (try to) make sure that it pleases most of the people most of the time.

In most modern economies, this process is the result of both private and public decisions acting through a combination of free markets and government action. The process is not always smooth – and budget negotiations have driven plenty of politicians to drink or despair – but it has delivered the highest living standards in world history.

Weighing pros and cons of government interventions

When analysing the ways in which modern economies and societies select a combination of goods and services to produce, you have to realise that current economic laws and institutions are the result of conflicting pressures about whether to leave markets to their own devices when turning resources into output or use the power of government to intervene in markets in order to secure a different set of outcomes.

Keep the following three factors in mind when considering the fight between leaving the markets alone and intervening:

✔ Modern economies are hugely complicated, with literally millions of goods and services produced using limited supplies of land, labour and capital. Markets handle this complexity easily, but government interventions usually don't – meaning that they often risk substantial reductions in productive and allocative efficiency.

✔ Some goods and services, such as coal-burning power plants and cocaine, have negative consequences. These negative consequences bring forth substantial pressure for government intervention in the economy because these markets, if left alone, produce a lot of these goods and services.

✔ Some people end up consuming a very large proportion of the goods and services produced, whereas others end up with very little. Such unequal distribution also brings forth a great deal of pressure for government intervention in the economy in order to equalise living standards.

These factors are both a consequence and a cause of the fact that our modern economies are largely a mix of market production and government intervention. For the most part, what to produce, how much of it to produce and who gets it is decided by voluntary transactions made by individuals and businesses. But sometimes, the government uses its coercive powers to achieve outcomes that wouldn't happen if individuals and businesses were left to their own devices.

In both cases, a huge apparatus of law and tradition governing economic transactions helps society produce a combination of output that is, hopefully, both productively efficient (so resources aren't wasted) and allocatively efficient (so the economy is producing the things that people want most).

The magic of markets: Going where no one person can ever go

Market production is the term that economists use to capture what happens when one individual offers to make or sell something to another individual at a price agreeable to both. Markets are very good at producing things for which people are willing to pay. In addition, markets tend to be very efficient if many providers of a good or service exist.

A *competitive market* is one in which many sellers compete against each other to attract customers. In such a situation, each seller has an incentive to sell at the lowest price possible subject to constraints imposed by their costs in order to undercut competitors and steal their customers. Because every firm has this incentive, prices tend to be driven so low that the businesses can just barely make a profit.

A competitive market also tends to guarantee productive efficiency because the best way for sellers to keep prices low is to make sure that they're using all their resources efficiently and that nothing is going to waste. Because competition is ongoing, the pressure to be efficient is constant. Sellers also have a big incentive to improve efficiency in order to undersell their rivals and steal their customers.

In terms of the PPF (which we discuss in the earlier section 'Graphing your production possibilities'), market production with a lot of competition tends to ensure not only that economies produce along the frontier, but also that they have frontiers that are constantly being pushed outward as firms improve efficiency.

Markets also have the benefit of working out, automatically, the things that people want. To grasp why this is so amazing, consider that we live in a world of nearly seven billion people.

It would be very hard for any one person to gather enough information to figure out what each of those nearly seven billion people most wants to buy.

But because production and distribution in modern economies aren't centralised, you don't need to know the big picture. In fact, the real magic of market economies is that they are just a collection of millions and billions of small face-to-face transactions between buyers and sellers.

For example, the person who sells you a TV at the local store has no idea about the total demand for TVs in the world, how many tons of steel or plastic are needed to produce them, or how many other things *weren't* produced because the steel and plastic needed to make the TVs were used for TVs rather than other things. All they know is that you're willing to pay them for a TV. And if they're making a profit selling TVs, they will take account of the greater potential sales by ordering more TVs from the factory. The factory, in turn, increases production, taking resources away from the production of other things. Reallocation of resources also occurs in markets because each resource has a price, and whoever is willing to pay the price gets the resource.

In fact, market economies are often called *price systems* because prices serve as the signals that allocate resources. Things in high demand have high prices, and things in low demand have low prices. Because businesses like to make money, they follow the price signals and produce more of what has a high price and less of what has a low price. In this way, markets tend to take our limited resources and use them to produce what people most want – or, at least, what people are most willing to pay for. And they do it all in a completely decentralised manner.

The misdeeds of markets

Markets aren't perfect. In particular, they suffer from two major problems:

- ✔ Markets produce whatever people are willing to pay for, even if these things aren't necessarily good for the people or the environment.

- ✔ Markets are amoral: they don't in any way guarantee fairness or equity.

The fact that illegal drugs are widely and cheaply available despite vigorous government programmes to stop their production and distribution is probably the best example of the robustness of markets. As long as there are profits to be made, you can be pretty certain that supply is going to rise to satisfy any demand. Illegal drugs are an excellent example of the fact that markets can deliver things without caring about their social value or their negative consequences.

The other big problem with markets is that they cater to those who have money to spend. The price system gives an incentive to produce only the things that people are willing and able to pay for. If someone is very poor, he can't give producers an incentive to provide him with even basic necessities like medicine and food. Under a pure price system, resources are instead directed toward producing things for those who have money to spend.

A related problem with markets is income and wealth inequality. Because market systems reward those who are best able to provide goods and services that people want to buy, some sellers end up becoming very rich because they're better at providing what people want. This invariably leads to large inequalities in wealth that many people find offensive, even when the money is honestly earned.

The case for government intervention

Many societies use their governments to intervene and address the problems that markets create or can't fix. Government interventions in the economy usually take one of three forms:

- ✔ **Penalties or bans on producing or consuming goods or services that are considered dangerous or immoral:** For example, governments may ban drugs or impose 'sin taxes' on things like alcohol and tobacco, which, though legal, are thought to be products whose use should be discouraged. However, prohibitions seldom work because the market, which need not be a *legal* market, still has large incentives to provide such goods and services.

- ✔ **Subsidies to encourage the production of goods and services that are considered desirable:** For example, most governments heavily subsidise the education of children and the provision of medical care. They do so because of the fear that insufficient education and inadequate medical care are likely to be provided without these subsidies.

✔ **Taxes on the well-off to provide goods and services to the less fortunate and to reduce inequalities in income and wealth:** Governments tax individuals and businesses in order to raise the money to provide things like good parks, clean air and art, as well as goods and services for the poor.

In terms of the PPF graph, each of these government interventions causes the economy to produce and allocate an output combination different from the one that society would end up with if the markets made all the production and allocation decisions.

Depending on the situation, the output combination produced by a government intervention may be better or worse than the market combination in terms of productive efficiency, allocative efficiency or both.

The case against government intervention

Government intervention is a powerful force for redirecting economic activity, but it doesn't necessarily make the economy better. Why not?

✔ Government programmes are often the result of special-interest lobbying that seeks to help some small group rather than to maximise the happiness of the general population. Special-interest lobbying takes resources away from other uses that often benefit numerous people in order to provide benefits to only a few.

✔ Government programmes often deliver poor service even when pursuing the common good, because they have no competition to create incentives to produce government goods and services efficiently.

✔ Government interventions usually lack the flexibility of the price system, which is able to constantly redirect resources to accommodate people's changing willingness to pay for one good rather than another. Government policies take years to pass, and laws are usually written in a very precise manner that doesn't allow for changing circumstances and rapid innovation – things that the price system handles with ease.

Although markets sometimes fail to deliver everything that society wants, government intervention isn't a panacea. Markets are very good at delivering the vast majority of things that people want, and they can usually do so at the lowest possible cost.

Opting for a mixed economy

In the real world, few societies opt for an extreme type of economy, such as one that is totally market-based or one that features constant and pervasive government intervention. Instead, most societies opt for some mixture of markets, government intervention and what economists refer to as *traditional production*. In their purest forms, these three types of economy can be defined as follows:

- ✔ **A market economy** is one in which almost all economic activity happens in markets with little or no interference by the government. Because of the lack of government intervention, this system is also often referred to as *laissez-faire,* which is French for 'let well alone'.

- ✔ **A command economy** is one in which all economic activity is directed by the government.

- ✔ **A traditional economy** is one in which production and distribution are handled along the lines of long-standing cultural traditions. For example, until the caste system was abolished in India during the last century, the production of nearly every good and service was permitted only by someone born into the appropriate caste. Similarly, in medieval Europe, people were usually unable to be part of the government or attain high military rank unless they were born into the nobility.

Because nearly every modern economy is a mixture of these three pure forms, most modern economies fall into the very inclusive category called *mixed economies.* With the exception of a few isolated traditional societies, however, the traditional economy part of the mixture has tended to decline in significance because most production has shifted to markets and because traditional economic restrictions on things like age and gender have become less important (and more illegal).

The result is that most mixed economies today are a mixture of the other two pure types: the command economy and the market economy. The mixtures that you find in most countries typically feature governments that mostly allow markets to determine what's produced, but that also mix in limited interventions in an attempt to make improvements over what the market would do if left to its own devices.

The precise nature of the mixture depends on the country, with the United Kingdom and the United States featuring more emphasis on markets whereas France and Germany, for example, feature more emphasis on government intervention. On the other hand, a few totalitarian states like North Korea still persist in running pure command economies as part of their all-encompassing authoritarian regimes. Command economies have all been dismal failures when we evaluate them in terms of productive and allocative efficiency, although plenty of people still feel nostalgia for them. Even well-intentioned governments can't gather enough information about production and distribution to do a good job of allocating resources. In fact, they do a much worse job than price systems.

Consequently, the opposite extreme, absolutely no government intervention, is an attractive option. Such laissez-faire systems were first suggested by French economists a couple of centuries ago in response to the habit of governments of that era to intervene very heavily in economic activity.

However, no pure laissez-faire economy has ever existed or is probably ever going to exist. The simple fact is that properly functioning market economies that use price mechanisms to allocate resources require a huge amount of government support. Among other things, market economies need governments to do the following:

- ✔ Enforce property rights so that people don't steal

- ✔ Provide legal systems to write and enforce contracts so that people can make purchases and sales of goods and services

- ✔ Enforce standardised systems of weights and measures so that people know they aren't being cheated

- ✔ Provide a stable money supply that's safe from counterfeiters

> ✔ Enforce patents and copyrights to encourage innovation and creativity

Notice that all these things must be in place in order for markets to function. Consequently, a more moderate, more modern version of laissez-faire says that government should provide the institutional framework necessary for market economies to function, and then get out of the way and let people make and sell whatever is demanded.

However, the vast majority of people want governments to do more than just set up the institutions necessary for markets to function. They want governments to stop the production and sale of things like drugs or subsidise the production of things that the market economy may not provide a lot of, such as housing for the poor. They often also want to tax well-off citizens to pay for government programmes for the poor.

 Many government programmes are so commonplace that you don't even think of them as being government interventions. For example, free public schools, safety features on cars, warning labels on medicine bottles, sin taxes on alcohol and tobacco and mandatory contributions to retirement systems are all government interventions in the economy. Because the government interventions such as these increase overall happiness, we can accept the fact that they are, strictly speaking, inefficient.

At the end of the day, all government interventions – both good and bad – are the result of a political process. In democracies, the amount of government intervention is, broadly speaking, a reflection of the will of the people.

Encouraging Technology and Innovation

One of the most important jobs of government is helping to promote the invention of new technologies so that we can enjoy higher living standards.

Technology is, in many ways, like any other good that a market can provide. If a profit incentive exists to inventing a new technology, businesspeople are going to figure out a way to invent it, just as they figure out ways to deliver all the other things that people are willing to pay for.

Businesses and governments spend hundreds of billions of research and development funds each year attempting to invent new technologies. Governments provide a good deal of direct support through research grants and university subsidies. But a crucial thing to understand about innovation is the indirect role that governments play not by subsidising new technology but by guarding it. In particular, the patents granted by governments provide a huge economic incentive for both individuals and businesses to innovate.

The fact that economic growth in western Europe and the United States took off 200 years ago, right after patents became widely enforced, is no coincidence. For the first time in world history, a secure financial incentive existed for using your brain to innovate.

Copyrights for literary, musical and cinematic works serve a similar purpose. A great deal more art is produced when artists know that they can make a living off their products. Along these lines, the easy duplication and distribution of digital media on the Internet is a troubling development because it may have weakened artists' ability to charge for the art that they work so hard to produce.

Governments also have a key role to play in encouraging education. Every rich country in the world has a policy of universal primary and secondary education, as well as strong universities. Smart new technologies require smart, well-educated researchers, and you don't get them without good educational systems.

Part II
Macroeconomics: The Science of Economic Growth and Stability

'I ignored the rumours about the recession sweeping the city, and now <u>I</u> am.'

In this part . . .

The chapters in this part introduce you to *macro-economics*, the study of the economy as a whole, which concentrates on economy-wide factors such as interest rates, inflation and the rate of unemployment. We explain what economists believe causes recessions, and we use the famous Keynesian model to illustrate the policies that economists believe can best be used to fight recessions. Finally, we touch upon the factors that economists believe are essential to promoting sustained economic growth and rising living standards.

Chapter 4

Measuring the Macroeconomy

* *

In This Chapter

▶ Measuring GDP: the total value of goods and services

▶ Deconstructing GDP into $C + I + G + NX$

▶ Understanding why free trade is good for you

* *

*M*acroeconomics studies the economy as a whole. Seen from on high, the production of goods and services is done by businesses or by the government. Businesses produce the bulk of what people consume, but the government provides many goods and services, including public safety, national defence and public goods such as roads and bridges. In addition, the government provides the legal structure within which businesses operate and also intervenes in the economy in order to do things such as regulate pollution, mandate safety equipment and redistribute income from the rich to the poor.

In order for economists to study the process of production, distribution and consumption with any real understanding, they need to keep track of exactly how much is being produced, as well as where it all ends up. Consequently, economists measure economic activity with the *National Accounts* (internationally known as *National Income and Product Accounts*, or NIPA). This system produces numerous useful statistics, including the famous *gross domestic product* (GDP), which measures the total quantity of goods and services produced in a country in a given period of time.

Using GDP to Track the Economy

Gross domestic product, or GDP, is a statistic that calculates the value of all goods and services produced in a given country in a given period of time. In the United Kingdom, the Office of National Statistics calculates and publishes this statistic regularly and revises it just as regularly as more data becomes available, giving us an idea of how much economic activity took place in the previous quarter or year.

GDP is very important because, other things being equal, richer people are happier people. We're not saying that money is the only thing that matters in life, but economists evaluate economies by how successfully they maximise happiness, and although money can't buy you love, it can buy you a lot of things that ought to make you happy, such as food, education and holidays. Consequently, a high and quickly growing GDP is preferable because it reflects lots of economic transactions that provide people with the goods and services they desire.

Because people like to consume goods and services, measuring GDP allows economists to quantify, in some sense, how well a country is doing at maximising its citizens' happiness given the country's limited resources. A rising GDP indicates that a country is working out ways to provide more of the goods and services that make people happy.

Tallying up what counts in GDP

Counting sales where money changes hands can get a little tricky because both a buyer and a seller are involved in every such transaction. The money that the buyer spends has to equal the money that the seller receives. Translated into economist lingo, income has to equal expenditure.

Consequently, you can measure GDP by totalling up all the expenditures in the economy or by counting up all the incomes in the economy. If your calculations are correct, both methods give you the same value for GDP.

When thinking about GDP, you also have to consider the goods and services that are being traded for money. Economists simplify life by saying that all the resources or

factors of production of a society – land, labour and capital –
are owned by households. *Households* can be made up of one
person or several – think in terms of individuals or families.
Firms buy or rent the factors of production from the households and use them to produce goods and services, which
are then sold back to the households. This process sets up a
circular flow for resources moving from households to firms,
and goods and services moving back the other way, as
Figure 4-1 shows.

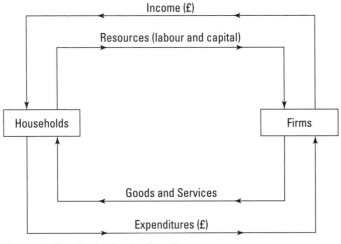

Figure 4-1: The simple circular-flow diagram.

Moving opposite to the flow of resources and goods are payments in pounds. When the firms buy factors of production
from households, they have to pay money to the households.
That money is income to the households. And when households buy goods and services from the firms, they pay for
those goods and services with money, which shows up in
Figure 4-1 as expenditures.

A key point to understand is that firms are owned by households, either directly, in the case of smaller businesses, or via
investment funding from banks or pension funds. In turn, any
money that a firm receives when it sells a good or a service
flows on as income to some individual or group of individuals. Because of this flow, incomes in Figure 4-1 have to equal
expenditures.

Considering flows of income and assets

Although you can use incomes or expenditures to measure GDP, economists prefer to use incomes because governments make both individuals and businesses keep track of every last penny of income they receive so that it can be taxed. This government requirement provides extensive, accurate data about incomes.

Tracing the flow of income

All the income in the economy flows into one of four categories:

- ✔ Labour receives wages
- ✔ Land receives rent
- ✔ Capital receives interest
- ✔ Entrepreneurship receives profits

You may recognise the first three of these categories as being the three traditional factors of production that we list in Chapter 3. Obviously, because you need land, labour and capital to make things, you have to pay for them. But in a dynamic, competitive economy, you also need people with a willingness to take on business risk and invest in risky new technologies. In order to get them to do so, you have to pay them, which is why some income must also flow to risk-taking entrepreneurs in the form of profits. Hence many economists like to think of entrepreneurship as a fourth factor of production – a factor that must be paid if you want to get stuff produced in a market economy.

Each of the four payments is a flow of money that compensates for a flow of services needed in production:

- ✔ Workers charge wages for the labour services that they provide.
- ✔ Owners of buildings and land charge rents to tenants for the services that real estate and physical structures provide.

✔ Firms wanting to obtain the services of capital, such as machines and computers, must pay for them. This payment is considered interest because, for example, the cost of obtaining the services of a £1,000 piece of capital equipment is the interest payments that a firm must make on a £1,000 loan to buy that piece of equipment.

✔ And, finally, the firm's profits must flow to the entrepreneurs and owners of the firm, who take on the risk that the firm may do badly or even go bankrupt.

Following the funds, around and around

The simple circular-flow diagram of Figure 4-1 captures the fact that an income exists for every expenditure. However, because the diagram divides the economy only into firms and households, it misses a lot of the action that goes on in the real world. In Figure 4-2, you can see a much more realistic and detailed circular-flow diagram that divides the economy into firms, households and the government, with these entities making transactions through the following three markets:

✔ **Markets for factors of production** are where money is exchanged to purchase or rent the land, labour, capital and entrepreneurship used in production.

✔ **Financial markets** are where people who want to lend money (savers) interact with those who want to borrow money (borrowers). In this market, the supply and demand for loans determine the *interest rate*, which is the price you have to pay to get someone to lend you their money for a while. Because most governments run deficits and have to borrow a lot of money, they're major players in the financial markets.

✔ **Markets for goods and services** are where people and the government buy the stuff that firms make.

In Figure 4-2, arrows show the flows of money throughout the economy. Firms make payments – rent, wages, interest and profits – to households to obtain the factors of production – land, labour, capital and entrepreneurship.

Households take the income they get from selling these factors and use it to pay for goods and services, to pay taxes or to save. The government buys goods and services using the tax revenues it takes in or the money it borrows in the financial markets. The financial markets also provide money for corporations to make investments. This money adds to what firms get from selling goods and services to households and the government.

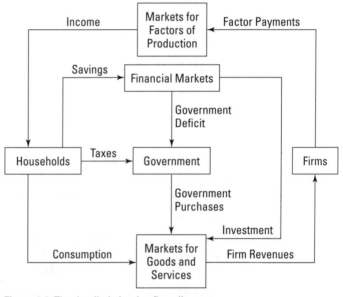

Figure 4-2: The detailed circular-flow diagram.

Note that not all transactions in the financial markets are relevant to the calculation of GDP. GDP measures currently produced output, and most transactions in the financial markets are trading property rights for stuff produced long ago. (As an analogy, a house that was built 30 years ago has nothing to do with current production, so the sale of the house doesn't factor into this year's GDP. Only the sales of newly constructed houses figure into this year's GDP.)

Counting stuff when it's made, not when it's sold

Newly produced output is counted as part of GDP as soon as it's produced, even before the output gets sold. That makes keeping track of the money associated with new production a little tricky.

For example, as soon as construction on a new house is completed, its market value of £300,000 is estimated and counted as part of GDP right then, even though the house may not be sold for months. Suppose construction was completed on 29 December 2008, adding £300,000 to 2008's GDP. If the house is subsequently sold on 21 February 2009, it doesn't count in 2009's GDP because double counting isn't allowed.

When sold, the house is considered old property and not new production. Economists just say that the property right to this (now old) house has changed hands from the builder to the new owner. Because trading old assets obviously involves no new production, it doesn't count in GDP.

This accounting convention applies to firms producing any sort of output good whatsoever. If Sony produces a TV on 31 December 2008, the value of that TV is counted in 2008's GDP, even though it won't be sold to a customer until the following year. A handy way to think about this is to imagine that Sony builds the TV and then, in effect, sells it to itself when it puts the TV into inventory. This 'sale' is what is counted in GDP for the year 2008. When the TV is later sold from inventory to a customer, the process is just an exchange of assets (trading the TV for cash).

The fact that output is counted when produced, rather than when sold, is a red flag when interpreting GDP statistics to gauge the health of the economy. High GDP means only that a lot of stuff is being produced and put into inventory, and not necessarily that firms are selling lots of stuff.

In fact, GDP can be high and the economy can be about to go into a recession, because inventories are piling up and managers are soon going to cut back on production in order to get

inventories back down to target levels. Consequently, economists who try to forecast where the economy is heading pay
much more attention to inventory levels than they do to last
quarter's GDP.

All things increase GDP

Generally speaking, higher GDP is better than lower GDP
because more output produced means higher potential living
standards, including better healthcare for the sick and more
money to aid the needy.

But higher GDP doesn't guarantee that happiness is increasing
because GDP often goes up when bad things happen. For example, if a major flood destroys a large section of a city, GDP goes
up as reconstruction kicks into gear and lots of new output is
produced to replace what was destroyed. But, of course, everyone would prefer that the flood not happen in the first place.

Similarly, higher GDP may be possible in certain situations
only if you're willing to tolerate more pollution or greater
income inequality. Countries experiencing rapid economic
development and quickly rising living standards often also get
dirtier environments, as well as more social unrest because
some people are getting richer much faster than others. The
GDP number doesn't reflect these negative conditions.

GDP also doesn't count the value of leisure. Many of your
favourite times have probably come about when you weren't
producing or consuming anything that would count in GDP –
sitting on the beach, climbing a mountain, taking a walk.
Moreover, an increase in GDP often comes at the price of
sacrificing these leisure activities – meaning that when you
see an increase in GDP, overall well-being or happiness hasn't
necessarily improved. So although policies that raise GDP are
generally beneficial for society, the costs involved in creating
the rising output must always be examined.

Introducing the GDP Equation

So far in this chapter, we've only *introduced* you to GDP. Now
we want you and GDP to make friends so that you can understand all GDP's little secrets – in particular, its constituent

parts and how they behave. This discussion is doubly useful because it makes the standard Keynesian macroeconomic model (which we introduce in Chapter 6) much easier to understand and manipulate.

The Keynesian model was first developed in 1936 by economist John Maynard Keynes in his book *The General Theory of Employment, Interest and Money*. His text was so influential, in fact, that it led to macroeconomics becoming a separate field of study for economists.

Earlier in this chapter, we explain that you can measure GDP by adding up all the expenditures made on purchasing goods and services or by adding up all the incomes that are derived from producing goods and services. The two numbers have to be equal. So this switch to counting up GDP using expenditure is totally legitimate.

The expenditure equation for totalling up GDP adds together the four traditional expenditure categories – consumption *(C)*, investment *(I)*, government *(G)* and net exports *(NX)* – to equal the value in pounds (or whatever currency a given country is using) of all goods and services produced domestically in that period, or the GDP *(Y)*. In terms of algebra, the equation looks like this:

$$Y = C + I + G + NX \tag{1}$$

Here's a quick look at the four expenditure variables that total up to GDP. As a group, they buy up every last bit of output produced in our country in a given period.

- ✔ *C* **stands for consumption expenditures** made by households on goods and services, whether domestically produced or produced abroad.

- ✔ *I* **stands for investment expenditures** made by firms on new capital goods including buildings, factories and equipment. *I* also contains changes in inventories, because any goods produced but not sold during a period have to go into firms' inventories and are counted as inventory investments.

- ✔ *G* **stands for government purchases of goods and services** (they've got to buy paperclips).

> ✔ *NX* **stands for net exports,** which is defined as all a country's exports *(EX)* minus all its imports *(IM)*, or *NX* = *EX* – *IM*. *EX* is the value in pounds of our output that foreigners are buying. *IM* is the value in pounds of their output that we're buying.

C is for consumption

Household consumption spending accounts for about 67 per cent of GDP – far more than the other three components combined. Many factors affect how much of their income households decide to spend on consumption and how much of it they decide to save for the future.

Macroeconomists model consumption very simply, as a function of people's after-tax, or disposable, incomes. You can derive disposable income algebraically using this handy three-step process:

1. **Start with *Y*, the total income in the economy.** In Keynes's equation, *Y* equals total expenditures, but because income equals expenditures, you can use it for income as well.

2. **Figure out how much tax people have to pay.** For simplicity, assume that the only tax is an income tax and that the income tax rate is given by *t*. For example, *t* = 0.25 means a tax rate of 25 per cent of people's incomes. Consequently, the total taxes that people pay, *T*, is given by $T = t \times Y$.

3. **Subtract people's taxes, *T*, from their incomes, *Y*, to figure out their after-tax incomes.** Economists refer to this amount as *disposable income* and write it algebraically as Y_D. Subtracting taxes from income looks like this:

$$Y_D = Y - T = Y - t \times Y = (1 - t) \times Y \qquad (2)$$

After you derive disposable income, you use a simple model to figure consumption expenditures made by households. The model says that consumption, *C*, is a function of disposable income and a couple of other variables, C_o and *c*.

$$C = C_o + c \times Y_D \qquad (3)$$

Lowercase c is called the *marginal propensity to consume,* or MPC, where c is always a number between 0 and 1 that indicates the rate at which you choose to consume income rather than save it. For example, if $c = 0.9$, you consume 90 pence of every £1 of disposable income that you have after paying taxes. (You save the other 10 pence.)

The actual value of the marginal propensity to consume, c, is determined by the individual and varies from person to person depending on how much of their disposable incomes they like to save. But what is C_o? Think of it as how much people consume even if they have zero disposable income this year. (If you assume that $Y_D = 0$ in the equation $C = C_o + c \times Y_D$, that equation reduces to $C = C_o$.) But where does the money come from to pay for C_o if you have zero disposable income? It comes from your personal savings, which you've piled up over the years. Economists call this dis-saving.

The overall equation $C = C_o + c \times Y_D$ says that your total consumption expenditure in an economy is your emergency level (when you have zero income) C_o plus a part of your disposable income given by $c \times Y_D$.

For the rest of this book, we assume that the equation $C = C_o + c \times Y_D$ is a good enough model of how consumption expenditures are determined in the economy. The equation isn't perfectly realistic, but it does show that consumption is reduced by higher tax rates and that people make a decision about how much of their disposable incomes to save or consume. The equation allows us to analyse the effects of policies that change tax rates and the effects of other policies that encourage people to spend higher or lower fractions of their incomes.

1 is for investment in capital stock

Investment is vitally important because the economy's capacity to produce depends on how much capital is available to make output. The capital stock increases when firms purchase new tools, buildings, machines, computers and so on to help produce consumption goods. Investment is a flow that increases the capital stock of the economy.

But, of course, capital wears out as it's used, by rusting, breaking down or being thrown away when it becomes obsolete. Economists call all these flows that decrease the capital stock *depreciation*. Naturally, firms must make some investments just to replace the capital that has depreciated. But any investment in excess of depreciation causes the overall size of the capital stock to increase, creating more potential output for people to consume.

The flow of investment spending over any period of time depends on the comparisons that firms make between the potential benefits and the costs of buying pieces of capital. The potential benefits are measured in terms of potential profits, and the costs of buying are measured by the interest rate, regardless of whether or not a firm borrows to buy a given piece of capital.

If a firm needs to borrow to buy capital, higher interest rates mean that the firm is less likely to borrow money because of the high loan-repayment costs. However, even if a firm has enough cash on hand to buy a given piece of equipment, higher interest rates force the firm to decide between using the cash to buy the equipment and lending it to someone else. The higher the interest rates, the more attractive lending the money becomes. Consequently, higher interest rates discourage investment regardless of whether firms have to borrow to fund investment.

Economists model the amount of investment expenditure that firms desire to make, I, as a function of the interest rate, r, which is given as a percentage. The equation that we use is typical of most introductory macroeconomics books:

$$I = I_o - I_r \times r \qquad\qquad (4)$$

This equation is similar in spirit to the consumption equation in the previous section except for the minus sign, which indicates that when the interest rate rises, I falls.

The parameter I_r tells you how much I falls in an entire economy for any given increase in interest rates. For example, suppose that r rises by one percentage point. If I_r is, say, 10 billion, you know that each one percentage point increase in interest rates decreases investment by £10 billion.

The parameter I_o tells you how much investment occurs if interest rates are zero. In truth, interest rates very rarely fall all the way to zero, but suppose that they do. Then the second term in the equation equals zero, leaving you with $I = I_o$.

The equation as a whole says that if interest rates were zero, investment expenditures max out at I_o. But as interest rates rise above zero and keep on rising, investment falls more and more. In fact, rates potentially rise so high that investment spending falls to zero.

The relationship between rates and investment is one reason why the government's ability to set interest rates has great bearing on the economy. By setting interest rates, the government can determine how much businesses want to spend buying investment goods. In particular, if the economy is in a recession, the government can lower interest rates in order to raise firms' expenditures on investment and (we hope) help improve the economy.

G whizz! Government, that is

In most countries, a huge portion of GDP is consumed by government. The size of that portion is a matter of some variation. According to the international Organisation for Economic Co-operation and Development, it stands at 42 per cent for the US and 48 per cent on average for the EU (it's 46 per cent in the UK). If you take away *transfer payments* – what gets paid out of tax revenues to transfer in, for example, benefits – which is what we do in this model, the figures are 23 per cent for the US and 27 per cent for the UK.

A government gets the money to buy all that output from taxation and borrowing. If a government's tax revenues are exactly equal to its expenditures, it has a *balanced budget*. If tax revenues are greater than expenditures, a government is running a *budget surplus*. But if expenditures exceed tax revenues, which can happen when a government borrows the difference on the financial markets, that government is running a *budget deficit*.

Governments borrow by selling bonds. A typical bond says that in exchange for £10,000 right now, the government promises to give you back £10,000 in ten years and, in the meantime, pay you £1,000 per year for each of the intervening years. If you accept the deal and buy the bond, you're in effect lending the government £10,000 right now and getting a 10 per cent per year return until the government returns your £10,000 in ten years.

Economists largely ignore the political machinations that go into determining government expenditures because the economic effects of government expenditure, G, depend on how big the expenditure turns out to be and not on how it got to be that size. Consequently, for the rest of this book, we make the simplifying assumption that government expenditures can be denoted as:

$$G = G_o \tag{5}$$

That is, G is equal to some number pre-determined by the political process, G_o.

G includes only government expenditures on newly produced goods and services, and doesn't include government expenditures that merely transfer money from one person to another. For example, when the government taxes you and gives the money to another person, that transaction has nothing to do with currently produced goods and services and consequently doesn't count as part of G. So when we talk about G, we're talking about only the government's purchases of currently produced goods and services.

NX: Exports less imports

When your country sells domestically made goods and services to someone or some firm in another country, such sales are called *exports*, or *EX*. When someone in your country buys something produced abroad, such purchases are called *imports*, or *IM*. *Net exports*, or *NX*, is simply the total value of all exports minus the total value of all imports during a given period of time. When using the expenditure method for totalling up GDP, you add in net exports, *NX*.

The whole point of totting up expenditures to get GDP is to figure out how many total pounds were expended on products made within your own country. Most of that expenditure is made by locals, but foreigners can also expend money on your products. That's exactly what happens when they pay you for the goods that you export to them. Consequently, you have to add in *EX* if you want to get a correct measure of expenditures made on stuff you produce domestically.

You have to subtract your imports of foreign goods because you must differentiate the total expenditures that domestic residents make on *all* goods and services from their expenditures on *domestically made* goods and services. Total expenditures on all goods and services, both domestic and foreign, are *C* (see the earlier section 'C is for consumption'). If you want to get just the part that's spent on domestically made stuff, you have to subtract the value of imports, *IM*, because all money spent on imports is money that's *not* spent on domestically made goods and services. So *C − IM* gives the amount of money that domestic residents spend on domestically produced output.

The result is that you can write your GDP expenditures equation that totals up all expenditures made on domestically produced output as follows:

$$Y = C - IM + I + G + EX \qquad (6)$$

But the equation is normally rearranged to put the exports and imports next to each other like this:

$$Y = C + I + G + EX - IM \qquad (7)$$

The reason for rearranging is because *EX − IM* quickly reveals your country's *trade balance*. When *EX − IM* is positive, you're exporting more than you're importing; when it's negative, you're importing more than you're exporting.

International trade is hugely important, and you need a good understanding of not only why a trade balance can be positive or negative, but also why you shouldn't necessarily worry if that balance is negative rather than positive.

The Effect of International Trade

Modern countries do a huge amount of trading with other countries – so huge, in fact, that for many countries imports and exports are equal to more than 50 per cent of their GDPs.

So, now is a good time to focus a little more deeply on the *NX* part of the GDP expenditure equation, $Y = C + I + G + NX$.

Understanding how international trade affects the economy is essential if you hope to have a complete understanding of macroeconomics. This section explains why trade deficits (negative values of *NX*) aren't necessarily bad and just why engaging in international trade – even when it means sustaining trade deficits – is typically hugely beneficial.

Trade deficits can be good!

If your exports exceed your imports, you have a *trade surplus*, whereas if your imports exceed your exports, you have a *trade deficit*. Unfortunately, the words *surplus* and *deficit* carry strong connotations that make it sound like surpluses are necessarily better than deficits, which is simply untrue – not that you'd know it from the rhetoric that politicians throw around. They make it sound as if trade deficits are always bad and always lead to calamity.

To understand why the politicians are wrong consider an example of two individuals who want to trade. Each person starts with $100, and each produces a product for sale. The first person grows and sells apples for $1 each. The second person grows and sells oranges, also for $1 each. Each of them produces 50 pieces of fruit.

Next, suppose that the apple grower really likes oranges and wants to buy 30 of them for $30, and that the orange grower wants to buy 20 apples for $20. Each person is happy to satisfy the other's desires, so the apple grower spends $30 buying oranges from the orange grower, and the orange grower spends $20 buying apples from the apple grower.

These trades shouldn't cause alarm bells to ring. When people start looking at the trades using the terms *trade surplus* and *trade deficit*, however, they often come to the false conclusion that only one of the growers benefits from the trades when, in reality, they were both quite eager to trade in this way.

To see where the confusion arises, notice that in the vocabulary of international trade, the apple grower exports only $20 worth of apples but imports $30 worth of oranges. At the same time, the orange grower exports £30 worth of oranges but imports only £20 worth of apples. As a result, the apple grower is running a £10 trade deficit and the orange grower is running a £10 trade surplus.

Does this mean that the apple grower is worse off than the orange grower? No. Each person started with £150 worth of stuff: their respective £100 cash piles plus £50 each worth of fruit. When they finish trading, they each still have £150 worth of stuff. The apple grower has £90 of cash plus £30 worth of apples and £30 worth of oranges. The orange grower has £110 of cash plus £20 worth of oranges and £20 worth of apples.

Saying that their trading has made one of them poorer is way off the mark. In fact, both of them are happier with their arrangements of wealth after trading than they were before trading because their trades were voluntary. If the apple grower would have been happier keeping his initial holdings of £100 cash and 50 apples, he wouldn't have traded for oranges. And the same applies with the orange grower.

As long as international trade is voluntary, all trades enhance happiness (that is, create gains, although those gains may not be equally divided). To concentrate on whether a trade deficit or surplus exists is to completely miss the point that international trade is simply a rearrangement of assets between countries that makes everyone happier. Even the country running the trade deficit is happier.

Considering assets

To people who hate trade deficits, the fact that the apple grower's cash pile falls from £100 before the trade to only £90 after the trade looks spooky, because these people focus totally on the fact that the apple grower is £10 poorer in terms of cash after the trading. And they're even more peeved because that £10 ends up with the orange grower, giving her a commanding £110 to £90 advantage in terms of cash piles.

This perspective misses the fact that the apple grower's overall wealth is still £150 and that he now has a distribution of assets that is more pleasing to him. But, if you point this out, deficit haters respond by asking you what happens after the apple grower eats his 30 apples and 30 oranges and after the orange grower eats her 20 apples and 20 oranges. In the end, all that the fruit growers have left are their respective cash piles. Because the apple grower has £20 less cash than the orange grower, he must be worse off by running a trade deficit.

Again, this reasoning misses the point that the apple grower was happier trading and ending up with £90 of cash than he would have been not trading and ending up with £100 in cash. If it weren't for trade, he'd have had a very boring diet of only apples.

Wielding a comparative advantage

The argument that even countries running trade deficits are better off because they get to consume a mix of goods and services they wouldn't get otherwise rests solely on the benefits of trading things that have already been produced. But an even better argument for international trade is the fact that it actually increases the total amount of output produced in the world, meaning that more output per person results, and overall living standards rise.

This argument, known as *comparative advantage*, was developed by the English economist David Ricardo in 1817 as a forceful rebuttal against import tariffs known as the *Corn Laws*, which heavily taxed imports of foreign-grown grain at the time. These laws kept the price of grain high, and so the nobility that owned the vast majority of farmland favoured retaining them. Naturally, the poor were opposed because the laws drove up the price of their basic food supply: bread.

Ricardo pointed out that abolishing restrictions on international trade would, in addition to helping England's poor, actually make England and all the countries it traded with richer by encouraging them to specialise in the production of goods and services that each of them was able to produce at the lowest possible cost. He demonstrated that this process of specialisation would increase total worldwide output and thereby raise living standards.

The logic behind the comparative advantage argument is most easily understood by thinking in terms of people instead of countries. Consider a lawyer named Heather and her brother Adam, who works as a bike mechanic. Heather is very good at filing patents for new discoveries, but she's also very good at repairing bicycles. In fact, she's faster at repairing them than her brother. On the other hand, Adam can also file patents, though not as quickly as Heather. Table 4-1 lists how many bike repairs and patent filings each of them can do in one day if they put all their efforts into only one of the activities.

Table 4-1 Productivity for Heather and Adam per Day

Person	*Patent Productivity*	*Bike Repair Productivity*
Heather	6	12
Adam	2	10

In one day's work, Heather can produce 6 patents or repair 12 bikes, whereas Adam can file 2 patents or repair 10 bikes. Heather is more efficient than her brother at producing both patents and bike repairs because she can convert one day's labour into more of either good than Adam.

Economists say that Heather has an *absolute advantage* over Adam at producing both goods, meaning that she's the more efficient producer of both; with the same amount of labour input (one workday), she can produce more than her brother. Before David Ricardo came along and explained comparative advantage, the only thing anyone knew to look at was absolute advantage. And when they saw situations like that of Heather and Adam, they concluded (incorrectly) that because Heather is more efficient than Adam at both tasks, she doesn't need to trade with him.

In other words, people used to believe, incorrectly, that because Heather is better than Adam at repairing bikes, she should not only work hard as a patent attorney filing lots of patents, but also fix her own bike whenever it breaks down. Ricardo pointed out that this argument based on absolute advantage is bogus and that Heather should, in fact, *never* fix bikes despite the fact that she's the most efficient bike repairer around. The nifty thing that Ricardo realised is that the world is better off if each person (and country) specialises.

The key insight of comparative advantage is that the proper measure of cost when considering whether Heather should produce one good or the other isn't how many hours of labour input it takes her to produce one patent or one bike repair (which is the logic behind absolute advantage). Instead, the true cost is how much production of one good you have to give up to produce a unit of the other good.

To produce one patent, Heather must give up the chance to repair two bikes. In contrast, to make one patent, Adam has to give up the chance to repair five bikes. So, Heather is the lower-cost producer of patents and, therefore, should specialise in filing patents. And Adam should specialise in bike repairs because he's the lower-cost producer of bike repairs.

On a larger scale, countries should specialise in the production of goods and services that they can deliver at lower costs than other countries. If countries are free to do this, everything that's produced comes from the lowest-cost producer. Because this arrangement leads to the most efficient possible production, total output increases, thereby raising living standards.

By letting comparative advantage guide who makes what, free trade increases total world output and thereby raises living standards. Under free trade, each country specialises in its area(s) of comparative advantage and then trades with other countries to obtain the goods and services it desires to consume.

Don't be tricked by absolute advantage. As you can see in this section's example, Heather has an absolute advantage at everything but has a comparative advantage only at filing patents. Having an absolute advantage means that you can make something at a lower cost as measured in inputs. (For example, Heather requires fewer hours of labour input to file a patent than Adam.) However, what matters in life isn't inputs but outputs – the things that people actually want to consume. By focusing on costs as measured in terms of alternative types of output that must be given up to produce something, comparative advantage ensures that you're focusing on being efficient in terms of what really matters: output.

Chapter 5

Inflation: More Money Isn't Always a Good Thing

• •

In This Chapter

▶ Risking inflation by printing too much money

▶ Measuring inflation with price indexes

▶ Adjusting interest rates to take account of inflation

• •

*I*nflation is the word economists use to describe a situation in which the general level of prices in the economy is rising. This situation doesn't mean that every price of every good is going up – a few prices may even be falling – but the overall trend is upward. Typically, the trend is for prices to go up only a small percentage each year, but people dislike even mild inflation because, face it, no one likes paying higher prices. Mild inflation also causes problems such as making retirement planning difficult. After all, if you don't know how expensive things are going to be when you retire, calculating with any certainty how much money you need to be saving right now is difficult.

Things can go from bad to worse if inflation really gets out of control and prices begin rising 20 or 30 per cent per month – something that has happened in more than a few countries in the last century. Such situations of *hyperinflation* usually accompany a major economic collapse featuring high unemployment and a major decrease in the production of goods and services.

The good news, however, is that economists know exactly what causes inflation and precisely how to stop it. The culprit is a money supply that grows too quickly, and the solution is simply to slow or halt the growth of the money supply. Unfortunately, some political pressure is always exerted in favour of inflation so that simply knowing how to prevent inflation doesn't necessarily mean it isn't going to develop.

In this chapter, we share some things about money and inflation that you may not already know, including why governments are often tempted to print a lot of money to pay for budget deficits, why doing so is actually a form of taxation and why certain groups encourage the government to print a ton of money. We also show you why printing lots of money causes inflation, how to measure inflation and how to measure the effect of inflation on interest rates.

The Risks of Too Much Money

We can't overstate how important money is to the proper functioning of the economy. Without money, you'd waste most of your time *bartering*, or arranging trades of one good for another – you know, like in primary school ('I'll trade you my apple for your cake!'). Bartering works well only in the rare circumstance that you run into somebody who has what you want and who wants what you have.

Money provides a medium of exchange so that you can still trade for the cake from the kid next to you, even if you don't have an apple. Money can be any good, object or thing, but its defining characteristic is that it's accepted as payment for all other goods and services. In today's economy, people pay for things using a wide variety of monies, including government-issued cash, cheques drawn on private bank deposits and electronic payments facilitated by credit cards and debit cards.

Balancing money supply and demand

As with everything in life, balance is essential. If a government prints too much money, prices go up and you get inflation. If a government prints too little, prices go down and you get deflation. But how much money is the right amount? And why does printing too much or too little cause inflation or deflation?

Basically, the value of money is determined by supply and demand (which we discuss in detail in Chapter 8):

- ✔ The *supply* of money is under government control, and the government can very easily print more money any time it wants to.

- ✔ The *demand* for money derives from its usefulness as a means of paying for things and from the fact that having money means not having to engage in barter.

For any given supply of money, supply and demand interact to set a value for each unit of money. If money is in short supply, each piece of money is very valuable; fewer pieces of money translate into fewer chances to avoid having to engage in barter. But if the government greatly increases the supply of money, each individual unit of money loses value because getting enough money together to avoid barter is easy.

Prices and the value of money are *inversely related*, meaning that when the value of money goes up, prices go down (and vice versa). To see this relationship, suppose that money is in short supply and is consequently very valuable. Because money's very valuable, it buys a lot of stuff. For example, imagine that £10 buys 1,000 grams of coffee (that is, you get 10 grams for 10 pence). But if money's very common, each unit isn't very valuable. In this case, say that £10 buys only 100 grams of coffee (that is, you get only 1 gram for your 10 pence and have to pay £1 to get your 10 grams). Therefore, the greater the supply of money, the higher the prices.

The demand for money tends to grow slowly over time; growing economies produce more stuff, and consumers demand more money with which to buy the available stuff. Depending on how a government reacts to consumer demand for more money, three scenarios are possible:

- ✔ If a government increases the supply of money *at the same rate* as the growing demand for money, prices don't change. In other words, if supply and demand for money grow at equal rates, the relative value of money doesn't change.

- ✔ If the government increases the supply of money *faster* than the demand for money grows, inflation results as money becomes relatively more plentiful and each piece of money becomes relatively less valuable. With each piece of money carrying less value, you need more of it to buy stuff, causing prices to rise.

✔ If the government increases the supply of money *slower* than the demand for money grows, deflation results because each piece of money grows relatively more valuable. Buying any given good or service requires less money.

You may be wondering if any way exists to know exactly how much inflation you can expect from printing any given amount of extra money. You're in luck! The *quantity theory of money* states that the overall level of prices in the economy is proportional to the quantity of money circulating in the economy. *Proportional* just means that things go up by equal amounts, so the quantity theory can also be stated this way: if you double the money supply, you double prices.

But *why* would any government want to cause inflation or deflation of any size whatsoever? For the answer to that question, read on!

Giving in to the inflation temptation

Inflation of prices is often explained by governments printing more paper money or producing a large amount of cheap-metal coins, which vastly increases the supply of money and makes each piece of money less precious. As sellers demand higher prices to make up for the fact that each piece of money is worth less, you get inflation.

So why in the world do governments ever print too much money? Good question. Historically, governments circulate more money in three circumstances:

✔ When governments can't raise enough tax revenue to pay their obligations

✔ When governments feel pressure from debtors who want inflation so that they can repay their debts using less valuable money

✔ When governments want to try to stimulate the economy during a recession or depression

As you find out more about these three reasons for increasing the money supply, keep in mind what we discuss in the previous section: if the supply of money increases faster than the demand for money, inflation results. Consequently, no matter what reason a government has for increasing the supply of money, it runs the risk of inflation. And that's true both for good reasons, such as wanting to help the economy out of a recession, and for bad reasons, such as helping debtors to repay their loans using less valuable money.

Heading for hyperinflation

Governments almost always have debts, and printing extra money can be a tempting way to pay them. Quite often, a government wants to spend more money than it's collecting in tax revenue. One solution is to borrow the shortfall, but another is simply to print up new bills to cover the difference.

Until very recently, printing new bills was difficult because most of the world's paper currencies were backed by a valuable metal, such as gold. Under this system, every piece of paper money circulating in the economy was convertible into a specific quantity of gold so that anyone holding cash was able to redeem their cash for gold any time they wanted. This so-called *gold standard* made it difficult for the government to devalue the currency by printing too much money because it first had to get more gold with which to back the new money. Because purchasing gold is expensive, governments were effectively restrained from increasing their money supplies.

A major break occurred in 1971 when, in order to pay for the escalating costs of the Vietnam War, President Nixon took the United States off the gold standard and put the US on the *fiat system*, in which paper currency isn't backed by anything. People just have to accept the currency as though it has value. In fact, *fiat* is Latin for 'Let it be done'. So when you say *fiat money*, you're basically referring to how a government creates money simply by ordering it into existence. The problem with a fiat money system is that nothing limits the number of little pieces of paper that the government can print up.

The trouble with printing money to pay your debts and obligations is that as soon as the money's out there, people spend it, drive up prices and cause inflation. And if you print more and more money, you end up with people offering shopkeepers and producers more and more money for the same amount of goods. The result is like a giant auction where everybody bidding on items keeps getting more and more money to bid with. The more money you print, the less each individual pound, euro, dollar, doubloon or whatever is worth.

If a government gets into the habit of rapidly printing new money to pay its bills, inflation can soon reach or even surpass 20 or 30 per cent per month, a situation referred to as a *hyperinflation*. Economists hate hyperinflations because they greatly disrupt daily life and ruin the investment climate.

Hyperinflation causes people to waste huge amounts of time trying to avoid the effects of rising prices. During the Weimar hyperinflation in Germany men working at factories were paid two or even three times a day because money lost its value so quickly. Their wives waited at the factories to take the money immediately to the nearest shops, trying to spend the pay before it lost most of its value.

Hyperinflation also destroys the incentive to save because the only sensible thing to do with money during a hyperinflation is to spend it as quickly as you can before it loses even more of its value. Those people whose life savings were in German marks during the Weimar hyperinflation soon found that what they had worked so hard to amass had become worthless. And people thinking about saving for the future were greatly discouraged because they knew that any money they saved would soon lose all value. The discouragement of saving causes major business problems because if people aren't saving, no money is available for businesses to borrow for new investments. And without new investments, the economy can't grow.

The politics of inflation

Even if the government isn't trying to use inflation to avoid tax increases, one group in particular always pressures it to circulate more money. You may even be a member of this group – they're called *borrowers*.

To understand the politics of inflation, you need to understand that one of the functions of money is as a *standard of deferred payment*. What does that mean? Imagine that you borrow £1,000 to invest on your farm, promising to pay the bank back £1,200 next year. For the past several years, prices in the economy have been stable, and, in particular, the pigs that you raise have sold for £100 each. Essentially, your loan lets you borrow the equivalent of ten pigs with the promise to pay back twelve pigs next year.

But you have an idea. You lobby your MP to lobby the government to print more money. In a collective rush of blood to the head, the Treasury agrees and instructs the mint to print a load more money. All that new money causes an inflation, after which the price of pigs rises to £200 each. Now you have to sell only six pigs to pay back the £1,200 loan, leaving you with more pigs, you pig!

Lenders, of course, oppose the inflationary desires of borrowers. If you were putting money in the bank, you'd do everything in your power to stop the inflation. If the change goes through, not only are your profits ruined, but also you're an outright loser. In the first year, your loan of £1,000 is the equivalent of ten pigs. But after the inflation, you get paid back the equivalent of only six pigs. You take a 40 per cent loss on the value of your loan. Too much inflation, and a lender ends up being a pig in a poke.

As long as economies use money, lenders and borrowers are always going to be lined up against each other, both trying to sway the government.

Stimulating the economy with inflation

A much more legitimate reason for governments to print more money has the very respectable name of monetary policy. *Monetary policy* refers to the decisions a government makes about increasing or decreasing the money supply in order to stimulate or slow down the economy.

The basic idea is that if the economy is in a recession, the government may print up some new money and spend it. All the goods and services it buys with the new money stimulate the economy immediately. In addition, all those businesses that received money from the government can now go out and spend that new money themselves. And whoever receives the money from them also goes out and spends it to buy things. In fact, this pattern can theoretically go on forever and stimulate a heck of a lot of economic activity – enough to lift an economy out of a recession.

If this result sounds too good to be true, that's because it is. And the reason is inflation. When people start spending all that new money, it drives up prices. Eventually, the only effect of the government's good intentions is that prices rise and no additional goods are sold. For example, if the government doubles the money supply, businesses double the prices they charge because each piece of money is worth half as much as before. Consequently, the total amount of goods and services sold is the same as before because, although twice as much money is being spent, prices are also twice as high.

The sad upshot is that an increase in the money supply stimulates the economy only when the increase is a surprise.

If the government can print the money and start spending it before people can raise prices, you get an increase in the amount of goods and services sold. Eventually, of course, people figure it out and raise prices, but until they do, the monetary stimulus works.

Unfortunately, continuing to fool people is difficult. You can surprise people once, but the second time is harder and the third time harder still. In fact, if the government keeps trying to surprise people, people begin to anticipate the government and raise prices even before the government prints more money. Consequently, most modern governments have decided against using this sort of monetary stimulus and now strive for zero inflation or very low inflation.

Tallying up the effects of inflation

In recent years in the UK, prices have risen only a small amount each year (about 2.5 per cent annually, although the figure has been much higher in the past). However, even moderate inflation causes problems by cutting into the practical benefits of using money instead of barter. You can get a better sense of this fact by looking at the four functions that economists generally ascribe to money and the ways in which inflation screws up each of them:

✔ **Money is a *store of value*.** If you sell a cow today for one gold coin, you should be able to turn around and trade that gold coin back for a cow tomorrow or next week or next month. When money retains its value, you can hold it instead of holding cows, or property or any other asset.

Inflation weakens the use of money as a store of value because each unit of currency is worth less and less as time passes.

✔ **Money is a *unit of account*.** When money is widely accepted in an economy, it often becomes the unit of account in which people write contracts. People start using phrases like '£50 worth of timber' rather than '50 square metres of timber'.

This practice makes sense if money holds its value over time, but in the presence of inflation, using money as a unit of account creates problems because the value of money declines. For example, if the value of money is falling fast, how much timber, exactly, is '£50 worth of timber'?

✔ **Money is a *standard of deferred payment*.** If you want a cow, you probably wouldn't borrow a cow with the promise to repay two cows next year. Instead, you'd be much more likely to borrow and repay in terms of money. That is, you'd borrow one gold coin and use it to buy a cow, after promising to pay back two gold coins next year.

The progressive devaluing of money during a period of inflation makes lenders reluctant to use money as a standard of deferred payment. Suppose a friend asks to borrow £100, promising to pay you £120 in a year. That seems like a good deal – after all, the interest rate is 20 per cent. But if prices are rapidly rising and the value of money is falling, how much are you going to be able to buy with that £120 next year?

Inflation makes people reluctant to lend money. They fear that when the loans are repaid, the repayment cash isn't going to have the same purchasing power as the cash that was lent. This uncertainty can have a devastating effect on the development of new businesses, which rely heavily on loans to fund their operations.

✔ **Money is a *medium of exchange*.** Money is a *medium* (literally meaning 'something in the middle') of trade between buyers and sellers because it can be directly exchanged for anything else, making buying and selling much easier. In a barter economy, an orange farmer who wants to buy beer may have to first trade oranges for apples and then apples for beer because the guy selling the beer wants only apples. Money can eliminate this kind of hassle.

But if inflation is bad enough, money is no longer an effective medium of exchange. During hyperinflations, economies often revert to barter so that buyers and sellers don't have to worry about the falling value of money. For example, in a healthy economy, the orange seller can first sell oranges for cash and then trade the cash for beer. But during a hyperinflation, between the time he sells the oranges for cash and buys the beer, the price of beer may have skyrocketed so high that he can't buy very much beer with the cash. During a hyperinflation, economies have to resort to cumbersome bartering. At the very least, if one currency becomes debased, people often tend to use a trusted foreign currency, usually the US dollar, as the medium of exchange.

Another effect of inflation is that it functions as a giant tax increase. This seems strange because you normally think of governments taxing by taking away chunks of people's money, not by printing more money. But a tax is basically anything that transfers private property to the government. Debasing the currency or printing more money can have this effect.

Suppose that the government wants to buy a £20,000 van for a village. The honest way to go about this is to use £20,000 of tax revenues to buy a van. But a sneakier way is to print £20,000 in new cash to buy the van. By printing and spending the new cash, the government has converted £20,000 of private property – the van – into public property. So, printing new cash works just like a tax. Because printing new money ends up causing inflation, this type of taxation is often referred to as an *inflation tax*.

Not only is the inflation tax sneaky, but also it unfairly targets the poor because they spend nearly all their income on goods and services, the costs of which go up greatly during an inflation. By contrast, because the rich have the opportunity to save a lot of their incomes instead of spending everything they take in, proportionately they're less affected by an inflation tax. By investing their savings in assets (like property) whose prices go up during inflation, the rich can insulate themselves from a great deal of the harm caused by inflation.

Measuring Inflation: Price Indexes

Inflation can cause lots of problems, so in order for the government to keep inflation under control, it needs a way to measure inflation accurately.

As we explain in the earlier section 'Buying an Inflation: The Risks of Too Much Money', the value of money is determined by the interaction of the *supply* of money with the *demand* for money. The supply of money is under the government's control, but the government can't directly ascertain the demand for money, so it has to look at how supply and demand interact in order to determine how much to increase or decrease the money supply:

- ✔ If an inflation is in effect, the government knows that the supply of money is increasing faster than the demand for money. If it wants to tame the inflation, it needs to reduce the supply of money.

- ✔ If a deflation is in effect, the government knows that the demand for money is increasing faster than the supply of money. If it wants to end the deflation, it needs to increase the supply of money.

Because inflation is a *general* increase in prices, the best way to look for it is to see whether the cost of buying a large collection of many different things changes over time. If, instead, you look at only one or two prices, you may end up confusing a *relative* price change for a *general* price change. (A relative price change is when one price goes up relative to the others, which remain unchanged.)

Economists arbitrarily define some large collection of goods and services and refer to this collection as a *market basket.* They then find out how much money is necessary to buy this basket at various times to measure inflation. In the UK several different measures have been used to try to capture the effect of inflation. Until recently the headline measure was the RPI-X; that is, the Retail Price Index less mortgage interest (to strip out the effect of interest rates, which otherwise complicate the picture too much). Recently, though, a new measure, called the CPI (Consumer Price Index), does roughly the same thing. The CPI captures the price of a basket of goods, and is often tweaked to take into account the change in consumer purchases over time. Other bodies such as the Organization for Economic Cooperation and Development (OECD) produce figures that are internationally comparable (that is, defined on the same basis across countries).

In the following sections, we show you how this process works by creating a market basket, seeing how this basket can be used to measure inflation and normalising it to a given base year so that calculating inflation rates between any two years is a piece of very agreeable cake.

Creating your very own market basket

The Consumer Price Index involves a large number of products and services – and is a big market basket. Understanding price indexes is easier if you create a simplified index with a very small market basket. In this section, we look at a *very* small market basket containing pizza, beer and textbooks. Because these three items are typical purchases of the undergraduate student population, we shall call it the Undergraduate Price Index.

For each of the three items in the Undergraduate Price Index, we create prices for 2007, 2008 and 2009 and list them in Table 5-1.

Table 5-1	The Undergraduate Price Index			
Item	*Number Bought*	*2007*	*2008*	*2009*
Pizza	10	£10	£9	£9
Beer	60	£2	£2	£2.25
Textbooks	1	£120	£160	£170

In 2007, one medium cheese pizza costs £10, a pint of subsidised student union brown ale £2 and an introductory economics textbook costs £120. The next year, the price of a medium cheese pizza actually falls to £9 because a new pizza outlet opens up next to the old one, causing a price war. Beer still costs £2, but the university bookshop raises the price of the textbook to £160.

In evaluating the index, you also have to track how many of each item the typical student buys each year. For the sake of simplicity, assume that a typical student buys ten cheese pizzas, 60 beers and one economics textbook each year.

Calculating the inflation rate

To calculate how much inflation your university economy has (or deflation, if the cost of living happens to go down), first total up how much the market basket costs each year. In 2007, it costs £340: £100 on pizza (ten pizzas at £10 each), £120 on beer (60 beers at £2 each), and £120 on economics textbooks (one textbook at £120). The cost of buying the same market basket in 2008 is £370. So the cost of buying the same market basket has gone up by £30.

Now that you've done the adding, you need to do some simple algebra. Economists use the capital letter P to denote how many pounds the defined market basket costs. So in this case, P_{2007} means the cost of buying the market basket in 2007 and P_{2008} is the cost of buying the market basket in 2008. We're going to use pi, the Greek letter π (pronounced 'pie') as shorthand for the rate of inflation.

To calculate the rate of inflation, you use a very simple formula:

$$\pi = (P_{Second\ Year} - P_{First\ Year}) / P_{First\ Year} \tag{1}$$

In this case, the formula becomes:

$$\pi = (P_{2008} - P_{2007}) / P_{2007} \tag{2}$$

Substituting in P_{2007} = £340 and P_{2008} = £370, you find that π = 0.088. Multiply by 100 to convert this number into a percentage, and inflation in the Undergraduate Price Index is 8.8 per cent between 2007 and 2008. So, on the basis of this number, a student needs 8.8 per cent more money in 2008 to buy the simple market basket.

Setting up a price index

The undergraduate market basket is a simple example, but when government statisticians compute the Consumer Price Index, they basically do the same thing, just using a lot more goods. They also introduce the concept of a *price index* (or *price level index*) to make calculating and interpreting inflation rates over several years much easier. To set up a price index, they first establish a base year, or index year. Continuing our example, suppose that 2007 is the base year for the Undergraduate Price Index. You can then make a handy mathematical transformation so that the price level in 2007 is fixed at the number 100 and the price levels of every other year are set up so that they're relative to the 100 of the base year.

To make P_{2007} = £340 your base year, divide it by itself. That, of course, gives you 1, which you then multiply by 100 to get 100 ($100 \times 1 = 100$). This may seem like an idiotic thing to do until you realise that if you do the same thing to the other years, you end up with something very useful. Divide P_{2008} by P_{2007} and then multiply that product by 100 to get 108.8. This number is easy to interpret: it's 8.8 per cent larger than 100. Or, put differently, the price level in 2008 is 8.8 per cent larger than the price level in 2007.

You can keep going, using the numbers for 2009 that appear in Table 5-1. For example, P_{2009} = £395. If you divide P_{2009} by P_{2007} and multiply by 100, you get 116.2; the price level in 2009 is 16.2 per cent bigger than the price level in 2007.

Working out the rate of inflation between 2008 and 2009 using these index numbers is also easy. Because the price index level for 2008 is 108.8 and the price index level for 2009 is 116.2, inflation is simply (116.2 – 108.8) / 108.8 = 0.068, or 6.8 per cent.

Figure 5-1 charts the actual values of the Retail Price Index from 1987 to 2006. The index was set to a level of 100 using prices that consumers paid on average over the two-year period ending January 1987.

You can see that the Retail Price Index grew from its initial level of 100 in 1987 to a level of 200 in 2006. That is, to buy what a typical household consumes, you would have needed double the money in 2006 compared to what was needed in

1987, with the worst of the increases occurring in the late 1980s and early 1990s. Or to put it another way, increases in the money supply doubled prices over this 20-year period.

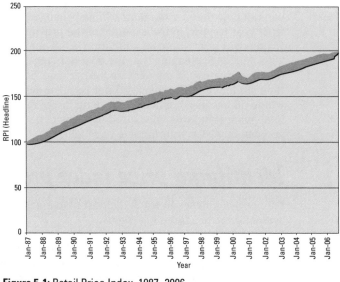

Figure 5-1: Retail Price Index, 1987–2006.

Determining the real standard of living with the price index

Beyond making inflation easy to measure and interpret, price indexes also make it simple to measure the very important difference between real prices and nominal prices. *Nominal prices* are simply money prices, which can change over time due to inflation. Because nominal prices can change, economists like to focus on *real prices*, which keep track of how much of one good you have to give up to get another good, no matter what happens to nominal prices.

For example, suppose that in 2008 you earn £10 an hour and the cost of a DVD is £20. The *real cost* of a DVD to you is two hours of work. Suppose that the next year, the prices of all goods double, but your wages also double so that you are earning £20 an hour and a DVD costs £40. The result is that you still have to work two hours to buy a DVD. So although the *nominal* price of a DVD has doubled, its *real* price in terms of labour – how much labour you have to give up to get a DVD – hasn't changed.

By constructing price indexes such as the CPI, economists can tell how the *real standard of living* changes for people from year to year. In the example of the previous section (using data from Table 5-1), inflation is 8.8 per cent between 2005 and 2006, meaning that the cost of living of a typical undergraduate student went up 8.8 per cent. So if at the same time student incomes rise by 5 per cent, students are actually worse off because costs have gone up faster than incomes. Real living standards, measured in terms of how much stuff you can buy with your income have fallen.

Identifying price index problems

Using price indexes to track the cost of living isn't a flawless system. Here are three big issues:

- ✔ **The market basket can never perfectly reflect family spending.** National Statistics tries to keep track of what a typical family of four purchases when calculating the Consumer Price Index (CPI). But families differ greatly, not only in terms of *what* they buy, but also in terms of *how many* of each thing they buy.

- ✔ **The market basket becomes outdated.** When to replace one product with another in the list is a fine judgement call. Suppose, for example, that National Statistics was deciding whether to include in the market basket DVD players instead of older VCRs. If Britain's national statisticians wait too long, they aren't capturing the change in purchases, but if they do it too soon, they may find that DVDs don't actually catch on and join the museum of dead technology in which case the figures would also be wrong.

- ✔ **The market basket can't account for quality.** Price isn't the only thing that matters to consumers. For example, what if a beer stays the same price but improves in quality from one year to the next? You're getting better beer for the same price, but this quality isn't reflected in the data. This problem is especially severe for things like computers, mobile phones and video games. For these products, quality improves dramatically year after year while prices stay the same or go down.

Each of these problems troubles government statisticians, who are constantly coming up with better price indexes and statistical methods to try to overcome them. The Federal Reserve Bank (the US government agency charged with determining the money supply) has recently come out with an estimate suggesting that the US CPI overstates inflation by 1 to 2 percentage points per year.

The main consequence of this overstatement is that the US government is overly generous with the cost-of-living increases it grants workers and retirees. Each year, government workers and retirees receive pay increases based upon increases in the CPI. These pay increases are designed to ensure that people's real incomes aren't eroded by inflation, but because the CPI is most likely overstating the rate of inflation each year, the cost-of-living increases are overly generous.

Pricing the Future: Nominal and Real Interest Rates

Because inflation erodes the value of a loan repayment, economists have to distinguish between *nominal interest rates* and *real interest rates*. Nominal interest rates are simply the normal money interest rates that you're used to dealing with; they measure the returns to a loan in terms of money borrowed and money returned. Real interest rates, however, compensate for inflation by measuring the returns to a loan in terms of units of stuff lent and units of stuff returned. This distinction is very important because what makes people want to save and invest is the *real* interest rate. After all, what lenders really care about isn't how much money they get back but how much stuff they can buy with it.

Suppose that you borrow £1,000 with the promise to pay £1,100 to the lender in a year. Your nominal interest rate is 10 per cent because you're paying back an additional £100, or 10 per cent more pounds than you borrowed. But if inflation occurs, the goods that £100 can buy decreases over time.

 Say a nice meal for two with a bottle of wine costs £100 right now but is going to cost £105 next year. Right now, the lender is giving up 10 of these very good meals (£1,000 divided by £100 per meal) in order to give you the loan. Next year, when she gets repaid £1,100, she can buy 10.47 meals at the price of £105. The lender is giving up 10 meals now in exchange for 10.47 meals next year, meaning that the real rate of interest on the loan is 4.7 per cent. Because of inflation, the real rate of interest on the loan is substantially less than the nominal rate.

When lenders and borrowers negotiate a nominal interest rate on a loan, they both try to estimate what the inflation rate is going to be over the period of the loan. This expected rate of inflation is denoted algebraically as πe. (Don't confuse expected inflation, πe, with actual inflation, π. The former is what people expect to happen ahead of time, whereas the latter is what actually ends up happening.) The following sections show you how to estimate and use this rate.

The Fisher equation

Economist Irving Fisher came up with a simple formula, known as the *Fisher equation*, which links nominal and real interest rates. Using i to denote the nominal interest rate and r to denote the real interest rate, the formula is as follows:

$$i = r + \pi^e \tag{3}$$

This equation simply says that the nominal interest rate is the real interest rate plus the expected rate of inflation. This relationship is very important to borrowers and lenders because although all loan contracts specify a nominal rate of interest, their goal is to achieve a specific real rate of interest, even after any subsequent inflation reduces the value of money. By using the Fisher equation, the borrowers and lenders can determine what nominal interest to charge now in order to achieve a given real rate of return, taking into account the expected rate of inflation.

To see how this works, suppose that a borrower and lender agree that 6 per cent is a fair real rate of interest, and they also agree that inflation is likely to be 3.3 per cent over the course of one year. Using the Fisher equation, they write the loan contract with a 9.3 per cent nominal interest rate. A year later, when the borrower repays the lender 9.3 per cent more money than was borrowed, that money is expected to have only 6 per cent more purchasing power than the borrowed money, given the expected increase in prices.

Predictions aren't perfect

Negotiations of the type described in the previous section depend crucially upon estimating the expected inflation rate, π^e, and lots of economists' job descriptions consist primarily of trying to predict future inflation rates. Their predictions are widely reported in the business media, but every person has his or her own inflation forecast. Some people listen to the experts, whereas others make estimates based on their own daily experiences.

Because forecasts aren't 100 per cent accurate, no one can say for sure what the real rate of return on the loan is going to be. For example, if the inflation rate turns out to be 9.3 per cent in the previous example, the real rate of return is 0 per cent. On the other hand, if the rate of inflation is 0 per cent, the lender gets back 9.3 per cent more money and can buy 9.3 per cent more stuff, meaning a real rate of return of 9.3 per cent.

Figure 5-2 plots actual inflation rates along with average expected inflation rates from a US study. The actual rates come from the monthly US CPI numbers, and the expected inflation rates come from a poll of consumers taken every month by the University of Michigan. Actual inflation between January 1980 and January 1981 was about 13 per cent. By comparison, consumers who were asked in January 1980 what they thought the rate of inflation would be over the next 12 months, on average, told researchers that they expected about a 10 per cent inflation rate. So in that particular instance, the inflationary expectations of typical consumers were off by about 3 per cent.

Since about 1980, the two sets of numbers have been remarkably close, meaning that people's guesses about inflation in the past two decades have usually been wrong by no more than about 1 per cent. Of course, this period also corresponds to a period in US history where the government was committed to low and stable inflation rates. You can see in the US case shown in Figure 5-2 that the two sets of numbers differ the most in the period of highest inflation in the late 1970s. The predictability gained from following a low and stable inflation policy is generally believed to help people and businesses make good guesses on their investment decisions, and therefore enable them to plan more effectively.

And because they can plan more effectively, people and businesses are more likely to increase their levels of investment. This reduced level of predictability, planning and investment is one of the reasons why Britain is held to have had a poorer investment performance than, for example, Germany (which has been more committed to low and stable inflation rates).

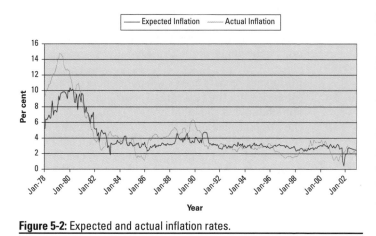

Figure 5-2: Expected and actual inflation rates.

Chapter 6

Understanding Why Recessions Happen

. . . .

In This Chapter

▶ Visualising the business cycle

▶ Hoping for the ideal: letting price adjustments eliminate recessions

▶ Dealing with reality: coping with sticky prices and lingering recessions

▶ Linking slow price adjustments to slow wage adjustments

▶ Introducing the Keynesian model

. . . .

*T*he biggest task of macroeconomists is to try to prevent – or at least shorten – *recessions*, those periods of time during which the economy's output of goods and services declines. Economists, politicians and most other people who work for a living despise recessions because of the high toll they exact in human suffering. When output falls, firms need fewer workers, and the typical result is massive layoffs, which cause significant increases in unemployment. Anticipating and preventing or at least lessening those consequences is one of the tasks currently occupying policy makers following the most recent recession. In this chapter, we use the *aggregate supply/aggregate demand* model to show you how economists analyse recessions. Typically, recessions begin with what economists like to call *shocks* – unexpected adverse events such as terrorist attacks, natural disasters, the introduction of bad government policies or sudden spikes in the cost of important natural resources like oil.

The first big lesson of this chapter is that if the prices of goods and services in the economy were free to adjust to changes in demand and supply caused by shocks, the economy would typically be able to recover quite swiftly. Unfortunately, however, the second big lesson is that not all real-world prices are totally free to adjust to shocks. Instead, some very important prices are quite slow to adjust – they are, as economists like to say, *sticky*. As a result, recessions can linger and cause a lot of harm unless the government intervenes to help the economy recover more quickly.

Throughout this chapter we use shocks to mean *negative* shocks – things and events that impact adversely on the economy. Bear in mind that shocks can be *positive* as well, that is, factors leading to sudden growth in demand in the economy such as the discovery of a new resource or a sudden and substantial tax cut.

Examining the Business Cycle

Economies go through alternating periods during which the output of goods and services expands and then contracts. (In Chapter 4, we explain that Y represents the total output of an economy, so we use Y in this section to conserve some words.) The alternating pattern of economic expansion and contraction, which is illustrated in Figure 6-1, is often called the *business cycle* because businesses are so greatly affected by the changes in output.

The solid line in Figure 6-1 represents how output, Y, varies over time. It alternates between troughs and peaks, which helps us identify periods of recession and recovery. Here's how we distinguish between the two:

- *Recessions*, or contractions, are the periods of time during which Y falls – that is, after a peak and before the next trough.

- *Recoveries*, or expansions, are the periods of time during which Y increases – that is, after a trough and before the next peak.

The dotted line in Figure 6-1 represents the long-run, average growth trend for Y. We draw Figure 6-1 with an upward sloping average growth trend for Y, to capture the fact that the economies of most countries now have sustained economic growth. In other words, on average, output tends to rise year after year. Because recessions still happen, however, the actual path of Y given by the solid line fluctuates around the long-run growth path given by the dotted line.

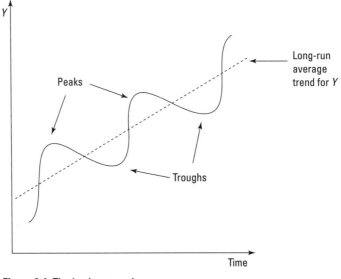

Figure 6-1: The business cycle.

Looking at Figure 6-1, you can see that macroeconomic policy has two very natural goals:

- ✔ **Making the long-run average growth line as steep as possible:** The steeper it is, the faster (on average) output and living standards rise.

- ✔ **Reducing the size of business-cycle fluctuations around the long-run average growth line.** Smaller distances between peaks and troughs translate into fewer people suffering through bouts of unemployment when output falls.

In Chapter 7, we explain the policies that economists think are best for achieving these two goals. But in order for Chapter 7 to make sense, we must first explain what causes the business cycle – especially recessions and the high rates of unemployment that accompany them.

Striving for Full-Employment Output

Before you can say whether an economy is doing well or doing poorly, you need some objective standard of what 'doing well' is. Economists use the concept of *full-employment output* (which is represented by the symbol Y^*) as their measure of how well an economy should be doing.

Full-employment output revolves around the concept of *full employment*, by which economists mean a situation in which everyone who wants a full-time job can get one. *Full-employment output* is how much output is produced in the economy when full employment exists in the labour market.

Please don't confuse full-employment output with the economy's *maximum output*, which is the larger amount of output that would be produced if everyone were forced to work as much as humanly possible.

Also, don't make the mistake of thinking that full employment is the same thing as having a zero unemployment rate. Even when everyone who wants a job can get one, some unemployment always exists as people voluntarily leave one job to search for a better job. For the duration of their job search, these people are counted as unemployed. Similarly, although the economy may be growing, *some* firms may be laying off workers, and those workers may be out looking for jobs. Economists call this situation *frictional unemployment*, as though the delay in finding a better job is due to some sort of friction slowing the process down.

As technology improves, full-employment output (Y^*) grows because better technology means that a fully employed labour force can produce more output. But to simplify their analyses, economists usually ignore the long-term growth trend and look only at whether actual output, Y, is currently above or below their best estimates of Y^* at that particular moment.

As we show you in this chapter, the economy naturally wants to adjust back to Y^* anytime it deviates from Y^*. If that adjustment process was rapid enough, you wouldn't have to worry about business cycles, recessions and unemployment. If the economy reverted back to Y^* fast enough, recessions would be too brief to cause any serious negative consequences. Unfortunately, the natural adjustment process can be very slow, and as a result, recessions can be quite lengthy and awful.

Returning to Y^*: The Natural Result of Price Adjustments

After an economic shock, such as a natural disaster or a spike in the cost of natural resources, price adjustments tend to return an economy to producing at full-employment output (Y^*). That's right, we said *price adjustments* – not the actions of government, the Chancellor of the Exchequer, the Governor of the Bank of England or even the European Central Bank.

Consider a situation in which the *aggregate* (total) demand for goods and services in the economy falls off: individuals, firms and the government demand and buy less output than the economy is currently producing. The result is an excess supply of output which, in turn, leads to lower prices. After all, what does any business do when it can't sell off all its products at the prices it's currently charging? It lowers prices and has a sale. The lower prices attract more buyers, and soon the business can sell off the rest of its output.

This process repeats itself all over the economy during an economic downturn. When aggregate demand falls off due to an economic shock, firms lower prices to sell off their outputs. This process leads to two outcomes:

- ✔ Prices all over the economy fall (more or less).
- ✔ The economy again produces at full-employment output, Y^*.

For this process to work well, prices must be able to change quickly; if they can, the economy very quickly returns to Y^*. If, however, price adjustments are slow, the economy may produce less output than Y^* for a significant amount of time. In other words, if prices don't adjust quickly, you can get a recession. And until prices do adjust, the recession lingers.

We've just given you the briefest overview possible of how the economy responds to an economic shock. The next section provides much more detail so that you can understand how and why the economy eventually gets back to Y^*.

Responding to Economic Shocks

Economists like to break the time period after an economic shock into two parts, which they call the *short run* and the *long run*. An easy way to get a handle on what these two parts mean for the macroeconomy is with the following:

✔ The *short run* refers to the period of time in which firms haven't yet made price changes in response to an economic shock.

✔ The *long run* refers to the period of time after which firms have made all necessary price changes in response to an economic shock.

These definitions are intentionally vague because the speed at which firms adjust prices varies from shock to shock. In this section, we show you that major differences exist between what happens in the short run and the long run.

We use a simple model that *holds constant* the money supply. Bear in mind that as the model gets more complicated, we can do away with some of these constraints.

Defining some critical terms

To see the difference between an economy responding to a shock in the short run versus the long run, begin by looking at Figure 6-2, which is a model of the macroeconomy. The horizontal axis measures the value of the output of goods and services sold in the economy (Y). This number is the same as a country's gross domestic product (GDP). The vertical axis measures the overall price level in the economy, P.

To understand the meaning of P, consider this: although each individual good and service has its own price, and some of those prices may be going up while others are going down, an overall trend in prices exists for the economy as a whole. P is simply a measure of how the prices of goods and services as a whole behave. If *P* goes up, on average prices are rising; if *P* goes down, on average prices are falling. And if prices stay the same, *P* (of course) stays the same.

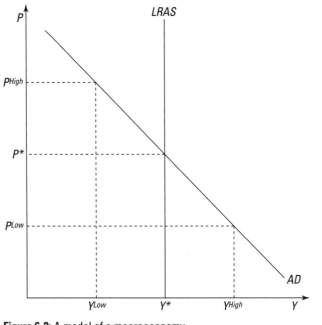

Figure 6-2: A model of a macroeconomy.

In Figure 6-2, you see the symbol P^*. This symbol represents the *equilibrium* level of prices. What does that mean? P^* is the price level at which consumers want to buy exactly the amount of full-employment output (Y^*).

How do economists determine P^*? That price level is determined by the intersection of what's called the *long-run aggregate supply curve (LRAS)* with the *aggregate demand curve (AD)*.

✔ The *aggregate demand curve* represents the total amount of goods and services that people want to buy.

Notice that in Figure 6-2, the *AD* curve slopes downward. That's because an inverse relationship exists between the price level and the amount of stuff that people want to buy. *Inverse relationship* simply means that at the higher price level (P^{High}), people want to buy a low level of output (Y^{Low}). But if prices fall to P^{Low}, people demand a much greater amount of output (Y^{High}). The downward slope of the *AD* curve captures the fact that at lower prices, people buy more.

✔ The *long-run aggregate supply curve* represents the amount of goods and services that an economy is going to produce when prices have adjusted after an economic shock.

In Figure 6-2, you can see that the *LRAS* is a vertical line drawn above the point on the horizontal axis that represents the full-employment output level, Y^*. Why? Because in the long run, changes in prices *always* return the economy to producing at the full-employment output level.

The Tao of P: Looking at price adjustments in the long run

Examine what happens if the economy starts out at a price level other than P^*. For example, look again at price level P^{High} and its corresponding aggregate demand level, Y^{Low}. Obviously, Y^{Low} is less than the economy's full-employment level of output (Y^*). That's important because firms would rather produce at output level Y^*. In fact, they've invested in factories and equipment that will be wasted if they produce at lower levels of output. Consequently, their response is to cut prices in order to increase sales. And they continue to cut prices until the overall price level in the economy falls down to P^*, because that's the price level at which consumers want to buy exactly Y^* worth of output.

Are you worried that all these price cuts will cause firms to lose money? Take heart: firms don't necessarily lose profits in this situation because their costs are falling at the same time. That's because when the economy is producing at less than Y^*, a lot of unemployed workers are available, as well as a lot of unused productive inputs such as iron and oil. Unemployment puts downward pressure on wages; in other words, having lots of labour readily available means you can hire people at lower wages. And the more piles of unused productive inputs that exist, the more their prices fall.

Okay, so the lower prices attract more customers, increase sales and cause the firms to hire back unemployed workers. Eventually, prices fall all the way to P^*, at which point the economy is operating at full employment again, meaning that all workers who want full-time jobs can get them.

In a similar fashion, prices can't remain below P^* for long. At price level P^{Low}, people want to buy Y^{High} worth of output. But that's more than firms can produce at full employment. The only way to produce that much output is if employees work longer than the standard working week. The only way to get them to do so is to pay them more, and the only way to give them higher wages is for firms to raise prices. So with demand exceeding supply, prices are raised until they reach P^*, at which price level the quantity demanded by consumers is exactly equal to the full-employment output level, Y^*.

As you can see, if prices have enough time to adjust, the economy always returns to producing at output level Y^*. Because we're calling the time required for prices to adjust the *long run*, it makes sense to call the vertical line above Y^* the *long-run aggregate supply curve*, because it shows how much output the economy will supply after prices have had enough time to adjust to equalise the supply and demand for goods and services.

Adjusting to a shift in aggregate demand

The previous section shows what happens if the prices of goods and services are, on the whole, too high or too low: they eventually adjust to the equilibrium price level (P^*), and so the economy can get back to producing at the full-employment output level (Y^*). But what causes the prices to be too high or too low in the first place? The usual cause is a shock to *aggregate demand* – the total amount of goods and services that people are willing to buy.

First, visualise what a shock to aggregate demand looks like: Figure 6-3 shows the aggregate demand curve shifting to the left from AD_o to AD_1. A leftward shift of aggregate demand is called a *negative demand shock*, and it may be caused, for example, by a decline in confidence in the economy that makes people want to save more and consume less. (A rightward shift of *AD* would be called a *positive demand shock.*)

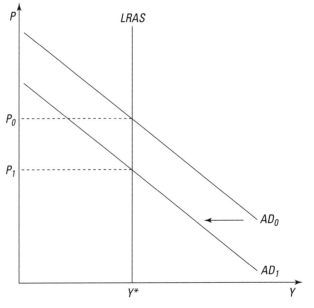

Figure 6-3: A negative shock to aggregate demand.

The original price level, P_o, was determined by where the original AD_o curve intersected the vertical *LRAS* curve. In the long run, after firms adjust to the demand shock, the new price level, P_1, is where the new AD_1 curve intersects the vertical *LRAS* curve.

The new price level (P_1) is less than the original price level (P_o). Why? Demand for goods and services decreases after the negative demand shock. The only way to entice consumers to again purchase full-employment levels of output (Y^*) is to lower the cost of buying that much output, so the price level has to fall. Firms may take some time to make the necessary price reductions, but when they do, the economy again produces at Y^* in the long run.

Therefore, in the long run, after prices have a chance to adjust to shocks, the economy again produces at the full-employment output level, Y^*. That's a huge contrast to what can happen in the short run before prices adjust.

Dealing with fixed prices in the short run

After an economic shock happens, prices eventually adjust to return the economy to full-employment output (Y^*). However, this process may take some time because in the short run, prices are essentially fixed. Even the managers of the most nimble firms need some time to decide how much to cut prices. And some firms aren't quite as nimble.

Suppose that a firm has printed up catalogues listing the prices of the things it sells. This firm distributes catalogues only once a year, which means it is committed to selling to customers at these prices until the next catalogue is sent out. In such a situation, a firm adjusts its production to meet whatever amount of demand happens to come along at these fixed prices. If a lot of people show up to buy at these prices, the firm increases production, typically by hiring more employees. If very few people show up to buy, it reduces production, typically by hiring fewer employees.

Figure 6-4 depicts a situation in which firms have committed to a fixed set of prices and can respond to changes in demand only by adjusting their production levels. The figure shows the horizontal *short-run aggregate supply curve (SRAS)*, which corresponds to price level P_o because the firms, in the short run, can't adjust their prices. Movements right and left along the *SRAS* curve capture the increases and decreases in output that firms have to make as demand for their products varies at the fixed price level.

In the short run, it makes sense to think of the firm as having more control over its production levels than its prices, which leads to modelling the *SRAS* curve as horizontal. In the long run, potential output is capped at a level given by a number of underlying long-run factors.

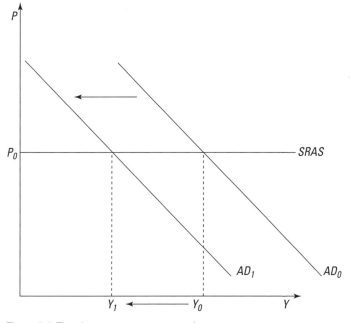

Figure 6-4: The short-run aggregate supply curve.

In between, we have a number of models of various degrees of elaborateness explaining what happens. Generally at some point, these models all agree: the *SRAS* first becomes upward sloping (implying that prices and output rise together) and then vertical. What we're going to do here is to skip the middle bit in the name of simplicity. Of course, in reality economies don't just jump from a horizontal *SRAS* to a vertical *LRAS*, from growth to recession, or from one price level to another. However, the model is simpler to understand, without losing the essential features of the analysis, if we pretend for the moment that this does happen to economies. For now, we're going to use only the initial horizontal curve and the final vertical curve, calling the former the *SRAS* and the latter the *LRAS*.

Figure 6-4 also has two aggregate demand curves, AD_o and AD_1, which again show what happens when aggregate demand is reduced as the result of a negative demand shock. The initial level of output that firms produce, Y_o, is determined by the intersection of the original aggregate demand curve, AD_o, with the *SRAS* curve. In other words, at price level P_o, people demand output level Y_o, and firms respond by supplying it.

When the negative demand shock strikes, it shifts aggregate demand leftward to AD_1. Reduced demand means that at the fixed price level, customers are willing to buy less output. Because firms can't change prices, their only recourse is to reduce production down to match the decrease in demand; this reduced level of output (Y_1) appears on the graph where the *SRAS* curve intersects AD_1. Because lower output means that firms need fewer workers, you end up with a recession: output falls and unemployment rises.

If you compare Figures 6-3 and 6-4, you can see that the left-ward shift in aggregate demand has very different effects in the short run and the long run:

> ✔ In the short run when prices are fixed, output falls and unemployment rises.

> ✔ In the long run, prices fall and output returns to the full-employment level.

Why the huge difference between the short run and the long run? Firms aren't forever stuck with their original catalogue prices. Eventually, they print new catalogues with lower prices. The lower prices entice customers to purchase more, and soon the economy can return to producing at the full-employment output level, Y^*.

Putting together the long and short of it

We now drive this subject home by putting the two very different responses together into one big picture.

Figure 6-5 lets you see how an economy adapts to a negative demand shock both in the short run and in the long run. The economy begins at point *A*, where the original aggregate demand curve, AD_o, intersects both the *LRAS* and the *SRAS* curves. At point *A*, the economy is in equilibrium because at price level P_o, the aggregate demand for output equals the full-employment level of output, Y^*. Neither a surplus nor a shortage exists that may cause prices to change.

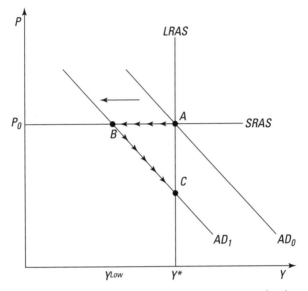

Figure 6-5: Short-run and long-run responses to a negative demand shock.

The *SRAS* curve is horizontal at price P_o to reflect the fact that after the economy reaches its equilibrium (where AD_o intersects the *LRAS* at output level Y^*), the prices that are determined at that level are fixed in the short run; they can't change immediately even if a demand shock happens to come along.

For example, suppose that the aggregate demand curve shifts left from AD_o to AD_1 because of a negative demand shock of some sort. Because prices are fixed in the short run at P_o, the economy's first response is to move from point *A* to point *B*. In other words, because prices are fixed, production falls from Y^* down to Y^{Low} as firms respond to decreased demand by cutting production.

At point *B*, the economy is operating below full employment, implying that there are a lot of unemployed workers. This high level of unemployment causes wages to fall. As wages fall, firms' costs also fall, allowing them to cut prices in order to attract more customers.

Falling prices cause increased aggregate demand for goods and services, which eventually moves the economy from point B to point C. When the economy reaches point C, it is once again producing at full employment, Y^*.

The short-run and long-run effects of a negative demand shock are basically total opposites of each other:

> ✔ In the short run, prices are fixed while output decreases.

> ✔ In the long run, prices decrease while output returns to Y^*.

If prices don't stay fixed for very long, the economy can quickly move from A to B to C. But if prices are slow to adjust to the negative aggregate demand shock, the economy can take a very long time to get from A to B to C. In such cases, a long-lasting recession results during which output remains below Y^* and many people are unemployed.

For these reasons, we need to figure out what affects the ability of prices to change quickly. The most important culprit is sticky prices, or more precisely, sticky wages.

Heading Toward Recession: Getting Stuck with Sticky Prices

When the economy encounters a negative demand shock like the one depicted in Figure 6-5, price flexibility (or lack of flexibility) determines both the severity and length of any recession that may result. If prices are infinitely flexible – if they can change within seconds or minutes after a shock – the economy immediately moves from point A to point C, and all is right with the world. But if prices are fixed for any period of time, the economy goes into a recession as it moves from point A to point B, before prices eventually fall and bring it back to full-employment output at point C.

In the real world, prices are slower to change, or, as economists like to say, prices are *sticky*. Interestingly, they tend to be stickier when going downward than upward, meaning that prices appear to have a harder time falling than rising.

The major culprit seems to be one particular price: wages. Wages are the price employers must pay workers for their labour. Unlike other prices in the economy, people are particularly emotionally attached to wages and how they change over time.

In particular, employees don't like to see their wages cut. They have a very strong sense of fairness when it comes to their wages and, as a result, usually retaliate against any wage cut by working less hard. (Not to mention that EU employment law has some pretty stern rules against firms cutting wages when workers have contracts!) As a result, managers typically find it counterproductive to lower wages even if a firm is losing money and needs to cut costs.

Cutting wages or workers

Suppose that a negative demand shock hits an economy and greatly reduces sales at a particular company. The firm is losing money, so managers need to figure out a way to cut costs. About 70 per cent of this company's total costs are labour costs (wages and salaries). Naturally, labour costs are an obvious target for cuts.

But the managers of the firm realise that if they cut wages, employees will get angry and work less hard. In fact, their productivity may fall off so much that cutting wages may make the firm's profit situation worse: output may fall so much that sales revenues decrease by more than the reduction in labour costs.

So, instead, the managers lay off a large chunk of their workforce in order to reduce labour costs. For example, if sales are down 40 per cent, the firm may lay off 40 per cent of the workforce. However, any workers who remain employed get to keep their old wages so that they aren't angry and their productivity doesn't fall.

For the reasons we're showing you here, what you see during a recession is a large increase in unemployment but little decrease in wage rates. The fact that managers are unwilling to cut wages, makes it very hard for firms to cut the prices of the goods and services they sell.

Adding up the costs of wages and profits

Obviously, firms need to turn a profit in order to stay in business. And that means making sure that the price per unit that they charge for their products exceeds the cost per unit of making them.

During a recession, lower aggregate demand means that firms reduce production and sell fewer units. As we discuss in the previous sections, wages are the largest component, a full 70 per cent, of most firms' costs. If a firm can't cut wages for fear of causing worker productivity to drop, it also can't reduce its per-unit production costs very much. In turn, the firm can't cut its prices very much because prices have to stay above production costs if firms are to make a profit and stay in business.

What does all this mean? When demand drops off, prices are typically sticky. They stay high despite the fact that less demand exists for output in the economy. That's an underlying reason for the economy moving horizontally from point *A* to point *B* in Figure 6-5 after the negative demand shock. Sticky prices means firms can't cut wages, the negative demand shock results in a recession with output falling and unemployment rising because so many workers get fired.

Unless prices can somehow begin to fall, the economy isn't able to move from *B* to *C* to get back to producing at the full-employment output level (Y^*). Prices do *eventually* fall, but this process can take a long time, meaning that the negative demand shock can cause a long-lasting recession.

Returning to Y^* with and without government intervention

Imagine that after the negative demand shock depicted in Figure 6-5 moves aggregate demand leftward from AD_0 to AD_1, the government doesn't wait for prices to eventually fall. Instead, it stimulates aggregate demand so that the aggregate demand curve shifts back rightward and returns to where it started, at AD_o. This action returns the economy to full employment without having to wait for prices to fall.

As we see in the previous sections, labour costs are slow to fall because firms don't want to alienate workers by cutting their wages. But because there are so many unemployed workers when the economy is at point B, wages eventually decline. Some firms hire unemployed people at lower wages, which reduces their costs, meaning that they can undersell firms that keep wages high. Eventually, competitive pressures mean that all firms end up cutting wages.

Other costs also decline, because during a recession, with output so much diminished, a significant portion of the economy's productive capacity is unused: unused factories, unused trucks, train cars and ships, as well as large amounts of unused lumber, iron, oil and other productive inputs.

The owners of these unused inputs lower their prices in order to try to sell them. As their prices fall, firm costs also fall, thereby allowing firms to reduce the selling prices of their output. And as these selling prices fall, the economy moves from point B to point C in Figure 6-5, restoring the economy to producing at the full-employment output level (Y^*).

Achieving Equilibrium with Sticky Prices: The Keynesian Model

Even if this book is the first on economics you've ever laid your hands on, you may have heard the name Keynes before.

John Maynard Keynes was the most influential economist of the 20th century. He was the first economist to realise that sticky prices (caused by sticky wages) are the culprit behind recessions. Keynes was led to the idea by the horrible state that the economy reached during the Great Depression of the 1930s. Just the name itself – *Great Depression* – gives you some idea how bad things got. Normal economic downturns are called *recessions*. Really bad recessions are called *depressions*.

The Great Depression started with a lingering recession from 1929 to 1933. This recession is most usually described as beginning with the infamous stock market crash of 1929 (the Wall Street Crash). To put the Great Depression in perspective, look at Table 6-1, which gives data for each of the seven recessions that the United States has experienced since 1960, plus (on the first line) the same data for the Great Depression. We use US data because its consistency over time makes seeing a clear picture a little easier: you can also plot a similar picture for the UK or many other countries.

Table 6-1	The Great Depression and US Recessions since 1960			
Start	*End*	*Duration (Months)*	*Highest Unemployment Rate*	*Change in Real GDP (%)*
8/1929	3/1933	43	24.9	−28.8
4/1960	2/1961	10	6.7	2.3
12/1969	11/1970	11	5.9	0.1
11/1973	3/1975	16	8.5	1.1
1/1980	7/1980	6	7.6	−0.3
6/1981	11/1982	16	9.7	−2.1
6/1990	3/1991	8	7.5	−0.9
3/2001	11/2001	8	6.0	0.5

Source: NBER, Economic Report of the President, Bureau of Labor Statistics

As you can see, the Great Depression was far, far worse than any normal recession. Nearly 25 per cent of the labour force was unemployed, and the initial downturn lasted about four times longer than the 10.7-month average duration of post-1960 recessions.

Total economic output as measured by real GDP (which we discuss in Chapter 5) also fell much more than in a normal recession. Because real GDP adjusts for inflation, it captures changes in the physical quantity of output produced. In recent recessions, output has fallen at most 2 or 3 percentage points. During the Great Depression, it fell 28.8 per cent!

In comparison, the misery of the Great Depression reached a peak in the UK in 1932. The rate of unemployment topped out at 22 per cent, although output measured by GDP fell by only about 5 per cent over the preceding years. The next worst recessions, in the early 1980s and 1990s, by contrast, were characterised by persistent high unemployment, peaking at 10 per cent, but falls in GDP of only 3 per cent and 1.5 per cent each.

As a witness to the Great Depression, Keynes obviously wanted to figure out what caused such a drastic economic downturn – and what may prevent such devastation from happening again.

Adjusting inventories instead of prices

Not only did Keynes figure out that sticky prices cause recessions, but he also developed a hugely influential model that's still presented in many macroeconomics textbooks. This model is a small part of a larger approach to managing the macroeconomy that came to be called *Keynesianism* – an approach that favoured large government interventions into the economy rather than the sort of *laissez-faire* policies of non-intervention preferred by other people.

To be fair, we have to point out that Keynesianism has attracted a lot of critics and is not the be-all-end-all of macroeconomics. But the part of it we present here is not controversial. This aspect of Keynesianism explains how an economy adjusts to *equilibrium* – a place where aggregate supply matches aggregate demand – in the extreme short run after an economic shock when prices can't change at all.

Look back at Figure 6-4 for a moment. The Keynesian model elaborates on exactly how an economy moves from producing at output level Y_o to producing at output level Y_1 when a shock to aggregate demand happens and prices are fixed at level P_o.

Keynes's model focuses our attention on firms' inventories of goods that have been made but not yet sold. According to Keynes, changes in inventories guide firms to increase or decrease output during situations in which prices are sticky and can't serve as signals of what to do.

To see the novelty of Keynes's inventory idea, understand that if prices were able to change, prices (not inventories) would guide firm decisions about how much to produce:

- ✔ If prices are rising, a firm knows that its product is popular and that it should increase output.

- ✔ If prices are falling, the firm knows that the product isn't doing well and that it should probably cut output (and maybe get into another line of business!).

In an economy with fixed prices, however, firms need some other way of deciding whether to increase or decrease production. Keynes realised that the guiding force would be changes in inventories.

Keeping an eye on target inventory levels

Inventories are constantly turning over, with goods flowing both in and out. New production increases inventories, while new sales decrease inventories. The two factors interact to determine whether inventories are rising, falling or staying the same. For example, if new production equals new sales, inventory levels stay constant. If new production exceeds new sales, inventories rise.

The interaction of new production and new sales is important because each firm has a *target level* of inventories that it likes to keep on hand to meet situations in which sales temporarily run faster than the firm can produce output. The target level is determined by the costs and benefits of having a bigger or smaller inventory on hand.

Having less inventory than the target level is dangerous because the firm may not be able to keep up with sales spikes. Having more inventory than the target level is wasteful because there's no point in having stuff sitting around unsold, year after year. Each firm weighs these costs and benefits to come up with its own target inventory level.

Keynes realised that aggregate demand shocks (which are, by definition, unexpected) would show up as unexpected changes in firm inventories.

- ✔ Unexpectedly low aggregate demand means that sales slow so much that inventories increase and reach levels higher than firms had planned on. Firms respond by cutting production. By reducing production rates to less than sales rates, inventories begin to fall down toward target levels.

- ✔ Unexpectedly high aggregate demand means that sales increase so much that inventories decrease and reach levels lower than firms had planned on. Firms respond by raising production. By increasing production rates to more than sales rates, inventories begin to rise toward target levels.

The changes in output levels caused by changes in inventories are hugely important because they determine not only whether output (Y) is increasing or decreasing, but also whether unemployment is rising or falling.

For example, if firms increase production because inventories have fallen below target levels, they need to hire more workers, and unemployment falls. If, on the other hand, firms decrease production because inventories rise above target levels, they need to lay off workers, and unemployment rises.

Adjusting inventories based on planned and actual expenditures

The Keynesian model differentiates between planned expenditures and actual expenditures as follows:

- ✔ *Planned expenditures* are the amount of money that households, firms, the government and foreigners want to spend on domestically produced goods and services.

- ✔ *Actual expenditures* are equal to gross domestic product (GDP),; they are what households, firms, the government and foreigners actually end up spending on domestically produced goods and services.

What happens when actual expenditures are different from planned expenditures? Inventories automatically change. For example, if more money is spent on goods and services than was planned, people are buying up more output than is currently being produced. This situation is possible because firms sell goods from their inventories that were produced in previous periods. On the flip side, if people spend less money on goods and services than was planned, firm inventories rise because firms have to store up all the output that they can't sell.

Keynes represented planned expenditures, *PE*, algebraically with the following equation:

$$PE = C + I^P + G + NX \qquad (1)$$

What do all these letters mean? We discuss them in detail in Chapter 4, but here's the short version:

- ✔ *C* stands for the amount of output that consumers want to consume.

- ✔ I^P stands for the amount of output that firms plan to buy as investment goods, such as new factories and equipment, as well as any inventory changes that firms plan to make.

  If, later on, firms have to increase or decrease inventories more than they planned, actual investment, *I*, doesn't equal planned investment, I^P.

- ✔ *G* stands for how much output the government wants to buy for things such as building schools or ensuring an adequate supply of paper for paperwork.

- ✔ *NX* stands for *net exports* – the value of our exports minus the value of our imports. *NX* tells us the net demand that the foreign sector of the economy has for stuff that we make domestically.

For actual expenditures, *Y*, Keynes used the same equation that we use to calculate gross domestic product (which we discuss in Chapter 4):

$$Y = C + I + G + NX \qquad (2)$$

Why can we use the GDP equation to calculate actual expenditures? As we explain in Chapter 4, actual expenditure is equal to national income because every penny of expenditure made in the economy is income to somebody. Furthermore, actual expenditure is also equal to the pound value of all goods and services produced in the economy because every bit of output produced is sold to someone. (This process is actually part of the way that stock is valued for accounting purposes:

any output that a firm makes but can't sell to customers is counted as being 'sold' by the firm to itself as that output is placed into inventory. These inventory changes are known as *inventory investment* and are totalled up in GDP as part of the total investment, *I*.)

Having three ways of looking at *Y* is actually very handy as you become familiar with the Keynesian model. Sometimes, understanding the model is easier if you think of *Y* as being actual expenditures; at other times understanding is easier if you think of *Y* as being national income or output. We switch between these three definitions whenever doing so helps make understanding the model easier.

The only difference between the right-hand sides of equation (1) and equation (2) is the investment variable, which is *planned investment (I^P)* in the first equation and *actual investment (I)* in the second. In other words, *Y* and *PE* differ only because of differences in investments caused by inventories increasing or decreasing unexpectedly when sales are more or less than planned.

Bringing some algebra into the mix

Algebra can be used to identify the Keynesian model's economic equilibrium. First, we need to define a *consumption function* – a way to calculate total consumption – that we can substitute into equation (1). In Chapter 4, we present the following formula for calculating consumption:

$$C = C_o + c(1 - t)Y \tag{3}$$

For all the details, look back at Chapter 4. For now, what you really need to know about this formula is that higher income *(Y)* leads to higher consumption *(C)*.

If you substitute equation (3) into equation (1), you get:

$$PE = C_o + c(1 - t)Y + I^P + G + NX \tag{4}$$

If you look carefully, you see that this equation shows that the total planned expenditure on goods and services in the economy *(PE)* depends on the total income in the economy *(Y)*. The higher the total income, the more money people are going to plan to spend.

A good way to simplify this equation is to create a variable called A and to define it as follows:

$$A = C_o + I^P + G + NX$$

When you do that, equation (3) looks a little more palatable:

$$PE = A + c(1 - t)Y \qquad (5)$$

The variable A stands for *autonomous expenditures*, by which economists mean the part of planned expenditures that doesn't depend on income (Y). The part of planned expenditures that does depend on income, $c(1 - t)Y$, is known as *induced expenditures*.

To understand induced expenditures, you need to realise that because t stands for the income tax rate, $(1 - t)Y$ is what people have left over to spend after the government taxes them. And of that amount, the fraction c gets spent on consumption, so that $c(1 - t)Y$ tells you how much expenditure is 'induced' by an income of size Y.

Figure 6-6 graphs equation (5) and labels it the *planned expenditure line*.

To find the specific equilibrium of the Keynesian model, understand that all possible equilibriums are captured by the following equation:

$$PE = Y \qquad (6)$$

This equation can be read as 'planned expenditures equal actual expenditures'. (Remember that Y equals both total income and total expenditure in the economy.)

Any situation where $PE = Y$ is an equilibrium. Why? Because if the economy can get to the point where $PE = Y$, nobody has any reason to change behaviour. Consumers are consuming as much as they planned to consume (C). The government is buying up as much output as it wanted to buy (G). Foreigners are buying as much stuff from us as they intended (NX). And, most importantly, firms are spending exactly as much on investment as they planned – implying that inventories aren't changing unexpectedly.

Planned Expenditures

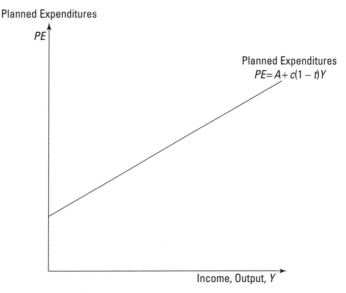

Figure 6-6: The planned expenditure line.

If planned expenditures equal actual expenditures, you truly have an equilibrium because everybody is getting what they want, and nobody has any incentive to change behaviour.

You can solve the equilibrium value of output, which we call $\tilde{y}$, by substituting equation (5) into equation (6). If you do so, you get the following:

$$= A + c(1 - t)Y \qquad (7)$$

Showing equilibrium graphically

If the last equation is confusing , stick with us because finding the Keynesian model's equilibrium graphically is much easier. To do so, you plot the $PE = Y$ equation on the same graph as the $PE = A + c(1 - t)Y$ equation, as we do in Figure 6-7. The point where the two lines cross is the equilibrium. At that point, planned expenditures equal actual expenditures in the economy.

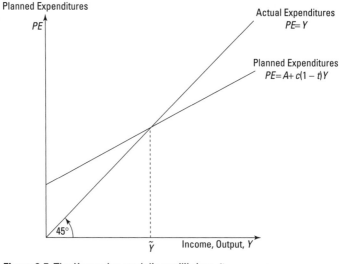

Figure 6-7: The Keynesian model's equilibrium, $\tilde{y}$.

This equilibrium is *stable*, by which we mean that if the economy starts out at any income level other than $\tilde{y}$, it soon moves back to $\tilde{y}$. The thing that returns the economy to $\tilde{y}$ is inventory changes.

To see why this is true, look at Figure 6-8, which exploits a nifty geometric trick about the $PE = Y$ line to show how the economy behaves when it's not producing at the equilibrium output level, $\tilde{y}$.

The trick is that the $PE = Y$ line shows up on the graph at a 45-degree angle, meaning that it can be used to draw squares – shapes whose sides have the same length. That means you can transpose any value of Y onto the vertical axis. To do so, take any value of Y, go straight up until you hit the 45-degree line, and then go straight sideways until you hit the vertical axis. The point you hit represents as many pounds vertically as Y represents horizontally.

For example, in Figure 6-8, start on the horizontal axis at output level Y_2, which is less than the equilibrium output level $\tilde{y}$. If you go up vertically to the 45-degree line and then to the left, you can plot output level Y_2 onto the vertical axis. Why is this useful? Because Y_2 can then be compared directly with the level of planned expenditures, PE_2, which you get by starting at output level Y_2 on the horizontal axis.

As you can see, $PE_2 > Y_2$, meaning that planned expenditures exceed output in the economy. This situation means that inventories are going to drop unexpectedly as firms sell part of their stockpiles of inventory to make up for the fact that people are buying up more stuff than firms are currently producing. This drop in inventories returns the economy to equilibrium.

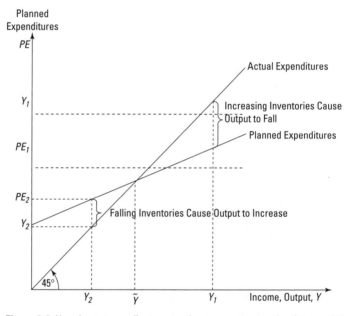

Figure 6-8: How inventory adjustments always move output back toward $\tilde{y}$.

As inventories fall unexpectedly, firms increase production. As a result, Y increases. Furthermore, Y continues to increase until it reaches $\tilde{y}$ because for any value of $Y < \tilde{y}$, you can see from the graph that planned expenditures continue to exceed output.

Inventory adjustments also return the economy to equilibrium if it starts out at an output level like Y_1, which is greater than $\tilde{y}$. As you can see in Figure 6-8, by using the 45-degree line, actual output, Y_1, exceeds planned expenditures, PE_1. In other words, people are buying less (PE_1) than firms are currently producing (Y_1), so inventories are going to start to rise.

Firms respond to increases in inventories by reducing output. They lay off workers and cut production. As a result, Y falls. Y continues to fall until it reaches $\tilde{y}$ because for any value of $Y > \tilde{y}$, you can see from the graph that output is going to continue to exceed actual expenditures.

Boosting GDP in the Keynesian model

Keynes didn't just invent his model to explain how economies with sticky prices reach a stable equilibrium. What he really wanted to do was to use it to show what governments can do during a recession to make things better.

For example, consider Figure 6-8 once again. Suppose that inventory adjustments have carried the economy to equilibrium income, $\tilde{y}$, but that $\tilde{y}$ is less than the economy's full-employment output level, Y^*. In such a case, Keynes asked, what – if anything – should governments do?

Governments can choose to do nothing. Eventually, because $\tilde{y}$ < Y^*, prices will fall and the economy will return to full employment (as it does moving from point B to point C in Figure 6-5). But Keynes argued that governments would be able to speed up the recovery by boosting planned expenditures.

For example, suppose that the government decides to increase G, government spending on goods and services. If it does so, PE in equation (4) clearly gets bigger. Because G is a part of autonomous expenditures (A), the increase in G means an increase in A in equation (5). Graphically, a larger A means that the planned expenditure line shifts vertically from PE_1 to PE_2, as shown in Figure 6-9. Given the fact that the actual expenditure line $(PE = Y)$ doesn't change, the vertical shift in the planned expenditure line causes equilibrium output to increase from $\tilde{y}_1$ to $\tilde{y}_2$.

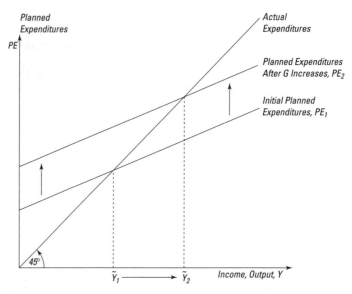

Figure 6-9: Increasing government expenditures increases equilibrium output from $\tilde{y}_1$ to $\tilde{y}_2$.

Keynes suggested using government policy to increase planned expenditures by whatever amount was necessary to increase the economy's short-run, sticky-price equilibrium, $\tilde{y}$, all the way to the full-employment output level, Y^*.

Chapter 7

Fighting Recessions with Monetary and Fiscal Policy

In This Chapter

▶ Using monetary and fiscal policy to stimulate the economy

▶ Facing the fact that too much stimulus causes inflation

▶ Realising that rational expectations can frustrate monetary and fiscal policy

▶ Getting the details behind monetary and fiscal policy

*M*onetary and fiscal policy are two of the most important functions of modern governments. *Monetary policy* focuses on increasing or decreasing the money supply in order to stimulate the economy, whereas *fiscal policy* uses government spending and the tax code to stimulate the economy.

Thanks to the development of good economic theory, governments these days have a fair idea of how to use monetary and fiscal policy to mitigate the duration and severity of recessions. This development is hugely important because it gives governments the chance to make a positive difference in the lives of billions of people. Good economic policy can make a nation prosperous, whereas bad economic policy can ruin it.

If you haven't read Chapter 6, we encourage you to do so before tackling this chapter. You may find it easier to tackle monetary and fiscal policy if you have a basic understanding of how recessions work, which is the focus of Chapter 6.

Stimulating Demand to End Recessions

We're going to look at monetary and fiscal policy separately and in detail. First, though, we're going to make an assumption about what each of them is for – altering the aggregate demand for goods and services. (The *aggregate demand* is the total demand for goods and services in an economy.) In particular, both policies can be used to increase aggregate demand during a recession.

Aiming for full-employment output

The ability to use monetary and fiscal policy to stimulate the economy is important because you always want to end a recession and return the economy to producing at the full-employment output level as quickly as possible.

The full-employment output level – symbolised by Y^* – is the amount of output the economy produces at full employment, which occurs when every person who wants a full-time job can get one. If the economy goes into recession and produces less than Y^* worth of output, millions of people lose their jobs because firms need fewer workers to produce the smaller amount of output.

Worse yet, the unemployment rate remains high until output returns to the full-employment level. Monetary and fiscal policy are useful precisely because they can help return the economy to producing at Y^* as soon as possible; they can shorten the period of frustration and misery that the unemployed endure.

Take a look at Figure 7-1, which shows how monetary and fiscal policy can be used to stimulate aggregate demand and return an economy to producing at Y^* as quickly as possible after the economy is hit with a negative demand shock.

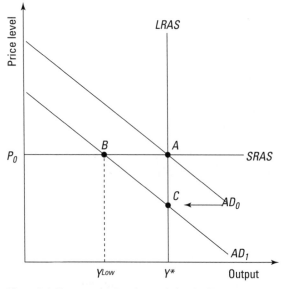

Figure 7-1: How a negative demand shock affects the economy.

In Figure 7-1, the economy begins in equilibrium at point A, where the downward-sloping aggregate demand curve, AD_o, intersects the vertical long-run aggregate supply curve, *LRAS*. Because prices in the economy are fixed in the short run, the short-run aggregate supply curve, *SRAS*, is horizontal at the initial price level (P_o), which is determined by the intersection of AD_o and *LRAS*.

When the negative demand shock comes along, here's what happens:

> ✔ The aggregate demand curve shifts left to AD_1, reflecting the reduction in spending on goods and services.
>
> ✔ With prices fixed at P_o in the short run, the economy's equilibrium shifts leftward from point A to point B, and output in the economy falls from Y^* down to Y^{Low}.
>
> ✔ As output falls, unemployment rises because firms don't need as many workers.

As you can see, the overall result of the demand shock is a recession: a period of falling output and rising unemployment.

Unfortunately, a recession can take a long time to resolve. If the government takes no action to end a recession, the only way for the economy to return to producing at the full-employment output level is for prices to drop so that the economy's equilibrium can slide down the AD_1 curve from point B to point C. That process is typically very slow because of sticky prices, and especially sticky wages. As a result, the economy has high unemployment and takes a long time to get back to producing at Y^* unless the government gets involved.

Putting people back to work

Monetary and fiscal policy accomplish the trick of increasing aggregate demand, which eliminates the need to endure the slow adjustment process that takes the economy from point B to point C (see Figure 7-1). The policies achieve this aim by shifting the aggregate demand curve to the right.

If the government was able to shift the aggregate demand curve from AD_1 back to AD_0, the economy would jump back to equilibrium point A. That's important because it gets the economy back to producing at Y^* without experiencing the slow adjustment process needed to get an economy to move from B to C. In human terms, unemployment ends much sooner for millions of workers who can once again find jobs and provide for themselves and their families.

Unfortunately, however, actually implementing aggregate demand shifts to fight recessions isn't easy. Several problems can creep up involving inflation and people's expectations about how increases in aggregate demand affect prices. So before we tackle the details about how monetary and fiscal policy can be used to increase aggregate demand, we first want to explain how inflation (and worries about inflation) can limit their effectiveness.

Generating Inflation: The Risk of Too Much Stimulation

The best way to begin to understand the limitations of economic policies that stimulate aggregate demand is to understand that in the long run, such policies can change only the price level, not the level of output. Why? No matter where the aggregate demand curve happens to be – no matter how much stuff consumers are willing (or unwilling) to buy – prices eventually adjust until the economy is again producing at full-employment output (Y^*). The economy simply doesn't want to stray from Y^* for too long.

We explain the economy's affection for Y^* in Chapter 6, and you can see it in Figure 7-1 as well. The negative demand shock shifts the aggregate demand curve from AD_0 to AD_1. If the government doesn't use some sort of stimulus, the economy slowly adjusts on its own from point A to point B to point C. At point C, the price level has fallen and output has returned to Y^*.

But even if the government applies some sort of stimulus to move the aggregate demand curve to the right of AD_1, the long-run result is that the economy comes to equilibrium at the point where the aggregate demand curve intersects the vertical long-run aggregate supply *(LRAS)* curve. that corresponds to the full-employment output level, Y^*.

*An exercise in futility: Trying to increase output beyond Y**

Because the economy always returns to producing at full-employment output (Y^*), the government can't keep the economy producing more output than Y^* for any significant period of time. To see why, suppose that the government uses monetary and/or fiscal policy to shift the aggregate demand curve from AD_0 to AD_1, as shown in Figure 7-2.

Before the shift, the economy is in equilibrium at point A, where the original aggregate demand curve, AD_0, intersects the long-run aggregate supply curve *(LRAS)*, which is a vertical line above Y^*. At initial equilibrium, the price level is P_0, and because prices are sticky in the short run, the short-run aggregate supply curve, $SRAS_0$, is a horizontal line at P_0.

When the government stimulates the economy and shifts the aggregate demand curve to the right from AD_0 to AD_1, the economy initially shifts from point A to point B. That is, because prices are fixed in the short run, the economy adjusts to a temporary equilibrium at B (where AD_1 intersects $SRAS_0$).

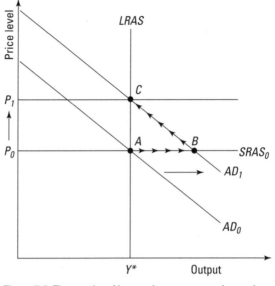

Figure 7-2: The results of increasing aggregate demand.

The economy's output level at point B is greater than the full-employment output level, Y^*. For this reason, point B is only a temporary equilibrium. That's because the economy can only produce more than Y^* by using more labour than is used at Y^*. In our simple model, only two ways exist in which this situation can happen:

- ✔ Firms convince existing workers to work overtime.

- ✔ Firms increase the total number of workers by tempting people such as retirees, who wouldn't normally be in the labour force, to take jobs.

Both ways of increasing the labour supply increase labour costs:

- ✔ To get existing workers to work overtime consistently, firms must pay them high overtime wages.

- ✔ To tempt people such as retirees to join the workforce, firms must increase wages (because, obviously, these people aren't tempted to work at the old wages).

Either way, production costs rise. And as they do, firms pass these costs on to consumers by raising the prices they charge for goods and services.

That's why the economy moves from point B to point C in Figure 7-2. Prices rise because wages are increasing, and therefore the economy moves up the AD_1 curve . Wages, and hence prices, continue to rise until the economy is again producing Y^* worth of output at point C. At that point, no need exists for further wage increases; the economy is once more producing at Y^*.

A temporary high: Tracing the movement of real wages

If you look at Figure 7-2 and consider the movement from A to B to C caused by the government's stimulus programme, you can see that the only long-run consequence is an increase in the price level from P_0 to P_1. After a period of increased production, the economy is back to producing at the full-employment output level, Y^*.

You can take two critical lessons away from this example:

- ✔ The government can't permanently keep output above Y^*.

- ✔ The government can't permanently keep more people employed than the number employed at Y^*.

These two lessons are true because of real wages. *Real wages* are wages measured not in terms of money, but in terms of how much stuff workers can buy with the money they're paid.

Real wages are crucial to understanding how government stimulus affects the economy, because people don't work hard for money in and of itself – they work hard for the things that money can buy. This distinction is important because as the economy reacts to the government's shifting of the aggregate demand curve from AD_0 to AD_1, real wages increase only temporarily. When real wages are higher, workers supply more labour. But when real wages fall back down to their original levels, workers go back to supplying their original amount of labour.

Raising nominal wages while prices are stuck

EXAMPLE

Confused? Stick with us. To see how the concept of real wages works, consider the situation of a banana-loving worker named Ralph. When the economy is at point *A* in Figure 7-2, Ralph is paid £10 per hour, and his favourite food, bananas, costs £1 per kilogram. This situation implies that his real wages – his wages measured in terms of what they can buy – are 10 kilograms of bananas per hour. At that real wage, Ralph is willing to work full-time.

When the government stimulates the economy and shifts the aggregate demand curve from AD_o to AD_1, workers like Ralph benefit at first because real wages initially rise. That's because in order to produce more output than Y^*, firms have to raise *nominal wages* (wages measured in money) in order to get workers to produce more. Because prices are initially sticky at price level P_o, the increase in nominal wages means an increase in real wages.

In Ralph's case, suppose that the price of bananas remains at £1 per kilogram because of sticky prices, but Ralph's nominal wage rises to £12 per hour because the company he works for needs more labour. Ralph's real wage increases from 10 kilograms of bananas per hour to 12 kilograms of bananas per hour.

This increase in real wages motivates workers to supply all the extra labour that's required to produce higher levels of output. (In Figure 7-2, this event is happening at point *B*.) Because nominal wages have gone up but prices haven't, the resulting increase in real wages causes workers to supply more labour, which in turn allows firms to produce an output level greater than Y^*.

Moving back to Y^* and to original real wages

Unfortunately, as firms begin to pass on the costs of increased wages as higher prices, real wages begin to fall. Suppose that because of higher labour costs, the price of bananas rises to £1.10 per kilogram. At that price, Ralph's real wage falls from 12 kilograms of bananas per hour down to 10.91 kilograms of bananas per hour. (To get 10.91, divide Ralph's £12 per hour money wage by the £1.10 per kilogram price of bananas.)

In Figure 7-2, the decrease in real wages happens as the economy moves along the aggregate demand curve from point *B* to point *C*. As prices rise, real wages fall. Prices are going to continue to rise until they reach the point where real wages return to where they originally were at point *A* before the government stimulated aggregate demand.

In Ralph's case, the price of bananas continues to rise until they cost £1.20 per kilogram. At that price, his higher nominal wage of £12 per hour again buys him 10 kilograms of bananas per hour; his real wage is back where it started.

This boomerang effect in the real wage makes total sense. Because the economy returns to producing at Y^*, you only need to motivate workers to supply enough labour to produce Y^*, not anything extra. Workers like Ralph were willing to supply that amount of labour at point *A* for a real wage of 10 kilograms of bananas per hour. After the economy moves to point *C*, they're once more willing to supply that amount of labour for the same real wage.

The idea is that if both wages and prices rise by 20 per cent, real wages remain unchanged and, consequently, the amount of labour that workers supply ends up unchanged.

This fact means that government stimulus policies, such as the one shown in Figure 7-2, which shift aggregate demand from AD_o to AD_1, can't permanently increase the amount of labour being employed by firms. Also, these policies can't permanently increase workers' real wages. These effects are at best temporary; they last only as long as the economy takes to adjust from *A* to *B* to *C*.

You may think that a temporary increase in employment and output is pretty good, however, and that the government should still go ahead and increase aggregate demand from AD_o to AD_1. Unfortunately, if people know about the stimulus ahead of time, the economy may adjust directly from *A* to *C* and eliminate the ability of the aggregate demand shift to stimulate the economy even temporarily.

Failing to stimulate: What happens when a stimulus is expected

In the previous section, we explain why an increase in aggregate demand that tries to increase output beyond Y^* can do so only temporarily, until prices adjust. In this section, we show you that prices may adjust so quickly that the stimulus may fail to increase output at all, even temporarily.

Respecting the importance of price stickiness

As we show in Figure 7-2, any increase in output after aggregate demand shifts rightward from AD_0 to AD_1 depends on prices being sticky in the short run. In other words, the economy moves from point A to point B along the horizontal short-run aggregate supply curve, $SRAS_0$, only if the price level is fixed at P_0 in the short run.

A lot of evidence shows that prices have a hard time falling during a recession. In particular, firms don't like to cut wages and insult their workers. If they cut wages, workers become angry and refuse to work as hard, and the resulting decline in productivity worsens the firm's profit situation.

As a result, a lot of *downward wage stickiness* is present in the economy – by which economists mean that nominal wages decline only rarely. Downward wage stickiness leads to *downward price stickiness*, because firms can't cut their prices below production costs if they want to turn a profit and stay in business.

Realising that prices aren't very sticky upward

In the previous section we talk only about *downward* stickiness; we don't say anything about prices or wages having trouble rising. In fact, very little in the economy seems to cause *upward* wage stickiness or *upward* price stickiness.

Quite the contrary, wages and prices seem quite free to rise if demand increases relative to supply. Business contracts and labour contracts may limit price and wage increases for a while, but as soon as these contracts expire, prices and wages are free to rise.

Anticipating (and undermining) a stimulus

The lack of upward price stickiness implies two very important things for any government attempting to stimulate the economy into producing more than the full-employment output level (Y^*):

- ✔ If prices and wages can rise quickly, the economy produces more than Y^* only very briefly. That is, it moves from A to B to C in Figure 7-2 very quickly – so quickly that the stimulus causes output and employment to rise above Y^* only very briefly.

- ✔ If people can see a stimulus coming, that stimulus (which attempts to increase output beyond Y^*) is likely to generate only inflation and no increase in output whatsoever. In other words, if people can anticipate an increase in aggregate demand, the economy may jump directly from point A to point C, so that the price level rises without even a temporary increase in output.

Suppose that the government preannounces a big stimulus package that's going to shift aggregate demand from AD_o to AD_1 in a few months' time (see Figure 7-2). Because workers and businesses can find out about macroeconomics just as well as the politicians running the government, they realise that the only long-run effect of the upcoming stimulus will be for prices to rise from P_o to P_1.

In addition, workers understand that real wages will remain unchanged in the long run, because both their nominal wages and their cost of living (given by the price level) will increase by equal amounts. As a result, they know that in the long run, the stimulus isn't going to help them at all. Indeed, their only hope for gains is based entirely upon the short run, when nominal wages should go up and the price level should stay the same. In other words, they hope to benefit from the movement from A to B in Figure 7-2.

But firms aren't stupid. They don't want to have their profits reduced because wages are rising while prices are fixed. So they simply anticipate everything. Because prices eventually have to rise from P_o to P_1 and wages eventually have to rise by an equal amount, firms get ahead of the wage increases by raising prices as soon as they can.

Nothing prevents firms from raising prices because nothing in the economy is causing upward price stickiness. So, if firms can see the stimulus coming ahead of time, they simply raise prices as soon as they can in order to make sure that prices and wages are going up at the same pace. As a result, the price level jumps from P_o to P_1.

Of course, at the same time, firms raise wages by an equal percentage in order to keep real wages the same. They want to keep workers motivated to supply the labour necessary to produce Y^* worth of output.

As you can see, if a government tries to stimulate the economy to produce beyond Y^*, and if the stimulus is understood and anticipated by everyone in the economy, the policy may not work at all. Prices and wages may simply jump from point A to point C, meaning that the stimulus fails to stimulate because output stays constant at Y^* while prices and wages go up simultaneously.

Having rational expectations

The phenomenon we describe in the previous section is an example of *rational expectations*, a term that economists use to describe how people rationally change their current behaviour in anticipation of future events. In this case, firms rationally decide to raise prices immediately when they find out that the government is going to increase aggregate demand from AD_o to AD_1 in the future.

Indeed, firms' only rational course of action is to raise prices immediately, because if they leave prices alone at P_o, they're volunteering for the decrease in profits that results when the economy moves from point A to point B (when nominal wages rise while prices stay constant). By immediately raising prices and shifting the economy directly from A to C, firms can avoid that situation altogether.

Rational expectations is one of the most important ideas in macroeconomics because it tells you that strong limits constrain the government's ability to control the economy. People don't just sit around like potted plants when the government announces a policy change. They change their behaviour. And sometimes, as in the case we describe in the previous section, their behavioural change completely ruins the government's ability to achieve its objective of stimulating the economy.

Figuring Out Fiscal Policy

Fiscal policy concerns itself with how governments tax and spend. This policy overlaps with macroeconomics because modern governments have many opportunities to increase aggregate demand by making changes in fiscal policy. These changes fall into two main categories:

- ✔ Increasing aggregate demand indirectly by lowering taxes so that consumers have larger after-tax incomes to spend on buying more goods and services
- ✔ Increasing aggregate demand directly by buying more goods and services

The first category involves decreasing government revenues, and the second involves increasing government spending. Because the government's budget deficit is defined as tax revenues minus spending, both types of fiscal policy are likely to increase government budget deficits. This fact is very important because large and ongoing government budget deficits may lead to many economic problems, including inflation.

Large budget deficits can limit the size of the aggregate demand shifts that a government can undertake. For example, if you look back at Figure 7-1, the government may want to use fiscal policy to shift aggregate demand rightward from AD_o to AD_1, but if doing so involves an overly large budget deficit, the government may have to settle for a smaller shift that moves the economy only part of the way back to producing again at full-employment output (Y^*).

Increasing government spending to help end recessions

If an economy gets into trouble, one of the options open to policymakers is to increase government spending. The idea is that if people are unemployed and unsold goods are sitting around gathering dust, the government can come in with a lot of money and buy up a lot of the unsold products. The result of this action is that the government generates so much demand that businesses start hiring the unemployed in order to increase output to meet all the new demand.

The hope is that this stimulus jumpstarts further demand. When people who were formerly unemployed start getting paid again, they start spending more money, which means that demand rises. When this happens, the economic recovery should be self-sustaining so that the government doesn't need to continue to spend so much money.

Paying for increased government spending

Politicians naturally like suggesting increases in government spending because such increases make them look good, especially if they can get some of the new spending earmarked specifically for their own constituents. However, nothing in life is free.

Only three ways exist to pay for increased government spending:

- ✔ The government can lower interest rates to expand the money supply.
- ✔ The government can raise taxes.
- ✔ The government can borrow more money.

Raising taxes is also problematic, because if you're trying to get out of a recession you want consumers to spend as much as possible on goods and services. If you raise taxes, consumers reduce their spending. You may offset some of the decreased private spending by immediately turning around and spending all the tax revenue, but clearly this approach is no way to stimulate aggregate demand in the long run.

Borrowing and spending: The most common solution

What governments need to do to combat recessions is figure out a way to increase their own spending without decreasing private spending. The solution is borrowing.

By borrowing and then spending money during a recession, the government can increase its purchases of goods and services without decreasing the private sector's purchases.

At any given moment in time, people want to save a certain part of their incomes. They can use these savings to buy many different kinds of assets, including stocks and bonds issued by corporations, real estate, mutual funds and annuities. But they can also use their savings to buy government bonds, which are, in essence, loans to the government.

By offering more bonds for sale, the government can redirect some of the savings that people are making away from purchases of other assets and into purchases of government-issued bonds. By selling bonds, the government can get hold of lots of money to spend on goods and services, thereby turning what would have been private spending on assets into public spending on goods and services.

Dealing with deficits

Increasing government spending and financing it through borrowing is clearly a good way to increase the overall demand for goods and services. But it has the potentially nasty side effect of creating a *budget deficit*, which is the amount by which government spending exceeds tax revenues during the current year. Any current budget deficit adds to the *national debt*, the cumulative total of all the money that the government owes lenders.

The problem with budget deficits and the national debt is that they have to be paid back someday. Consider a ten-year bond that pays a 6 per cent rate of return. When you buy the bond from the government, you give it, for example, £1,000. In return, the government promises to do two things:

✔ To give you back your £1,000 in ten years

✔ To give you £60 per year (a 6 per cent return) until you get your £1,000 back

So, the government gets $1,000 right now to spend on goods and services to boost the economy, but it needs to figure out where to get $60 per year to provide your interest payments, and also where to get $1,000 in ten years when the bond matures.

Relying on the security of future tax revenues

Obviously, people are only willing to lend the government money by buying bonds because they believe that the government is eventually going to pay them back. They have confidence in that happening because governments have the exclusive right to tax things. Essentially, future tax revenues secure all government borrowing.

But the link between taxes and bond repayments isn't direct. In other words, just because a government has a lot of bonds coming due doesn't necessarily mean it has to raise taxes suddenly to get the money to pay off the bonds. Instead, governments often refinance the bonds that are coming due; they simply issue new bonds to get enough cash to pay off the old bonds. This process is referred to as *rolling over the debt* and is routinely practised by governments everywhere.

The only reason that investors are willing to participate in a rollover is that they have confidence that the government can always use its tax powers to pay off its debts. Investor confidence allows governments to keep on borrowing, whether to fund new borrowing or to roll over old debt. When investors don't have that confidence, the effect can be catastrophic.

Paying the debt by printing money: A devastating choice

Sometimes, investor confidence in the government turns out to have been misplaced. Governments have another (rather diabolical) way to pay off their bonds besides using tax revenues: they can expand the money supply. Responsible governments generally don't take this action any longer, but it has happened, and it's really worth being aware of the possibility.

A $1,000 bond obligates the government to pay you back $1,000 worth of money. The bond doesn't say where that $1,000 comes from. So the government is free to print $1,000 worth of new bills and hand them to you. But when you and all the other bond holders with newly printed cash go out into the economy and start spending that new money, you drive up prices and cause inflation.

We have seen that high inflation destroys economic activity. During high inflation, prices lose much of their meaning, and people are much more mistrustful and reluctant to engage in long-term contracts or make long-term investments because they don't know how much money will be worth in the future.

Knowing the potential horrors of inflation, people tend to worry any time they see a government running large budget deficits or piling up a very large debt. They worry that the government may find itself in a position in which it can't raise taxes high enough to pay off its obligations (or is unwilling to anger voters by raising taxes that high). Investors worry that if this situation occurs, the government may resort to printing money to pay off its debts. And doing so ruins the economy.

Printing money to pay government debts also badly hurts most bondholders because most of them get their cash after prices have gone up, meaning that their cash doesn't buy much stuff. Consequently, when people really begin to worry that a government may start printing money to pay off its debts, the government finds getting anyone to buy its bonds harder and harder. In such a situation, to get anyone to buy its bonds, the government offers higher and higher interest rates to compensate for people's worries that the money they're eventually going to get back isn't going to be worth much. These higher interest rates then make the government's situation even more desperate, because any debt rollovers have to be done at the higher interest rates.

Furthermore, because inflation affects all bonds, not just the ones issued by the government, interest rates all across the economy rise if people fear inflation is coming. This situation can have bad economic consequences *immediately*, because higher interest rates dissuade consumers from borrowing money to buy things like cars and houses, and also discourage firms from borrowing money to buy new factories and equipment. Consequently, just the expectation that a government may print money at some point in the future to pay off its bonds can cause immediate harm to the economy.

Dissecting Monetary Policy

Monetary policy is the manipulation of the money supply and interest rates in order to stabilise or stimulate the economy. In modern economies, monetary policy has come to be regarded as the most powerful mechanism that governments have at their disposal to fight recessions and reduce unemployment – even more powerful than fiscal policy.

Monetary policy is put into practice by first changing the supply of money in order to manipulate interest rates. Because interest rates affect everything from the demand for home mortgages by consumers to the demand for investment goods by businesses, they have a huge and pervasive effect on stimulating or depressing economic activity.

To give you a complete picture of how monetary policy functions, we first review what money is. We then show you that an economy can have too much money, and that this fact is related to interest rates and inflation. In turn, this information gives you the necessary insight to understand how the government can affect interest rates by changing the amount of money that's floating around in the economy.

Identifying the benefits of fiat money

Money is an *asset*, meaning that it holds its value over time. Other assets include real estate and property, precious metals like gold and financial assets like stocks and bonds. But money is usually held to be a better medium of exchange than any of the above.

To keep things simple, we've referred to the concept of printing money a lot. The thing to remember, though, is that 'money' does not just mean the cash and coins in circulation, but has a wider definition that includes cash deposits in banks, credit and loans, and government bonds of varying degrees of tradeability. As a result, we also talk about *expanding the money supply*, which means doing something that increases the supply of all of the above.

Money makes an economy much more efficient because it eliminates the need to engage in barter. But governments always face the temptation to print more money in order to pay off old debts or buy lots of newly produced goods and services.

Historically, one way to limit governments' ability to print up more money to pay off bills was to put them on a *metallic standard*. Under such a system, governments were unable to print more bills without backing them with a precious metal, like gold.

For monetary policy, this situation meant that the government was unable to increase the supply of paper money arbitrarily because if it wanted to print new bills, it had to buy an ounce of gold with which to back them. The high cost of buying gold limited the money supply.

Such a system is great for preventing high inflation because the only way you ever get high inflation is if the government prints a huge amount of new money.

Preventing inflation is a good thing, but using a metallic standard turns out to have some large drawbacks. Using a metallic standard causes the supply of money to be pretty much fixed over time, meaning that even if the economy needs a little bit more or a little bit less money to make it work better, the government can't do anything because the supply of money is fixed by the amount of gold the government has in its vaults.

In particular, the metallic standard means that you can't use monetary policy to stimulate your economy if it gets into a recession. One of the reasons that the Great Depression was so bad everywhere around the world was that nearly every country was on a gold standard when the calamity began. This arrangement meant that governments were unable to increase their money supplies in order to help their economies. This situation also explains why the countries that quit their gold standards earliest had the shortest and mildest recessions; after they quit, they were free to print new money to stimulate their economies. On the other hand, countries like the United States and the United Kingdom that stubbornly stuck to their gold standards had the most prolonged and painful economic downturns.

This was obviously a problem andled to the adoption of a system called *fiat money*. Under a fiat money system, the government simply prints up as many bills as it likes, declares them to be money, and puts them out in the economy. (*Fiat* means 'let it be' in Latin.) The great benefit of this system is that the government can arbitrarily increase or decrease the money supply in whatever way best helps to stimulate the economy.

For the rest of this chapter, we use M to denote the total supply of money floating around the economy. For example, M = £1.3 trillion means that the sum of the face values of all the bills and coins in the economy is £1.3 trillion.

Realising that you can have too much money!

Monetary policy works by manipulating the supply of money in order to change the price of borrowing money, which is the interest rate. The key to making monetary policy work is the fact that the demand for money depends on the interest rate.

Imagine that we hand you £1 million, and you can do whatever you want with it. Suppose that you're frugal and decide to save every last penny, at least for a year, because you think that's going to give you enough time to figure out how to best blow the money.

Our question to you is: should you keep all your new wealth in cash?

The correct answer is 'NO!'.

Holding your wealth in cash is, to be blunt, really stupid because cash earns no interest. Even if you put the money into a standard current account, you get at least a tiny bit of interest. Even 1 per cent of interest on a million pounds is £10,000. Why would you give that up? Even better, if you use the cash to buy government bonds, you may get 5 or 6 per cent. That's £50,000 or £60,000 more than if you keep your wealth in the form of cash.

Clearly, the higher the interest rate you can get on other assets, the more incentive you have to convert your cash into other assets. In fact, the only thing preventing people from converting all their wealth to other assets and never holding any cash is the fact that money lets them buy things. Beyond that function, money is no better than any other asset; in fact, it's worse in terms of its rate of return because the rate of return on cash is always zero.

In Figure 7-3, we create a graph that demonstrates how much money people demand to hold at any particular interest rate. We denote money demand as M^D. The nominal interest rate, i, is on the vertical axis. The horizontal axis is measured in currency, which in the UK means pounds.

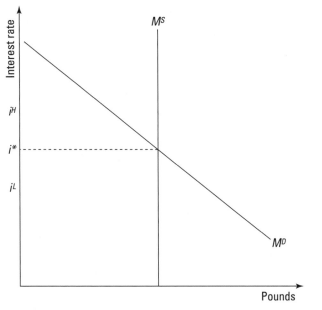

Figure 7-3: The equilibrium interest rate is determined by the intersection of the money demand curve with the money supply curve.

As you can see from the downward slope of the money demand curve, the higher the interest rate, the less money people want to hold. This graph simply represents the idea that cash, with its zero interest rate, is a worse and worse place to park your wealth if you can get higher and higher returns in alternative assets. In other words, the higher the interest rate on other assets, the more you're going to want to economise on your cash holdings.

Figure 7-3 also contains the vertical money supply curve, where M^S stands for money supply. This curve is vertical because the government can decide how much money it wants to print and circulate without regard to the interest rate.

The M^D and M^S curves cross at interest rate i^*. This interest rate is the *equilibrium* interest rate, because it's the only rate at which the total amount of money that people want to hold is equal to the total amount of money that the government has circulated.

More importantly, i^* is a *stable equilibrium*, meaning that if interest rates ever deviate from it, market forces are going to push them back to i^*. But before this fact is going to make sense, we need to explain how interest rates are determined in the bond market. Pay close attention because bond markets are *the* place where interest rates for the whole economy are determined. Bond markets have a huge effect on everything else that goes on in the economy.

Getting to know bonds

A *bond* is a financial asset for which you pay a certain amount of money right now in exchange for a series of payments in the future. Two kinds of payments exist, face value payments and coupon payments:

- The *face value payment* is printed on the face of the bond certificate and comes on the date the bond expires.

- The *coupon payments* are typically made twice per year until the bond expires. They're called *coupon payments* because before computerised recordkeeping, you literally clipped a coupon off the bottom of the bond certificate and mailed it in to receive your payment.

Typically, bonds expire after one, five, ten or twenty years.

Bonds don't guarantee any sort of rate of return. They promise only to make the coupon and face value payments on time. The rate of return depends on how much you pay for the right to receive those payments.

Imagine a really simple kind of bond called a *zero-coupon bond* (so named because no coupon payments apply). The only payment this bond ever makes is the face value payment that comes when the bond expires. And to make things really simple, suppose that it pays its owner exactly £100 exactly one year from now.

If you're the bond owner, you have to understand that the rate of return the bond pays depends on how much you pay for it right now. Suppose that you were naive enough to pay £100 for the bond right now. Your rate of return would be zero per cent, because you paid £100 for something that's going to give you £100 in a year.

On the other hand, suppose that you pay only £90 for the bond right now. Your rate of return is going to be about 11 per cent, because (£100 – £90)/£90 = 0.111, or 11.1 per cent. If you were able to buy the bond for only £50, your rate of return would be 100 per cent, because you'd double your money in a year's time.

You can work through to the result, but it's really useful to state again here that the rate of return on a bond *varies inversely* with how much you pay for it. Because the amount of money you get in the future is always fixed, the more you pay for it right now, the less your rate of return. Higher bond prices imply lower rates of return.

Seeing the link between bond prices and interest rates

The fact that bond prices vary inversely with interest rates is the key to understanding why i^* is a stable equilibrium in Figure 7-3. In this section, we explain the link.

First, consider interest rates that are higher than i^*, such as i^H. When interest rates are higher than i^*, the amount of money supplied exceeds the amount of money demanded. This situation means that people have been given more of the asset called money than they want to hold. So they try to reallocate their portfolio of assets by using the excess money to buy other assets.

One of the things that people buy is bonds. But with all this new money being thrown at the limited supply of bonds, the price of bonds rises. When bond prices rise, interest rates fall. That's why if you start out at an interest rate that's higher than i^*, interest rates fall back down toward i^*. Excess money drives up the price of bonds, which lowers interest rates.

On the other hand, for interest rates like i^L that are lower than i^*, the amount of money demanded exceeds the amount of money supplied. Because people want more money than they have, they're going to try to get it by selling non-cash assets like bonds in order to convert those assets cash.

Imagine that everybody tries to sell his or her bonds to achieve this aim. With all the selling, bond prices fall, meaning that interest rates *rise*. In fact, bond prices continue to fall and interest rates continue to rise until they are back at i^*, because that's the only rate of interest at which people are satisfied holding the amount of money, M^S, that the government has decided to circulate.

You need to understand that the movements back to the equilibrium interest rate, i^*, are very quick. Any excess money demand or excess money supply never lasts very long because rapid adjustments in the price of bonds move the interest rate to its equilibrium.

If interest rates adjust very quickly, it follows that a government could expand the money supply simply as it wishes. This could give the government a useful tool to manage the economy. However, if people know that the government can do this, they simply factor that into their guesses about the future and behave as if the government has already done so. Thus, the usefulness of this policy would be reduced. This is one of the underlying reasons for governments delegating monetary policy to some other authority (such as the Bank of England).

Changing the money supply to change interest rates

Monetary policy works because governments know that interest rates adjust in order to get people to hold whatever amount of money the government decides to print. The interest rate is, in some sense, the price of money, and it reacts in a way similar to other prices. That is, if the money supply suddenly increases, the price of money falls, and vice versa.

You can see this fact graphed in Figure 7-4, in which the government increases the money supply from M^S_o to M^S_1. This action shifts the vertical money supply line to the right and lowers the equilibrium nominal interest rate from i^*_o to i^*_1.

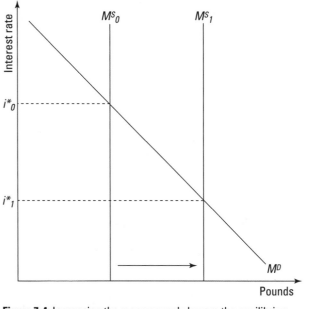

Figure 7-4: Increasing the money supply lowers the equilibrium nominal interest rate.

The system in the UK works as follows. The Bank of England controls the supply of money because it has a *legal monopoly* to do so. In general, the way the Bank changes the money supply is not by telling the mint to print more or less of the coin of Her Majesty's realm, but by setting something called the *base rate*, which is the lowest possible interest rate that commercial banks can use to borrow from the government – in other words, doing everything we talked about earlier but backwards! Another possibility, and one that's worth discussing, is using a slightly more subtle method called *open-market operations*. We look at this method now using a notional central Bank, as most of this is internationally standard these.

The term *open-market operations* refers to the central bank's buying and selling of government bonds. That is, open-market operations are transactions that take place in the public, or open, bond market. Depending on whether the Bank buys or sells bonds, the money supply out in circulation in the economy increases or decreases:

- ✔ If the Bank wants to increase the money supply, it buys bonds because in order to buy bonds the government must pay cash, which then circulates throughout the economy.

- ✔ If the Bank wants to decrease the money supply, it sells bonds because the people to whom the Bank is selling the bonds have to give the government money, which reduces the amount in circulation.

By buying or selling bonds in this way, the amount of money out in circulation (M^S) can be very precisely controlled, meaning that the government can, in turn, keep tight control over interest rates.

Lowering interest rates to stimulate the economy

Now that you understand the actual mechanics by which the Bank of England (or similar institutions in other countries) manipulates interest rates, you're ready to see how monetary policy affects the economy.

The basic idea behind monetary policy is that lower interest rates cause both more consumption and more investment, thereby shifting the aggregate demand curve to the right. Here's how:

✔ Lower interest rates stimulate consumer consumption spending by making it more attractive to take out loans to buy things such as cars and houses.

✔ Lower interest rates stimulate investment spending by businesses because at lower interest rates, a larger number of potential investment projects become profitable. That is, if interest rates are 10 per cent, businesses are only willing to borrow money to invest in projects with rates of return of more than 10 per cent. But if interest rates fall to 5 per cent, all projects with rates of return higher than 5 per cent become viable, and so firms take out more loans and start more projects.

When trying to remember how monetary policy works, keep in mind that it's actually a very simple three-step process. If a central Bank wants to help increase output, it initiates the following chain of events:

1. **The Bank buys government bonds in order to increase the money supply.**

2. **The increased money supply causes interest rates to fall because the prices of bonds get bid up.**

3. **Consumers and businesses respond to the lower interest rates by taking out more loans and using the money to buy more goods.**

Understanding how rational expectations can limit monetary policy

The government's ability to use increases in the money supply to stimulate the economy is limited by rational expectations and the fears that people have about inflation. Specifically, investors understand that increases in the money supply can cause inflation (as we discuss in Chapter 5). This understanding means that whenever a central Bank increases the money supply in order to lower nominal interest rates, it has to do so with some moderation, in order to avoid causing inflationary fears that can offset the stimulatory effect of increasing the money supply.

Graphing the results of money supply increases

Take a look at Figure 7-5, which shows an economy in recession at point A where aggregate demand curve AD_0 intersects short-run aggregate supply curve $SRAS_0$, which is fixed at price level P_0. The Bank then increases the money supply to lower interest rates and stimulate the economy, which causes the aggregate demand curve to shift rightward to AD_1.

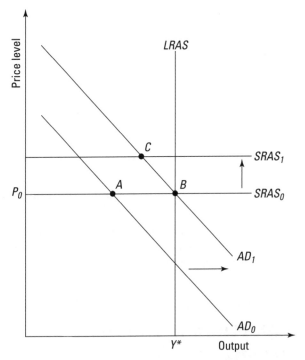

Figure 7-5: The result of increasing the money supply depends on inflationary expectations.

At this point, two things can happen, depending on people's inflationary expectations:

>   ✔ If people believe that the price level is going to remain fixed at P_0, the rightward shift in aggregate demand moves the economy's equilibrium rightward along the $SRAS_0$ curve from point A to point B.

   ✔ If people believe that the price level is going to jump in response to the increase in the money supply, the short-run aggregate supply curve shifts up vertically by the amount that the price level is expected to increase. Therefore, the economy's equilibrium moves from *A* to *C*, where AD_I intersects the new short-run aggregate supply curve, $SRAS_I$.

Because output increases less if the economy moves from *A* to *C* than if it moves from *A* to *B*, the Bank obviously has to be careful about inflationary expectations when trying to stimulate the economy by increasing the money supply. If people expect inflation to occur, their actions can offset some of the stimulus that an increased money supply is expected to bring.

Realising how inflationary expectations affect interest rates

The underlying problem is that the Bank has partial control over interest rates. In particular, the Bank controls money supply but not money demand. This causes a problem: if people think that an increase in the money supply is going to cause inflation, they increase their money demand because they're expecting to need more cash to buy things at higher prices.

So although the increase in the money supply tends to lower interest rates, as shown in Figure 7-4, the increase in money demand caused by inflationary fears tends to increase interest rates. As higher interest rates tend to decrease investment, any increase in interest rates caused by inflationary fears works against the stimulus that the Bank is attempting to apply to the economy.

This decrease in the effectiveness of monetary stimulus is why the big shift in aggregate demand in Figure 7-5 doesn't shift the economy all the way back to producing at Y^*. If people expect inflation, part of the stimulus ends up causing inflation rather than stimulating the economy.

So how does the Bank set monetary policy if it seems to have little or no effect? In fact, two hidden mechanisms are at play.

✔ **Precommitment:** By establishing a credible commitment to a monetary policy, the Bank is able to keep everyone else honest. If the Bank says, 'I will act to ensure that inflation is no higher than 5 per cent', you know that it will act to prevent inflation rising any higher. As a result, people will factor the Bank's policy into their decisions and act as if the Bank had already done so.

✔ **Advantage:** The Bank knows what it may do when we can only guess, so if it thinks our expectations are out of line with policy, it can pull a surprise move and generate a short-run stimulus or contraction before we know it.

Part III

Microeconomics: The Science of Consumer and Firm Behaviour

'Are you hiding something from us, Mr Dingwall?'

In this part . . .

*M*icroeconomics focuses on the decision-making behaviour of individual people and individual firms. In this part, we show you that economic models assume that individuals make decisions in an attempt to maximise happiness, and firms make decisions in an attempt to maximise profits. The pleasant but surprising thing is that in the context of competitive markets, firms pursuing profits and individuals pursuing happiness end up using society's limited pool of resources in the most efficient manner possible – meaning that properly functioning competitive markets produce the best combination of goods and services from society's limited pool of resources.

Chapter 8

Supply and Demand

● ●

In This Chapter

▶ Weighing the effects of higher prices on supply and demand

▶ Examining supply and demand curves

▶ Focusing on market equilibrium

▶ Identifying policies that prevent market equilibrium

● ●

*M*odern economies continually trade goods for other goods, either directly or via the medium of money. All this activity can get very complicated, so we need a simple model to help make sense of it all. This chapter introduces you to just such a simple model, called the *supply and demand model*, to help you make sense of how the quantity of a good sold is related to the price of the good.

We begin this chapter by introducing you to markets. We then explain supply and demand separately and show you how to draw and manipulate supply curves and demand curves; the demand curves capture the behaviour of buyers, whereas the supply curves capture the behaviour of suppliers. The next step is to watch the curves interact to see how markets function both when left to their own devices and when subject to government regulation or intervention.

Making Sense of Markets

In the modern economy, most economic activity takes place in *markets*, places where buyers and sellers come together to trade money for a good or service. A market doesn't have to be an actual (physical) place; in fact, many markets nowadays are fully computerised and exist only in cyberspace (online music stores, for example). But no matter what sort of institutional arrangement governs markets, they all tend to behave in the same way, which means we can study markets in general instead of having to study each one separately.

We use a very simple model called *supply and demand*, which relates the number of people producing or buying a good to its price – holding other things constant. This model logically separates buyers from sellers and then summarises each group's behaviour with a single line on a graph. The buyers' behaviour is captured by the demand curve, whereas the sellers' behaviour is captured by the supply curve. By putting these two curves on the same graph, economists can show how buyers and sellers interact to determine how much of any particular item may be sold, as well as the price at which to sell it.

Deconstructing Demand

People want to buy things, and economists refer to that desire as demand. When they say *demand*, economists mean how much of something people are both *willing and able* to pay for. So although you may want a bajillion scoops of ice cream, that desire isn't a demand in the economic sense. Your *demand* is three scoops because you're willing and able to buy three scoops at the price that the local ice cream shop charges.

Getting our terms straight

To be precise in terminology, we need to distinguish between two slightly different concepts. The ice-cream scoop scenario actually describes *quantity demanded*, which refers to how much you demand at a specific price *given your income and preferences*. In contrast, when an economist uses the word *demand*, he or she means the whole range of quantities that a person with a given income and preferences demands at various possible prices.

This may seem like hair splitting, but the difference is crucial and prevents us from getting confused between the two concepts: just remember that *demand* is general across all prices and preferences, and *quantity demanded* is specific to one price.

To get a better handle on the difference between these two concepts, you have to understand that economists divide everything that can possibly affect the quantity demanded into two groups: the price and everything else. The two groups have different effects.

Prices have an *inverse relationship* with the quantity demanded. In other words, the higher the price, the less people demand (if all the other things that may possibly affect the quantity demanded are held constant).

Other things that we hold constant include such important factors as tastes, preferences and incomes. For example, no matter how low the price of a ticket gets, Spurs supporters aren't going to buy a single seat to watch Arsenal, because they don't value having a seat. At the same time, however, many thousands love Arsenal so much that even if the price gets very high, they're still willing to buy a seat.

No matter how much a seat at Arsenal costs, the people who love the team have a higher quantity demanded than Spurs fans. Because this remains true for every possible price, we say that Arsenal fans have a higher demand for this particular product than Spurs fans.

Another important factor is income. As you get richer, you increase your purchases of certain goods that you've always liked and can now afford to buy in larger quantities. These goods are called *normal goods*. On the other hand, you decrease your purchases of things that you were buying only because you were too poor to get what you really wanted. These goods are called *inferior goods*. For example, new cars are normal goods, whereas really old, poorly running used cars are inferior goods. Similarly, freshly made organic salads are normal goods, whereas three-day-old discounted bread is an inferior good.

Given the complexity of variables such as preferences and income, why do economists insist on dividing everything that can possibly influence your quantity demanded into only two groups, the price and everything else? They do so for two reasons:

✔ When you don't separate prices from everything else, things get confusing, and economists want to concentrate on prices.

✔ When you translate the concept of demand into a graph and create a demand curve, prices have a very different effect than the other variables. This point is what we show you next.

Graphing the demand curve

If we add up the demands from different consumers in a market, we get the *demand curve* for the market. A demand curve is shown in Figure 8-1. Suppose that this demand curve represents the demand for cabbages. On the vertical axis is the price of cabbages, measured in pounds sterling. The horizontal axis is the number, or quantity, of cabbages that are demanded at any given price.

You get the total revenue gained from selling a given number of units at a given price by reading off the price and quantity demanded. For example, at point A you sell five cabbages at a price of £2 per cabbage, and therefore you receive a total of £10.

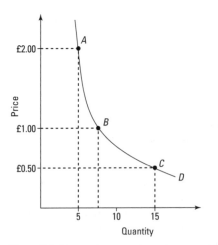

Figure 8-1: Demand curves slope downward because when prices fall, people buy more.

As Figure 8-1 shows, the demand curve slopes downward, reflecting an inverse relationship between the price of cabbages and the number of cabbages people want to buy. For example, consider point *A* on the demand curve. At a price of £2 per cabbage, people demand five cabbages. However, as point *B* demonstrates, if the price drops to £1 per cabbage, people demand eight cabbages. And if the price drops to only 50 pence per cabbage, they demand 15 cabbages.

Price changes: Moving along the demand curve

When you consider the relationship between the price and the quantity demanded at each price, you need to understand that increases or decreases in price simply move you along the demand curve, so that you just read off the price and quantity at a new point on the same curve.

In the previous section, we mention that economists divide all the variables that can affect demand into two groups, price and everything else. Geometrically, this division is reflected in the fact that price changes move you along the demand curve, whereas the other variables combine to determine the curve's exact location and shape. For example, if people hate cabbages, you aren't going to find them buying five when the price is £2, as they do at point *A* in Figure 8-1. If people hate cabbages, they buy none at all, no matter what the price, and the demand curve looks very different.

Other changes: Shifting the demand curve

Since the non-price factors determine the location and shape of the demand curve, any change in these factors causes the demand curve to shift its location.

For example, suppose that a government health study comes out saying that cabbages make people irresistible to other people. Naturally, the demand for cabbages increases, *at any given price*. Using our graphs, the effect is to shift the demand curve to the right. We illustrate this effect in Figure 8-2, where point *D* indicates the demand curve before the study is announced and *D'* indicates the demand curve after the study is announced.

Whenever a demand curve moves, economists say that a *shift in demand* has occurred. In this case, you can say that demand has increased, whereas if the curve shifted to the left, you say that demand decreased.

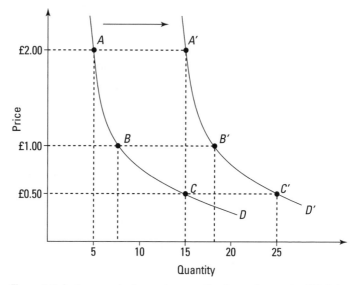

Figure 8-2: An increase in demand causes the demand curve to shift right from point *D* to point *D′*.

Making sure we're clear, in this way of describing the movements, the quantities demanded increase or decrease *while holding prices constant*. We need to emphasise this point: you *have* to distinguish between changes in quantities demanded that occur because the price changes (movements along a given curve) and changes in quantities demanded that occur because something other than the price changes (shifts of the entire curve).

To see the difference, compare point *A* and point *A′* in Figure 8-2. Both points share the same price of £2 per cabbage, but thanks to the recently released government study, people now demand fifteen cabbages at that price (point *A′*) rather than five cabbages at that price (point *A*). Because the price is the same for the two points, you *know* that the change in the quantity demanded was caused by something other than price. Similarly, you can look at what happens to the quantity demanded while holding the price constant at £1: the quantity increases from eight before the study to eighteen after, moving from point *B* to point *B'*.

Remember that anything other than the price that affects the quantity demanded shifts the demand curve. In our example, a positive research study causes people to demand more cabbages. But many other factors may influence people's demand, including changes in their income or wealth and changes in their tastes or preferences. Whenever any of these non-price factors changes, the demand curve shifts left or right.

Determining the slope of the demand curve

The slopes of demand curves depend on how people view the trade-offs that changing prices force them to make. For instance, imagine that the price of a good you currently buy falls from £10 down to £9. How do you respond? Well, that depends on how you feel about the good in question relative to other goods you can spend your money on:

- ✔ You may buy a lot more of the good in question because extra units bring you a lot of happiness, and you're consequently grateful to be able to purchase them for £9 instead of £10.

- ✔ You may barely increase your buying because, although you like being able to buy the good for £9 rather than £10, extra units just don't make you all that much happier. In such a situation, the best thing about the price cut is that it frees up money to buy more of other things.

In terms of demand curves, these different reactions lead to different slopes. The person who buys a lot more when the price falls has a flat demand curve, whereas the person whose purchases barely budge when the price falls has a steep demand curve.

Consider Figure 8-3, where we show two separate demand curves on two separate graphs. The one on the left is your demand for sherbet lemons. The one on the right is your friend's demand for sherbet lemons.

Notice that your demand curve has a very steep slope whereas your friend's demand curve is very flat. The difference is completely the result of differences in how you react to price changes.

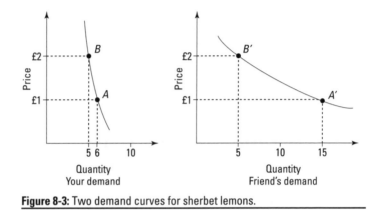

Figure 8-3: Two demand curves for sherbet lemons.

You can see this by comparing your quantity demanded at point *A* with your quantity demanded at point *B*. Even though the price doubles from £1 per bag of delicious sherbets to £2 per bag, your quantity demanded falls only from six bags to five bags. In contrast, when the price doubles from £1 per bag to £2 per bag, your friend's quantity demanded falls hugely, from fifteen bags to only five bags.

Defining demand elasticity

Economists have repurposed the word *elasticity* to describe how changes in one variable affect another variable. When they say demand elasticity, they mean a concept called the *price elasticity of demand* – how much the quantity demanded changes when the price changes. In Figure 8-3, your demand curve has a lot less demand elasticity than your friend's because the same change in price causes your quantity demanded to fall much less than your friend's quantity demanded.

Extreme cases of demand elasticity are illustrated in Figure 8-4 using two demand curves, the first being perfectly vertical and the second being perfectly horizontal.

The vertical demand curve, *D*, is said to be perfectly inelastic, because exactly *Q* units are demanded, no matter what the price. You may be wondering just what sort of a good has such a demand curve, and one answer is lifesaving drugs. If you need exactly *Q* units to keep living, you're willing to pay any price asked. Ransoms in kidnappings are also likely to be perfectly inelastic, because people are willing to pay any price to get their family members back. In fact, any good has a demand curve like this when your valuation for the good is so extreme that you're willing to pay anything for it.

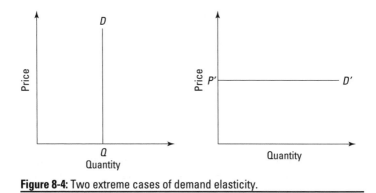

Figure 8-4: Two extreme cases of demand elasticity.

On the other hand, the horizontal demand curve, *D'*, is said to be perfectly elastic. To understand this name, try to imagine a very gradually sloping demand curve that's almost – but not quite – horizontal. On such a very shallowly sloped demand curve, even a small change in price causes a big change in the quantity demanded. Indeed, the flatter a demand curve becomes, the greater is the change in the quantity demanded for any given price change. For instance, look at Figure 8-3 one more time. Compare how a £1 change in the price of sherbets causes a much bigger change in your friend's quantity demanded on her flatter demand curve than on your steeper demand curve.

You can think of a perfectly horizontal demand curve as being the most extreme case of this phenomenon, so that even the tiniest change in price brings forth an infinite change in quantity demanded. That is, when prices are above *P'* in the right-hand graph in Figure 8-4, you buy nothing, whereas when prices are at *P'* or just a penny less, you buy a whole lot. (Infinite is a whole lot.)

Suppose you work for a large restaurant chain and have to buy tons of tomato ketchup. Your options are brand X and brand Y, but because they taste exactly the same, the only thing that matters is the price. Consequently, when the price of brand X is even the slightest bit lower than brand Y, you buy tons of brand X and none of brand Y. When the price of X is even slightly higher than that of brand Y, you buy tons of Y and none of X. Or to put it another way, when brand X is easily substituted with brand Y, the demand for brand X tends towards being perfectly elastic too.

In this case, an interesting thing applies when you're on the supply side of the market: if you know the elasticity, you can tell whether you're wise to raise prices. Remember that the demand curve maps a price to a quantity. Multiply that price by that quantity and you have the revenue you can make from a product being bought at that price. The result is the area of a box drawn between the demand curves and that price and quantity.

Now, if you changed the price of the good, you get another box with an area equal to the revenue to be made from selling at the new price. You can compare the size of the two boxes to tell whether you're better off at the higher or lower price. (Holding all other things constant, of course.)

Of course, perfectly elastic or perfectly inelastic demand curves aren't very common. Nearly all demand curves slope downward, meaning that moderate changes in prices cause moderate changes in quantities demanded.

Sorting Out Supply

We now move on to how economists view the supply of goods and services. The key underlying concept is that supplying things is costly. As any business owner knows, you have to pay people to supply the things you want. Even more interesting, though, is the fact that the more you want them to supply, the higher their costs of supplying each additional unit.

Because production costs rise as you produce more output, if you want producers to make more, you have to pay them more. This fact implies that supply curves slope upward.

Graphing the supply curve

Using cabbages again as an example, imagine that a farmer named Babbage grows cabbage. In Figure 8-5, we graph Mr Babbage's supply of cabbages and label that supply as *S*.

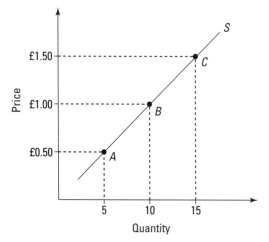

Figure 8-5: Supply curves have an upward slope because of increasing production costs.

The horizontal axis gives the number of cabbages supplied, whereas the vertical axis gives the price per cabbage that you have to pay Mr Babbage to supply you any given number of cabbages. Thus, point *A* says that you have to pay Mr Babbage 50 pence for each cabbage if you want him to supply you with five cabbages.

Because Mr Babbage's production costs rise as he tries to grow more and more cabbages, you have to pay him £1 per cabbage if you want him to grow you ten cabbages, as shown by point *B*. And you have to pay £1.50 per cabbage if you want 15 cabbages, as shown by point *C*.

Keep in mind that the points on the supply curve don't represent the prices that Mr Babbage wants to receive for any given amount of cabbages – obviously, he wants to receive as much as he can get for each one. Instead, each amount in pounds on a supply curve represents the minimum that you can pay him and still get him to produce the desired amount.

At point *A*, you can get him to produce five cabbages if you pay him 50 pence for each cabbage; if you offer him 49 pence, he refuses. Why? Because he has costs (such as land, fertiliser, labour, tractors and other things farmers need to buy), and he can cover them when he gets 50 pence for each cabbage but not 49 pence.

Separating sales price and production cost

As with demand curves, economists split all the things that can affect the quantity supplied into two groups: the price and everything else. The things that go into everything else relate to the costs of supplying the good in question.

When you see a particular supply curve, imagine that it derives from a particular production technology used by the supplier. (When an economist says *a technology*, he or she means a particular way of combining inputs to make outputs.) Because each possible technology creates its own unique relationship between output levels and costs, some technologies give rise to steeply sloped supply curves, whereas others generate fairly flat supply curves.

Price changes: Moving along the supply curve

Varying the price of an item moves you along a given supply curve because the supply curve represents the minimum payment you need to give the supplier in order for him or her to supply the amount of output you want.

To see how this works, think about cabbages again. Consider what happens if you offer to pay Mr Babbage £1 per cabbage, and then you let him choose how many cabbages he wants to produce. Given his supply curve in Figure 8-5, he wants to produce exactly ten cabbages and no more, because for cabbages one to nine the cost of production is less than you're paying him. For example, consider point *A* in Figure 8-5. At point *A*, Mr Babbage's production costs are 50 pence per cabbage, meaning that if you pay him £1 per cabbage for five cabbages, he makes a nice profit. Similarly, because his cost per cabbage for producing six cabbages is also less than £1 per cabbage, he's going to want to produce a sixth cabbage. The same is true of cabbages seven, eight and nine.

At ten cabbages, Mr Babbage is indifferent, because his cost per cabbage is £1 and you're offering him £1. Mr Babbage will supply up to this point. But notice that Mr Babbage doesn't produce at point *C* if you offer him £1 per cabbage, because his cost of production is £2 per cabbage.

So think about the supply curve and how it responds to price changes in this way: suppliers look at whatever price is being offered and produce as many units as are profitable, but no more. Therefore, raising or lowering prices moves you along the supply curve as the suppliers' quantities supplied respond to changing prices.

Cost changes: Shifting the supply curve

Because a supplier's cost structure determines the location and slope of the supply curve, changes in the cost structure cause changes in the supply curve. In Figure 8-6, Mr Babbage's costs of production increase because the government imposes a new organic farming law under which he's required to grow cabbages without using pesticides. In response, he has to hire lots of extra workers to kill pests with tweezers instead of simply spraying cheap chemicals.

Because his costs of production have increased, the minimum you have to pay him to produce any given level of output also goes up. Consequently, his supply curve can be thought of as shifting upward vertically from S_0 to S_1.

We draw the shift in Figure 8-6 to show that Mr Babbage's cost of production is 50 pence higher for each cabbage no matter how many cabbages are produced. Compare points *A* and *A'*. Before the new regulation, Mr Babbage was willing to produce five cabbages if you paid him 50 pence for each cabbage. After the policy change, you have to pay him £1 per cabbage when you want him to grow you five cabbages.

Similarly, points *B* and *B'* show that before the regulation, he's willing to grow you ten cabbages if you offered him £1 per cabbage. Now, you have to offer him £1.50 per cabbage when you want him to grow ten.

The important thing to remember is that anything that changes producers' costs structures shifts their supply curves. Things that make production more costly shift supply curves up, whereas things that lower costs shift supply curves down.

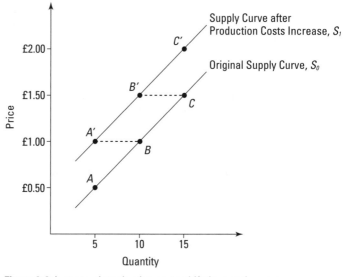

Figure 8-6: Increased production costs shift the supply curve.

Keep in mind that thinking about supply curves as moving left and right when cost structures shift is perfectly kosher. For example, consider the quantity supplied at a price of £1 both before and after the cost increase. Before the cost increase, Mr Babbage is willing to supply you with ten cabbages for £1 each, putting you at point B on the original supply curve. But after the cost increase, he's willing to supply you only five cabbages for £1 per cabbage, putting you at point A' on the shifted supply curve. Similarly, at a price of £1.50 per cabbage, Mr Babbage was previously willing to supply you with 15 cabbages (point C), whereas after the cost increase he's willing to supply only 10 cabbages at that price (point B').

You can quite accurately say that the supply curve shifted left when costs increased. And you can quickly surmise that a decrease in costs shifts the supply curve to the right.

Extreme supply cases

Two extreme supply curves help to illustrate how production costs and prices combine to determine the quantity to be supplied at any particular price. We illustrate these two cases in Figure 8-7.

The graph on the left shows a vertical supply curve and illustrates what economists call *perfectly inelastic supply*. The graph on the right with a horizontal supply curve illustrates what economists call *perfectly elastic supply*. We talk about each curve in the next two sections.

Paying any price: Perfectly inelastic supply

The left graph of Figure 8-7 illustrates a situation in which the price has no effect on the quantity supplied. As you can see in the graph, no matter how low or how high the price, the quantity Q is supplied. Because the quantity supplied is completely unresponsive to the price, economists call this situation *perfectly inelastic*, and supply situations that look like this are usually referred to as situations of *perfectly inelastic supply*.

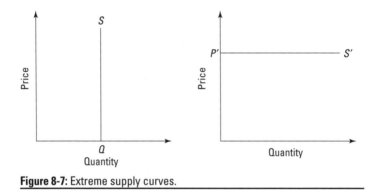

Figure 8-7: Extreme supply curves.

We expect you're curious about what things have perfectly inelastic supply curves. The answer is unique things that can't be reproduced. Examples include:

- ✔ **The Hope Diamond:** Because only one Hope Diamond can exist, no matter how much anyone wanted to pay, its supply curve is vertical.

- ✔ **Land:** As comedian Will Rogers said back in the early 20th century, 'Buy land. They ain't making more of it.'

- ✔ **The electromagnetic spectrum:** Only one set of radio frequencies exists, and we all have to share because making more frequencies is impossible.

An interesting thing about unique situations is that no production costs are involved. Because of this, offering the owner a price is not an incentive as it may be when you pay a producer enough to make something for you. Instead, the price serves solely to transfer the right of ownership and usage from one person to another.

Producing however much you want: Perfectly elastic supply

The right-hand graph in Figure 8-7 illustrates the polar opposite case, where the supply curve is perfectly horizontal. The idea here is that the supplier is producing something with non-increasing costs. No matter how many units you want, the supplier's cost remains only P' pounds to make a unit. Consequently, whether you want one unit produced or one jillion units produced, you pay only P' pounds per unit.

In the real world, perfectly elastic supply curves are rare to the point of non-existence, because production costs typically rise with output levels (as we explain in Chapter 10). However, in the virtual world they are common. For example, it costs Google a negligible amount to supply an extra search. One problem associated with that is that it proves to be very difficult to charge direct users for their searches.

Interacting Supply and Demand to Find Market Equilibrium

In previous sections we discuss demand and supply curves separately. Now we bring them together so that they can interact to show you how markets determine the amounts, as well as the prices, of goods and services sold.

Finding market equilibrium

In Figure 8-8, we show a demand curve and a supply curve on the same axes, labelled D and S, respectively. Remember three things about the demand and supply model when looking at this graph:

✔ The *equilibrium* of the supply and demand model is where the demand and supply curves cross.

✔ The price and the quantity where the curves cross are, respectively, how much the good or service in question costs and how much of it gets sold. This price and this quantity are known as the *market price* and the *market quantity*.

✔ The market price and market quantity represent a stable equilibrium such that market forces always push the price and quantity back to these values. Consequently, the market price and market quantity are also called the *equilibrium price* and the *equilibrium quantity*.

We label the market price and market quantity as P^* and Q^*, respectively. What makes this price and this quantity special is that at price P^*, the quantity that buyers demand is equal to the quantity that producers want to supply.

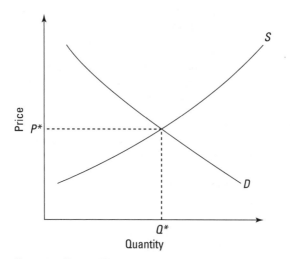

Figure 8-8: The equilibrium price and quantity happen where the demand curve crosses the supply curve.

Put slightly differently, you can see starting at price P^* and moving to the right horizontally along the dotted line that buyers demand Q^* at that price and sellers supply Q^* at that price. Because demand equals supply, both producers and consumers are content. The consumers get exactly the quantity that they want to buy at price P^*, and the producers sell exactly the quantity that they want to sell at price P^*.

Even more interesting is that at any price other than P^*, buyers or sellers always bring some sort of pressure to bear to return the model to the market equilibrium price and quantity. The pleasant result is that no matter where the market starts, it always ends back at equilibrium.

Demonstrating the stability of the market equilibrium

The market equilibrium is called a stable equilibrium because no matter where the demand and supply model starts off, it always gravitates back to the market equilibrium – just so long as we don't introduce any outside forces! This inherent stability is great because it means that markets are self-correcting, and when you know where the demand and supply curves are, you know where prices and quantities are going to end up. Especially gratifying is the fact that the actions of the market participants – buyers and sellers – move the market towards equilibrium without the need for any outside intervention, such as government regulations.

We want to prove to you that the market equilibrium is indeed stable. In the next section we focus on the fact that when prices start higher than P^*, they fall down to P^*. After that, we show you that when prices start lower than P^*, they rise up to P^*. The fact that prices always move toward P^* indicates that the market equilibrium is stable.

Excess supply: Reducing prices until they reach equilibrium

In Figure 8-9, you can see what happens when you have a price like P^H that starts out higher than the market equilibrium price, P^*. At price P^H, the quantity demanded by buyers, Q^D, is less than the quantity supplied by sellers, Q^S. (We use dotted lines to show where P^H intersects the demand and supply curves.) Economists refer to such a situation as excess supply, and it can't be an equilibrium because sellers aren't able to sell everything they want to sell at price P^H.

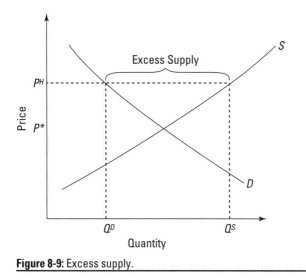

Figure 8-9: Excess supply.

Of the total amount that sellers want to sell, Q^S, only the amount Q^D is sold, meaning that the surplus, $Q^S - Q^D$, remains unsold unless something is done. Sellers see the huge pile of unsold goods and do what any store does when it can't sell something at current prices: they have a sale.

Sellers lower the price until supply no longer exceeds demand. You can see in Figure 8-9 that this means sellers keep lowering the price until it falls all the way down to P^*, because P^* is the only price at which the quantity demanded by buyers equals the quantity that sellers want to supply.

Excess demand: Raising prices until they reach equilibrium

Figure 8-10 shows a situation opposite to the one in the preceding section. The initial price, P^L, is lower than the market equilibrium price, P^*. You can see that in this case, the problem is not excess supply, but rather excess demand, because at price P^L the amount that buyers want to buy, Q^D, exceeds the amount that suppliers want to sell, Q^S.

In other words, a shortage exists that equals $Q^D - Q^S$ units. As a result, buyers start bidding the price up, competing against each other for the insufficient amount of the good.

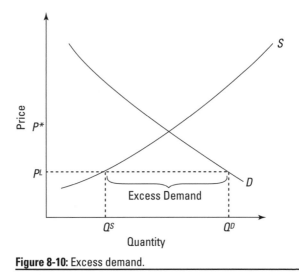

Figure 8-10: Excess demand.

As long as the price is less than P^*, some degree of shortage exists, and the price continues to be bid up. This means that whenever you start out with a price less than P^*, the price is pushed back up to P^*, returning the market to its equilibrium – the only place where neither a shortage nor a surplus exists.

Adjusting to New Market Equilibriums When Supply or Demand Changes

As shown in the previous sections, for any given supply and demand curves, market forces adjust until the price and quantity correspond to where the demand and supply curves cross. When they reach that point – the market equilibrium – the price and quantity don't change. They stay right there as long as the demand and supply curves don't move.

In this section, we show you how prices and quantities do adjust when the demand and supply curves change. We illustrate this adjustment by showing you a demand curve shift and then a supply curve shift.

Reacting to an increase in demand

Take a close look at Figure 8-11, which shows what happens when the demand curve shifts to the right from D_o to D_1 while the supply curve S stays the same. Before the shift, the market equilibrium price is P^*_o, and the market equilibrium quantity is Q^*_o. When the demand curve shifts to the right to D_1, the price momentarily stays the same at P^*_o. But this price can't last because with the new demand curve, an excess demand now exists: that is, at price P^*_o, the quantity demanded, Q^D_1, exceeds the quantity supplied, Q^*_o.

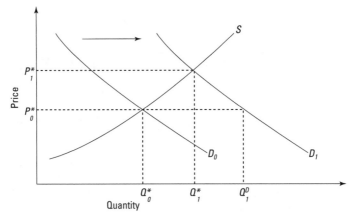

Figure 8-11: A rightward shift of the demand curve re-establishes market equilibrium.

The result of the shortage is that the price rises and until it reaches P^*_1, the price where demand curve D_1 crosses supply curve S.

Note that when moving from the first equilibrium to the second, the equilibrium quantity increases from Q^*_o to Q^*_1. This result makes good sense because if demand increases and buyers are willing to pay more for something, you expect more of it to be supplied. Also, the price goes up from one equilibrium to the other because to get suppliers to supply more in a world of rising costs, you have to pay them more.

Much more subtle, however, is that the slope of the supply curve interacts with the demand curve to determine the size of the changes in price and quantity. Refer back to the perfectly vertical supply curve of the left-hand graph of Figure 8-7. For such a supply curve, any increase in demand increases the price *only*, because the quantity can't increase. On the other hand, if you're dealing with the perfectly horizontal supply curve of the right-hand graph of Figure 8-7, a rightward shift in demand increases the quantity *only*, because the price is fixed at P'.

Thinking through these two extreme cases hammers home that in a situation like Figure 8-11, neither demand nor supply is in complete control. Their interaction jointly determines equilibrium prices and quantities and how they change if the demand curve or the supply curve shifts.

Reacting to a decrease in supply

To show you how the market equilibrium changes when the supply curve shifts, consider Figure 8-12 in which the supply curve shifts from S_0 to S_1 because of an increase in production costs.

The shift in supply causes the market equilibrium to adjust. The original equilibrium is at price P^*_0 and quantity Q^*_0, which is the point where the demand curve D and the original supply curve S_0 cross. When production costs increase, the supply curve shifts to S_1.

For a moment, the price remains at P^*_0. But this price can't continue because the quantity demanded at this price, Q^*_0, exceeds the quantity supplied, Q^S_1. This situation of excess demand causes the price to be bid up until reaching the new equilibrium price of P^*_1, at which price the quantity demanded equals the quantity supplied at Q^*_1.

When you compare this situation of increasing costs with the situation of increasing demand in the previous section, you notice that in both cases the equilibrium price rises. However, make sure to note that the equilibrium quantities go in opposite directions. An increase in demand causes an increase in equilibrium quantity, but an increase in costs causes a reduction in equilibrium quantity.

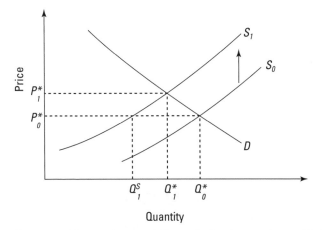

Figure 8-12: The supply curve shifts vertically when market equilibrium resets.

Equilibrium quantity falls because the increase in production costs doesn't just affect the producer. In order to stay in business, the producer has to pass along the cost increase. But when he or she passes the increase along, it tends to discourage buyers. The result is that the equilibrium quantity falls because some buyers aren't willing to pay the higher costs. Those who still want to buy are willing to pay the higher costs – as reflected in the increased market price.

Constructing Impediments to Market Equilibrium

Left to its own devices, a market always adjusts until the price and quantity are determined by where the demand and supply curves cross. The equilibrium price has the great property that everyone who wants to buy at that price can do so, whereas everyone who wants to sell at that price can also do so.

Remember, the market price is not always the politically expedient price, and governments often interfere in the market to prevent the market equilibrium from being reached. Such interventions happen because politically influential buyers think the market price is too high, or because politically influential sellers think the price is too low.

Unfortunately, when the government intervenes to help the people who are complaining, it can create a whole new set of problems and, in some cases, even hurt the very people that the intervention was designed to help. To explain how this happens, we first explain price ceilings and then price floors. Price ceilings prevent prices from rising to the market equilibrium, whereas price floors keep prices from falling to the market equilibrium.

Raising price ceilings

Sometimes the government intervenes in a market so that the price stays below the market equilibrium price, P*. Remember, prices below the market equilibrium normally rise, and therefore these policies are called *price ceilings*, because they prevent the price from rising as high as it may have gone if left alone. Prices hit the ceiling and then go no higher.

To see how this policy works, and the problems it creates, look at Figure 8-13, in which the price ceiling P^C lies below the market equilibrium price of P^*. To make clear that we have a ceiling above which the price can't rise, we draw a solid horizontal line starting from P^C and extending right.

The problem in Figure 8-13 is that at the ceiling price, the quantity demanded, Q^D, far exceeds the quantity supplied, Q^S. This situation may not look like a big problem, but you have to deal with the shortage somehow. You have to figure out a way to allocate the insufficient supply among all the people who want it. The result is that people end up queuing to get the limited supply.

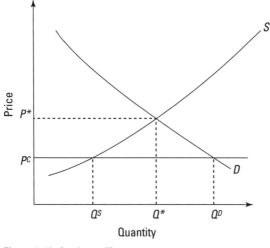

Figure 8-13: A price ceiling.

Propping up price floors

The opposite sort of market intervention is a *price floor*, by which the government keeps the price above its market equilibrium value. An example of this is shown in Figure 8-14, where the floor price, P^F, is greater than the market equilibrium price, P^*. To make it clear that prices can't fall below P^F, we draw a solid horizontal line at that price.

The problem in Figure 8-14 is that at price P^F, the quantity supplied, Q^S, is greater than the quantity demanded, Q^D. The normal response to excess supply is for the price to fall. To prevent the price from falling, the government steps in and buys up the excess supply to prop the price up.

In other words, of the total amount Q^S supplied at price P^F, regular consumers demand and purchase Q^D. The remainder, $Q^S - Q^D$, must be purchased by the government. This situation doesn't sound too bad until you read about price floors in agriculture, which proponents usually refer to euphemistically as *price supports*.

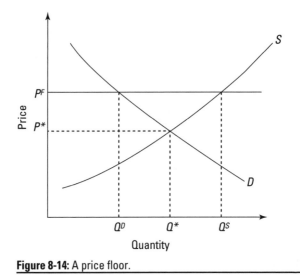

Figure 8-14: A price floor.

Therefore, as regards both price ceilings and price floors, remember that mischief is typically caused when you interfere with the markets. This reasoning doesn't mean that governments should *never* intervene in the operation of a market, but rather that they need to be smart enough not to intervene in ways that they know are going to lead to perverse results.

Chapter 9

Getting to Know the Utility-Maximising Consumer

In This Chapter

▶ Studying how people maximise their happiness

▶ Taking account of diminishing marginal utility

▶ Watching how people weigh alternatives

▶ Choosing exactly the right amounts within a limited budget

*T*his chapter gets behind the demand curve by showing you how people choose the things they choose. This decision-making process is very important because human wants drive the economy. Firms don't randomly produce goods and services; they produce the things that people want to buy.

The thing that makes studying this process hard is the fact that people have so many different things on which they can spend their money. What's impressive is that economists have come up with a way to explain how you're going to spend £100 in a shop that has hundreds or even thousands of items for sale. In fact, an economist can explain not only which items you're going to buy, but also how many of each you're going to buy. In other words, economists can explain not just *what* you demand, but also the *quantities* you demand, which is where demand curves come from.

Measuring Happiness: Utility

In order for people to choose between the exceedingly different goods and services available in the economy, they must have a way of comparing them all. Comparing costs is pretty easy; you just compare prices. But how do you compare the benefits of various goods and services? How do you assess whether spending £20 on Swiss chocolate bars or on a cotton shirt is better? In what ways are chocolate and shirts even comparable?

Obviously, people do manage to make the comparison and rank the two options. Economists imagine that people do this by assigning a common measure of happiness to each possible thing they can buy and use. Economists call this common measure of happiness *utility*, and they imagine that if they were able to get inside your brain and measure utility, they'd do so using a unit that they very uncreatively call a *util*. However, making such strong claims about how people measure happiness is not necessary.

Some people very naturally object to assigning specific numbers of utils to different things – for example, 25 utils to the pleasure associated with eating a brownie, or 75 utils to the pleasure associated with watching a sunset. Making such specific assignments is called *cardinal utility* (like cardinal numbers: 1, 2, 3 . . .). The objections to cardinal utility centre on doubts about whether people even make such assessments – after all, how many utils do you think you receive from a sunny day or a baby's smile?

A much less objectionable thing to do is to think in terms of *ordinal utility,* a system in which you simply rank things. For example, instead of saying that the sunset has a utility of 75, which makes it preferred to the brownie with a utility of 25, you can simply say that sunsets are preferred to brownies. This system has a much more intuitive feeling for most people and eliminates the need to try to measure things using the imaginary unit called the util.

Using the cardinal utility system is a much easier way to explain the crucial concept of *diminishing marginal utility*. So although it may seem a bit unrealistic, the cardinal utility system really is the best way to convey this incredibly important idea.

Diminishing Marginal Utility

People get bored even with things they like and get tired of repetition. Economists have to take account of this tendency when studying how people choose to spend their money.

If you love your pizza, and you haven't had any pizza in a long time, you get a great big rush of utility from eating a slice. But eating that first slice dampens the thrill of pizza, and so if you eat a second slice, it may taste good, but not as good as the first. And if you have a third slice, that's not as good as the second. And by the time you get to your third 13-inch stuffed-crust slice of pizza, you're likely to start to get sick and experience pain rather than pleasure.

This phenomenon isn't limited to pizza; it applies to nearly everything. Unless you're addicted to something, you get tired of it the more you have it, and each additional unit brings you less happiness than the previous unit.

To make this phenomenon clearer, look at Figure 9-1, which shows the cumulative total utility of a pizza lover who eats more and more slices of pizza. For example, total utility after eating one slice of pizza is 20 utils, after eating two slices, 36 utils and after three slices, the total utility is 50 utils.

When you look at these numbers, you notice that the extra utility each additional slice brings is decreasing:

- **First slice:** Total utility increases by 20 utils (0 to 20).

- **Second slice:** The increase is only 16 utils; total utility increases from 20 utils to 36 utils.

- **Third slice:** Total utility increases 14 utils (36 to 50).

Economists refer to this phenomenon as *diminishing marginal utility* because the extra utility, or *marginal utility*, that each successive slice brings decreases relative to the marginal utility brought by the previous slice. Diminishing marginal utility is simply a reflection of the fact that people get fed up or bored with things. Or, in the case of food and drink, their appetite decreases with each unit they consume.

Look at what happens in Figure 9-1 after slice number eight. Total utility actually goes down, because slice number nine can make even the most rabid pizza lover feel a little sick. Add on slice number ten, and total utility falls again.

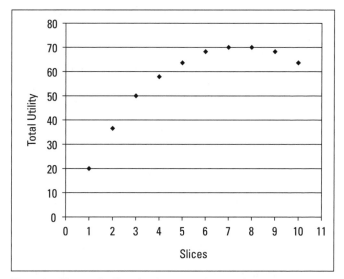

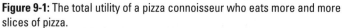

Figure 9-1: The total utility of a pizza connoisseur who eats more and more slices of pizza.

This decrease in total utility implies that marginal utility must be negative for slices nine and ten. Look at Table 9-1, which gives both the total and marginal utilities for each slice. As you can see, the data matches Figure 9-1 and shows that although total utility increases for slices one through seven, it stalls at slice number eight and falls for slices nine and ten.

The right column shows the diminishing marginal utility that comes with eating more and more slices of pizza, because the marginal utility that comes with the next slice is always less than that of the previous slice. Although marginal utility is 20 utils for the first slice, it falls to 0 utils for slice eight and then actually becomes negative for slices nine and ten because eating them makes just about anyone ill.

Table 9-1	Total and Marginal Utility of Eating Ten Slices of Pizza	
Slice	**Total Utility**	**Marginal Utility**
1	20	20
2	36	16
3	50	14
4	58	8
5	64	6
6	68	4
7	70	2
8	70	0
9	68	−2
10	64	−4

In Figure 9-2, we plot out the marginal utility for each slice of pizza. You can see quite clearly from the downward slope of the points that marginal utility diminishes as one eats more and more slices of pizza.

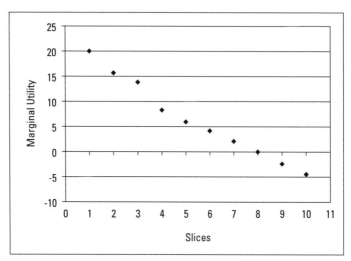

Figure 9-2: The marginal utility derived from each slice of pizza.

You have to be careful not to confuse diminishing marginal utility with *negative* marginal utility. As you see in Table 9-1 and Figure 9-2, diminishing marginal utility for all slices of pizza starts with the second, because each successive slice has a smaller marginal utility than the previous one. But the marginal utilities are still positive for all slices up to slice seven, and they become negative only for slices nine and ten.

That fact implies that you enjoy eating every slice up to and including the seventh slice because doing so brings you an increase in utility (happiness). So don't think that just because marginal utility is diminishing for a particular slice, you don't want to eat it. Marginal utility can be diminishing but still positive. The only slices you want to avoid outright are the ninth and tenth.

Choosing Among Many Options When Facing a Limited Budget

The phenomenon of diminishing marginal utility makes studying human choices very interesting because whether you prefer chocolate ice cream or vanilla ice cream can't be determined in the abstract. Instead, your preference depends on what you've already eaten.

If you haven't had any ice cream for months, you may choose chocolate. But if you're asked whether you want chocolate or vanilla after you've just eaten a gallon of chocolate, you're probably going to say vanilla because you've already more than satisfied your chocolate cravings.

So the answer to the question 'Chocolate or vanilla?' isn't as straightforward as it seems. Your preferences exhibit diminishing marginal utility, and even something that you normally like a lot doesn't bring you much marginal utility (additional happiness) if you've just indulged in it a lot.

This fact ends up leading to a very simple formula about how people make decisions when faced with limited budgets. But before we state the formula, we give you an example that helps explain it.

Trying to buy as much (marginal) utility as you can

In this example, you have £10 to spend and, because you're going to the local student bar, the only two things you can spend the money on are pints of beer and slices of pizza. You're now thinking about how to best spend your £10, and the intelligent thing to do is to think in terms of buying up as much utility as you can with your limited budget. Both beer and pizza make you happy, but your goal isn't just to be happy; you want to be as happy as possible given your limited budget. So you want to make sure that every pound buys you the maximum possible amount of utility.

Keep in mind that you don't care where utility comes from. One util from beer makes you just as happy as one util from pizza; all you care about is buying up as many utils as possible. To do that, the key concept turns out to be the price of utility. Beer and pizza clearly have prices measured in pounds, but what is the price of a util?

Well, it depends. Take a look at Table 9-2. The first three columns repeat the data from Table 9-1 that give total and marginal utilities for ten slices of pizza. But the final two columns include new data and are labelled 'MU per pound at £1 per slice' and 'MU per pound at £2 per slice' respectively. (*MU* stands for *marginal utility*.)

Table 9-2   Determining the Price of Utility for Pizza

Slice	Total Utility	Marginal Utility	MU per Pound at £1 per Slice	MU per Pound at £2 per Slice
1	20	20	20	10
2	36	16	16	8
3	50	14	14	7
4	58	8	8	4
5	64	6	6	3
6	68	4	4	2
7	70	2	2	1

(continued)

Table 9-2 *(continued)*

Slice	Total Utility	Marginal Utility	MU per Pound at £1 per Slice	MU per Pound at £2 per Slice
8	70	0	0	0
9	68	–2	–2	–1
10	64	–4	–4	–2

What we've done in these last two columns is to calculate how much it costs to get some additional happiness (marginal utility) if buying slices of pizza is the way you're getting it.

Consider the fourth column, which assumes that each slice of pizza costs £1. If you buy one slice, it brings you a marginal utility of 20 utils at a cost of £1. So the MU per pound of the first slice is 20.

But now consider spending a second pound to buy a second slice of pizza. Because that second slice brings with it a marginal utility of only 16 utils, the MU per pound spent here is only 16. And because diminishing marginal utility continues to decrease the marginal utility of each additional slice of pizza, each additional pound you spend buys you less additional utility than the previous pound.

The final column of Table 9-2 shows you that the MU per pound that you get from pizza depends on how much each slice of pizza costs. If pizza costs £2 per slice, each pound spent brings you less marginal utility than when pizza cost only £1 per slice.

For example, because each slice now costs £2, when you buy the first slice and it brings you 20 utils, you're getting only 10 utils per pound spent. Although the second slice still brings you 16 additional utils of happiness, because it now costs you £2 to get those utils, your MU per pound is only 8 utils.

In Table 9-3, we give you the same sort of information as in Table 9-2, but this time for total utility, marginal utility and MU per pound when drinking beer that costs £2 per pint.

Table 9-3   Determining the Price of Utility for Beer

Pint	Total Utility	Marginal Utility	MU per Pound at £2 per Pint
1	20	20	10
2	38	18	9
3	54	16	8
4	68	14	7
5	80	12	6
6	90	10	5
7	98	8	4
8	104	6	3
9	108	4	2
10	110	2	1

As you can see from the third column, you exhibit diminishing marginal utility with regard to beer, as your MU for each beer falls from 20 utils for the first pint down to only 2 utils for the tenth pint. As a result, your MU per pound spent in the fourth column falls from 10 per pound for the first pint down to only 1 per pound for the last pint.

Allocating money between two goods to maximise total utility

Tables 9-2 and 9-3 show you how much utility you can get by spending money on pizza or beer. The trick now is to see how you can get the most possible utility for your limited budget of £10. As a first attempt, consider the two extreme options: blowing all the money on pizza or blowing all the money on beer. (Pizza costs £1 per slice, and beer costs £2 per pint.)

If you spend all £10 on pizza, you can buy ten slices of pizza, which gives you a total utility of 64 utils. On the other hand, if you spend all £10 on beer, you can buy five pints at £2 each and thereby get 80 total utils. If these were your only two options, you'd clearly prefer to spend all your money on beer because it brings you more utils than buying only pizza.

However, you can do a much better thing. You can get even more total utility if you wisely mix up your consumption a bit and spend some of your money on beer and some on pizza.

The way you get the most utility possible out of your £10 is simple: take each of the ten pounds in turn and spend it on whichever good brings more utility. Don't think of your task as buying slices of pizza or pints of beer, but bear in mind that your job is buying utility. For every pound spent, you want to buy as much utility as possible, and you don't care whether that utility comes from beer or pizza.

The only thing complicating this process of spending each pound on whichever good brings the most utility is the fact that you have diminishing marginal utility for both beer and pizza, meaning that the amount of utility you're able to buy with each extra pound spent depends on how much beer or pizza you've already bought. But given the information in Tables 9-2 and 9-3, you can work out the best thing you can do with each pound:

- **Pound 1:** How do you spend your first pound? From the fourth column of Table 9-2, you can see that if you spend that pound on pizza, you can buy 20 utils of utility. On the other hand, the fourth column of Table 9-3 tells you that if you spend that first pound on beer (along with a second pound because pints cost £2), you get only 10 utils of utility. So, the obvious thing to do with the first pound is to buy pizza rather than beer.

- **Pound 2:** If you use your second pound to buy a second slice of pizza, you get 16 utils of utility. If you buy beer with that second pound (along with a third pound because the price of a pint is £2), you get only 10 utils for that second pound because it's going to be spent on buying the first pint. So once again, you're better spending this pound on pizza rather than beer.

- **Pound 3:** You also want to spend the third pound on pizza rather than beer because you get 14 utils of marginal utility rather than 10 utils. (Remember, this pound would buy the *first* pint of beer, which brings 10 utils of utility.)

- **Pounds 4 and 5:** At pound number four, everything changes, because if you spend a fourth pound on pizza, it brings 8 utils. However, if you spend that fourth pound (along with the fifth pound) on a pint, you get an MU per pound of 10 utils (for each of those pounds). So, you're best spending pounds four and five on buying the first pint of beer.

✔ **Pounds 6 and 7:** You should also spend pounds six and seven on beer, because you get an MU per pound of 9 utils for your second pint, whereas you get only 8 utils if you spend the sixth pound on a fourth slice of pizza.

✔ **Pounds 8, 9 and 10:** For pound number eight, the MUs per pound are tied. If you use this pound to buy a fourth slice of pizza, you get 8 utils. You get the same by spending the pound on a third pint of beer. So what you should do is spend your last three pounds on buying a fourth slice of pizza and a third pint of beer.

In Table 9-4, we list how to spend each of your ten pounds. Notice that the total utility you can purchase with your ten pounds is 112 utils. That's much better than the 64 utils you get spending all the money on pizza or the 80 utils you get spending it all on beer. By spending each pound in sequence on whichever good brings the most utility, you've done much better than spending the money on only one good or the other.

Table 9-4	How to Spend Each Pound Optimally on Pizza and Beer	
Pound	**Good Chosen**	**MU per Pound**
1	Pizza	20
2	Pizza	16
3	Pizza	14
4	Beer	10
5	Beer	10
6	Beer	9
7	Beer	9
8	Pizza	8
9	Beer	8
10	Beer	8
Total utils		**112**

Also notice that you end up buying four slices of pizza and three pints of beer. Given this budget and these prices, your quantity demanded of pizza is four slices and your quantity demanded of beer is three pints. The process of maximising utility is also the basis of demand curves and the relationship between quantity demanded and price.

Equalising the marginal utility per pound of all goods and services

In the previous section, we go through a rather tedious process to determine how to best spend £10 on beer and pizza. Making these decisions doesn't always take so long. In this section, we explain a simple formula that guides people to maximise the total utility they can get out of spending any budget, no matter how many goods are available to choose from or how much they each cost.

To keep things simple, we begin by showing you the version of the formula that applies to deciding how to best spend your budget when you have only two goods or services to choose from. When you get the hang of the two-good version, the multi-good version is effortless.

We call the two goods X and Y. Their respective prices are P_X pounds for each unit of X and P_y pounds for each unit of Y. Also, their respective marginal utilities are MU_X and MU_y. The formula looks like this:

$$\frac{MU_x}{P_x} = \frac{MU_y}{P_y}$$

This equation means that if a person has allocated their limited budget optimally between the two goods, the marginal utilities per pound of X and Y are equal at the optimal quantities of X and Y.

This relationship holds true in the example in the previous section. Look back at Table 9-4. When you optimally spend your £10 on beer and pizza, the optimal amounts of each are four slices of pizza and three pints of beer. From the third column of Table 9-4, you can see that marginal utilities per pound for the fourth slice of pizza and the third beer are indeed equal at 8 utils per pound, just as the formula in equation (1) dictates.

Now, we demonstrate *why* marginal utilities per pound have to be equal if you want to maximise your utility with a limited budget. If marginal utilities per pound aren't equal, you want to keep rearranging your purchases until they are.

First, imagine that you choose some other quantities of each good, so that for the final unit of X and the final unit of Y that you purchase:

$$\frac{MU_x}{P_x} > \frac{MU_y}{P_y}$$

For example, let pizza be X and beer be Y. From Tables 9-2 and 9-3, you can see that if you purchase four pints of beer and two slices of pizza, the MU per pound for the fourth pint of beer is 7 utils, while the MU per pound for the second slice of pizza is 16 utils. Clearly, the MU per pound of pizza is much bigger than the MU per pound of beer if you spend your limited budget in this way.

But this way of spending your budget isn't optimal. The reason is that the money you're spending on what is currently the final unit of X (pizza) buys more marginal utility than the money you're currently spending on the final unit of Y (beer). If you can get more utility by spending a pound on X than you can on Y, take money away from spending on Y in order to spend it on X. And as long as the inequality in equation (2) holds true, continue to take money away from Y in order to increase spending on X.

Consider a more extreme example. Suppose that you spend all £10 buying five pints of beer. You can see from Table 9-3 that the marginal utility per pound of the last pound spent on beer is only 6 utils. By contrast, if you took that pound away from beer and used it to buy a first slice of pizza, the pizza brings you 20 utils (see Table 9-2). Clearly, you need to reduce your beer buying in order to increase your pizza buying.

Continue to buy fewer beers and more pizza until you arrive at the combination of four slices of pizza and three beers.

That is, rearrange your spending until the marginal utilities per pound of both beer and pizza are equal, as in equation (1).

The same rule applies if you start out spending all your money on pizza. If you buy ten slices of pizza, you can see from Table 9-2 that the marginal utility of the tenth slice is actually –4 utils. Meanwhile, the marginal utility per pound of the first pound spent on beer is 10 utils. Clearly you need to take money away from pizza and use it to buy more beer.

Deriving Demand Curves from Diminishing Marginal Utility

Diminishing marginal utility is one reason that demand curves slope downward. You can get a hint of this from Figure 9-2, where you see that the marginal utility that comes with each successive piece of pizza decreases. If your goal is to use your money to buy up as much utility as possible in order to make yourself as happy as possible, you're willing to pay less and less for each successive piece of pizza, as the next piece of pizza brings with it less utility than the previous piece.

However, Figure 9-2 is not a demand curve, for two reasons:

✔ It doesn't take into account the effect that prices have on the quantity demanded.

✔ It looks at only one good in isolation, whereas the quantity demanded of a good is determined by finding the solution to the more general problem of allocating a limited budget across all available goods in order to maximise total utility.

Seeing how price changes affect quantities demanded

In the example we use in this chapter, you need to decide how to best spend £10 when your choices are slices of pizza or pints of beer. Now we make one change to that example: imagine that pizza now costs £2 per slice rather than £1 per slice. We want to show you how this price change affects the quantity demanded of both pizza and beer.

The changes in quantities demanded result from the fact that the new, higher price of pizza reduces the marginal utility per pound for pizza. Doubling the price of pizza means that the marginal utility per pound spent on each slice of pizza is exactly half of what it was before. You can see this by comparing the fourth and fifth columns of Table 9-2. Because the increase in price lowers the marginal utility that each pound spent on pizza buys, naturally this affects where you spend your limited budget of £10.

As you may expect, a higher price of pizza leads you to eat less pizza and drink more beer. You can prove this to yourself by spending, in order, each of your pounds so that you buy whichever good has the higher marginal utility. The results of doing so are summarised in Table 9-5.

Table 9-5   Optimally Spending Your Budget When Pizza Costs £2

Pound	Good Chosen	MU per Pound
1	Pizza	10
2	Pizza	10
3	Beer	10
4	Beer	10
5	Beer	9
6	Beer	8
7	Beer	8
8	Beer	8
9	Pizza	8
10	Pizza	8
Total utils		**90**

By comparing Table 9-5 with Table 9-4, you can see that raising the price of pizza from £1 to £2 has reduced the quantity of pizza you'd order, though since you can't divide slices or pints in this model it doesn't yet affect the quantity demanded of beer. You can now only afford two slices of pizza and three pints of beer. If we were to raise the price of pizza further, you'd reallocate so that you'd only buy one slice of pizza and four pints of beer. At £3 per slice, you'd be completely out of the pizza market altogether, as the utility gained from spending all £10 on five pints of beer would be higher than the utility gained from consuming any pizza. In other words, you'd substitute towards the cheaper good to get yourself as much utility as possible overall. Economists call this the *substitution effect* of a price change.

To see why, think about it like this. We've given you a choice of two things to spend your money on, and because you've decided to choose your purchases so as to get as much utility as possible, you'll substitute towards the good that gives you the best bang for your buck in terms of maximising your utility. So as the price of one goes up and you get less utility per pound from buying it, you'll substitute *towards* the good that gives you more utility per pound spent.

The increase in the price of pizza has also made you poorer in the only sense that really matters: you're less happy. Due to the price increase, the total number of utils that you can purchase with your £10 budget has fallen from 112 down to only 90. Despite rearranging your quantities consumed of beer and pizza to make the most of the new situation, the price increase still hurts you overall. This is what's called the *income effect*.

Forming a demand curve

You can use the information about how your quantity demanded changes when price goes up to plot out two points on your demand curve for pizza: four slices demanded at a price of £1, and two slices demanded at a price of £2. In Figure 9-3, we plot these two points and sketch in the rest of the demand curve. As you look at the figure, keep in mind two things:

- ✔ The downward slope of the pizza demand curve derives in part from the diminishing marginal utility of pizza, but . . .

- ✔ As the price of pizza changes, the quantity demanded of pizza doesn't change in isolation; it changes as the result of rearranging the quantity demanded of both beer and pizza in order to maximise total utility.

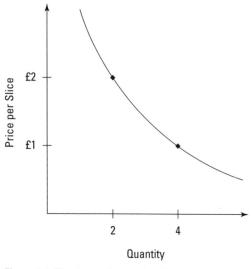

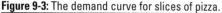

Figure 9-3: The demand curve for slices of pizza.

Demand curves for individual goods aren't made in isolation. Certainly, a relationship exists between a good's price and its quantity demanded. However, when the good's price changes, that change affects the entire budgeting decision – not just for that good, but for *every* good. The resulting change in the good's quantity demanded is just part of the overall rearrangement of spending that strives to keep maximising total utility given the new price.

Consider how the increase in the price of pizza affects the demand curve for beer. As we increase the price of pizza from £1 to £3 per slice, consumption of beer rises from three to five slices. But the price of beer was unchanged. This means that the demand curve for beer must have *shifted*.

We illustrate this shift in Figure 9-4. Point *A* on demand curve *D* shifts over to become point *A'* on demand curve *D'*. Events like this, where changes in the price of one good affect the quantity demanded of another good, are called *cross-price effects*. By contrast, when a change in a good's own price affects its own quantity demanded, you have *own-price effects*.

Please note that whereas cross-price effects cause demand curves to shift, own-price effects cause movements along given demand curves.

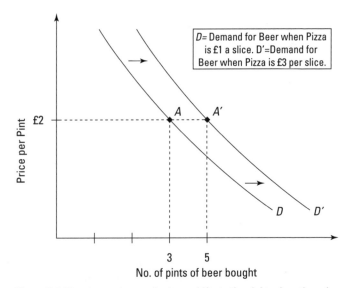

D= Demand for Beer when Pizza is £1 a slice. D'=Demand for Beer when Pizza is £3 per slice.

Figure 9-4: The demand curve for beer shifts to the right when the price of pizza changes, holding the price of beer constant.

The direction of a cross-price effect depends on the situation. In this chapter, we allow consumers to purchase only two goods, beer and pizza. The result is that when the price of pizza goes up, they switch some of their purchasing power over to buying beer – or, as economists say, they *substitute* from one good to the other. That's why when the price of pizza goes up, the demand curve for beer in Figure 9-4 shifts to the right.

But in the real world, where many other consumption goods are available, the demand curve may very well shift in the other direction. For example, some people like drinking beer only when they eat pizza. For them, an increase in the price of pizza may decrease *both* the amount of pizza eaten and the amount of beer drunk.

Such people think of beer and pizza as a complementary bundle. An increase in the price of one good of the bundle increases the price of the entire bundle. These people buy less of each good of the bundle in order to free up money to spend on the many other consumption goods available. For consumers with these preferences, when the price of pizza goes up, the demand curve for beer shifts left.

Chapter 10

The Core of Capitalism: The Profit-Maximising Firm

In This Chapter

▶ Considering competition

▶ Deconstructing a firm's cost structure

▶ Determining a firm's profit-maximising output level

▶ Seeing how costs determine a firm's supply curve

▶ Understanding how firms react to losing money

*I*n modern market economies like the UK, some sort of business enterprise made nearly everything you eat, drink, wear, drive, ride, fly or use. So, naturally, economists devote a huge amount of effort to studying how businesses behave.

In this chapter, we show you how economists model a firm that's a member of a competitive industry; a firm that's just one of many firms competing against each other for your business. You need to understand how firms behave in competitive industries for two reasons:

✔ Most firms in the real world face a lot of competition because they are members of industries in which firms can enter and exit relatively freely. Therefore, firms have to worry about competitors already in the industry and those that may potentially come into the industry.

✔ All firms – even those that don't face much competition – behave in remarkably similar ways.

Above all, firms like to maximise profits. And, even more importantly, all firms go about maximising profits in the same way: by producing exactly the level of output at which the cost of producing one more unit just equals the increase in revenue that the firm gets from selling that unit.

Maximising Profits Is a Firm's Goal

People create firms in order to produce things. That statement may prompt you to ask a fundamental question: *why* do people bother creating firms to make things? One reason may be altruism. Another may be that making things is fun. Another may be that the people who start a firm are bored doing other things. But economists think the answer is much simpler.

Economists assume that the overriding goal of all firms is to make as big a profit as possible.

To put it a bit more bluntly, if you don't make at least some profits in the long run, you aren't going to have a business for very long. Even if your personal goals for your business aren't about making yourself a nice big retirement fund, you're going to have to worry about making profits at some level.

Facing Competition

Firms may or may not face a lot of competition from other firms. At one extreme lies *monopoly*, in which a firm is the only firm in its industry and faces no competition. At the other extreme lies what economists call *perfect competition*, a situation in which a firm competes against many other firms in an industry in which they all produce an identical good. And in between the extremes lie two situations: *oligopoly*, where two, three or (at most) a few firms are in an industry; and *imperfect (monopolistic) competition*, in which many competitors exist, but each produces a good that is unique – at least in some way – to competing products.

In this chapter, you find out how firms behave under perfect competition. This situation is the simplest case to understand, because in an industry in which many competitors are producing identical products, none of the firms has any control over the price they charge.

Listing the requirements for perfect competition

To know why firms engaging in perfect competition have no control over the prices they charge, you have to understand that perfect competition assumes three things about the firms in an industry:

- ✔ Each firm is one of many in the industry.

- ✔ Each firm represents a very small part of the industry.

- ✔ Each firm sells identical or nearly identical products.

Once upon a time, people used to do their shopping in markets, and a market comes close to fulfilling the three criteria above. Individual stallholders are gathered together so that each has only a small share of the industry (in this case, a market). This situation means that individual stallholders are *price takers*, that is, no single stallholder can affect the price that consumers are willing to pay for their produce. A nice shiny apple is therefore likely to cost the same no matter which vendor you buy it from!

Commodity markets also have this property. A *commodity* is something that has a defined quality, such as a metal. For example, something either is gold or it is not gold. The gold that's traded on commodity exchanges in London either satisfies this definition or it's something else.

To see why these things together mean that individual miners have no control over the price of gold, start with the fact that they are producing a nearly identical product. Because the gold from one place is identical to the gold from any other place, the only way an Angolan producer can entice you to buy from him rather than from a Russian producer is to offer you a lower price. Because all the gold is identical, all that producers have to compete on is price and price alone.

With price jumping to the fore as the key factor in the commodity market, we can use supply and demand analysis to figure out what the price is going to be. As we describe in Chapter 8, where the *market demand curve* for gold crosses the *market supply curve* for gold determines the price. How are these curves determined?

- ✔ To determine the *market demand curve* for gold, add up the individual demand curves of all the people who want to buy gold.
- ✔ To determine the *market supply curve* for gold, add up the individual supply curves of all the individual gold producers.

The first two assumptions of perfect competition come into play here: so many producers of gold exist and each producer produces such a very small part of the total supply of gold that the market supply curve for gold is basically unaffected by the presence or absence of any given individual supply curve of any particular gold producer. If a trillion troy ounces of gold are sold every year, the market price is unaffected by whether a small producer with only 1,000 ounces to sell bothers showing up to the market or not. He's just too small a player to cause the market price to change.

If every player is too small to cause the market price to change, each one has to take as given whatever price is generated by market demand interacting with market supply.

Acting as price takers but quantity makers

When the three assumptions of perfect competition are met, they produce a situation in which individual firms have no control over the prices they can charge. If that's all true, the individual firms can justly be called price takers.

Because firms have no control over their prices under perfect competition, the only thing that price-taking firms can control is how much to produce.

Firms choose to make whatever quantity maximises their profits. This fact is mathematically convenient because it turns out that the quantity of output that a firm chooses to produce controls each of the two things that determine profits: total revenues and total costs.

To understand this fact more clearly, you have to know that a firm's profit is simply defined as its total revenue minus its total costs. Put into algebra,

$$Profit = TR - TC \qquad (1)$$

where *TR* stands for total revenue, and *TC* stands for total costs.

The total revenue for a competitive firm is simply the quantity, *q*, of its output that it chooses to sell times the market price, *p*, that it can get for each unit:

$$TR = p \times q \qquad (2)$$

For example, if a market vendor can sell 37 apples for £1 each, his total revenue is £37. But notice that because the price at which the vendor can sell *(p)* is out of his hands if he's a price taker, the only way he can control total revenue is by deciding how many apples to sell. So a firm's decision about how big or small to make *q* determines its total revenue.

Much of this chapter is devoted to showing you that the firm's total costs, *TC*, are also determined by how big or small *q* is. But, interestingly, although each extra unit of *q* sold brings in *p* pounds of revenue, the cost of each unit of *q* manufactured depends on how many units of *q* have already been made. Costs tend to increase as firms produce more and more, so each successive unit costs more than the previous unit.

For example, suppose that the apple vendor can sell as many apples as he wants for £1 each. The first apple costs 10 pence to produce, the second one costs 20 pence, the third one costs 30 pence, and so on. In such a case, he's willing to produce no more than ten apples. Why? Because for each of the first nine apples, he makes a profit, but for apple ten (which costs £1 to produce), he only breaks even. If he produces any more apples, he sustains a loss. (Apple number 11, for example, costs £1.10 to produce, but he gets only £1 for selling it.)

Consequently, you can see that the firm's choice of q determines both the TR and TC terms in profit equation (1). The only thing left to figure out is exactly how big to make q in order to maximise profits. Fortunately a ridiculously simple formula exists that gives the solution.

But before we get to the formula, we need to clarify a major source of confusion caused by the fact that economists use the word *profit* to mean something slightly different from conventional usage.

Distinguishing between accounting profits and economic profits

To an economist, the terms *profit* and *loss* refer to whether the gains from running a business are bigger or smaller than the costs involved. If the gains exceed the costs, you're said to be *running a profit*, whereas if the costs exceed the gains, you're said to be *running a loss*. If the two are just equal, you're said to be *breaking even*.

Things get complicated, however, because although accountants and economists agree on what counts as revenue, they disagree on what to count as costs.

Taking account of opportunity costs

Consider a business that sells lemonade. Both the accountant and the economist agree that the firm's revenues are simply how much money it makes from selling lemonade. However, they differ on what to count as costs:

> ✔ Accountants consider costs to be only actual monies spent in running the business: how much the firm pays its workers, how much it pays to buy lemons and so on. If the firm has revenues of £10,000, and it spends £9,000 to make those revenues, the accountant concludes that the firm's profit is £1,000. This number is the firm's *accounting profit* – the type of profit that is reported every day in financial statements and newspaper articles.

> ✔ Economists prefer a subtler concept, referred to as *economic profit*. Economic profit takes into account not just the money costs directly incurred by running a business, but also the *opportunity costs* incurred.

As we explain in Chapter 2, opportunity costs are what you have to give up in order to do something. Think about the entrepreneur who starts this lemonade business. After paying for materials and employees' wages, the accounting profits are £1,000. But is that really a good deal?

Suppose that this person left a job as a computer programmer to open up the lemonade business, and in the same amount of time that it took the lemonade business to turn a £1,000 profit, she would have made £10,000 in wages if she had stayed at her old job. That is, she gave up the opportunity to earn £10,000 in wages to open up a business that makes only a £1,000 accounting profit. She actually sustains an *economic loss* of £9,000. When you know this fact, her decision to switch careers doesn't seem like such a good idea.

Being motivated by economic profits

Economists like to concentrate on economic profits and losses rather than accounting profits or losses because the economic profits and losses are what motivate people. In our example, you can imagine that when other computer programmers see what happened to their former colleague after she switched careers, they're not going to follow her.

For the rest of the chapter, whenever you see any costs listed, assume that they are *economic costs*; that is, they include not only money directly spent operating a business, but also the costs of other opportunities foregone in order to operate the business. Likewise, whenever you see a profit or a loss, assume that this is an economic profit or an economic loss.

The most important application of this concept is to determine how much output a firm needs to produce. If producing the 12th unit of a product produces an economic profit, obviously the firm wants to produce it. But if increasing production to a 13th unit results in an economic loss, obviously the firm doesn't want to produce it.

Analysing a Firm's Cost Structure

To understand how costs and revenues interact to determine economic profits or losses, we can break up a firm's total costs into two subcategories: fixed costs and variable costs.

- ✔ *Fixed costs* are costs that have to be paid even if the firm isn't producing anything. For example, after a rent contract is signed for the firm's headquarters, that rent must be paid whether the firm produces anything or not. Similarly, if the firm has taken out a loan, it's legally required to make its debt payments whether producing zero units of output or a billion units of output.

- ✔ *Variable costs* are costs that vary with the amount of output produced. For example, if you are in the lemonade-making business and you choose to produce nothing, you obviously don't have to buy any lemons. But the more lemonade you do produce, the more you spend buying lemons. Similarly, producing more lemonade requires more workers, so your labour costs also vary with the amount of output you produce.

Fixed costs can be represented as *FC* and variable costs as *VC*. Together, they sum up to a firm's total costs, or *TC*:

$$TC = FC + VC \tag{3}$$

As you look at equation (3), keep in mind that it deals with the economic costs facing the firm and therefore captures the opportunity costs of the firm's expenditures on both fixed costs and variable costs.

Focusing on costs per unit of output

Economists distinguish between fixed and variable costs because they have very different effects on a firm's decision of how much to produce. Take a look at Table 10-1, which gives data on LemonAid Ltd, our lemonade producer. To keep things simple, we're varying only the amount of labour involved in producing a bottle.

Table 10-1 The Cost Structure of LemonAid

Workers	Output	Fixed Costs	Average Fixed Costs	Variable Costs	Average Variable Costs	Total Costs	Average Total Costs	Marginal Costs
0	0	100	–	0	–	100	–	–
1	50	100	2.00	80	1.60	180	3.60	1.60
2	140	100	0.71	160	1.14	260	1.86	0.89
3	220	100	0.45	240	1.09	340	1.55	1.00
4	290	100	0.34	320	1.10	420	1.45	1.14
5	350	100	0.29	400	1.14	500	1.43	1.33
6	400	100	0.25	480	1.20	580	1.45	1.60
7	440	100	0.23	560	1.27	660	1.50	2.00
8	470	100	0.21	640	1.36	740	1.57	2.67

When LemonAid gets started, it buys a juicer machine for £100, which gives it fixed costs of £100. It then has to decide how much to produce, which in turn determines how many workers it needs to hire. In the first column, the number of workers varies from zero to eight. If the firm hires no workers, you can see in the top entry of the second column that no output is produced. But if it hires workers, output increases as you move down the second column. More workers mean more output.

Studying increasing and decreasing returns

Pay attention to the fact that the amount of additional, or marginal, output produced by each additional worker is not constant: that is, if you go from no workers to one worker, output increases from nothing to 50 bottles of lemonade. However, as you go from one worker to two workers, output increases from 50 bottles to 140 bottles. Put into economic jargon, the second worker's *marginal output* is 90 bottles, whereas the first worker's marginal output is only 50 bottles.

Now look at these facts in terms of costs and benefits. If you have to pay each worker the same wage of £80 per day (£10 per hour for 8 hours of work), you're going to like the fact that whereas the first worker produces 50 bottles for his £80 pay, the second worker produces 90 bottles for her £80 pay.

Economists refer to situations like this as *increasing returns*, because the amount of return you get for a given amount of input (one more worker) increases as you add successive units of input. But if you look farther down the second column, you find that increasing returns don't last forever.

Indeed, in the case of LemonAid, increasing returns end almost immediately. Consider what happens to output when you add a third worker. Output does increase, but only by 80 units, from 140 bottles to 220 bottles. And things get even worse the more workers you add. Adding a fourth worker increases output by only 70 bottles, and adding a fifth increases output by only 60 bottles.

Economists call situations like this *diminishing returns*, because each successive unit of an input, such as labour, brings with it a smaller increase in output than the previous unit of input.

Determining the cause of diminishing returns

Diminishing returns exists because LemonAid bought only one juicer machine for squeezing the juice out of lemons.

The first worker can use the machine to squeeze enough juice for 50 bottles by carrying lemons to the machine and then operating the machine. But it turns out that two workers together can do even better by dividing up the work: one brings lemons to the machine, and the other operates it. Working together, they can produce a total of 140 bottles – more than double the 50 bottles that one worker can produce working alone.

However, a third worker doesn't increase output nearly as much as a second because the two major tasks – carrying and operating – have already been taken care of. At best, he can just help the first two workers do these tasks a little faster. The same holds true for all successive workers: having them is helpful, but each one adds less to output than the previous one because things start getting crowded and little room is left for improvement.

Examining average variable costs

Variable costs are affected by the fact that additional workers first bring increasing returns but then decreasing returns. In the case of the LemonAid example in Table 10-1, the variable costs are all labour costs, with each worker having to be paid £80 per day. You can see these variable costs increase as you move down the fifth column.

But what's much more interesting is looking at *average variable costs (AVC)*, which are defined as variable costs divided by quantity *(VC/q)*. For example, because one worker produces 50 bottles of output at a variable cost of £80, the average variable cost is £80/50 = £1.60 per bottle. When two workers together cost £160 in variable costs but produce 140 bottles, the average variable cost for two workers is only £160/£140 = £1.14 per bottle.

The decrease in average variable costs is the result of increasing returns: when moving from one worker to two workers, variable costs double (from £80 to £160) but output more than doubles (from 50 bottles to 140 bottles).

When diminishing returns set in, average variable costs start to rise, which you can see as you move down the sixth column of Table 10-1. This happens because although each additional worker costs an extra £80, each additional worker after the second worker brings a smaller increase in output than his predecessor. Each successive £80 wage payment brings with it fewer and fewer additional bottles produced, so the average variable cost per bottle must rise.

LemonAid's average variable costs show up as a subtle U shape when you plot them on a graph, which we do in Figure 10-1. (We also show the company's average fixed costs and average total costs.) This average variable cost curve is going to have a huge effect on how many bottles the firm's managers want to produce in order to maximise firm profits.

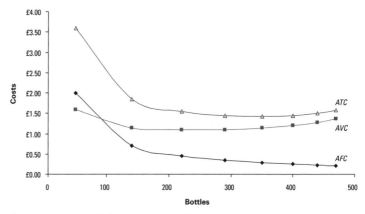

Figure 10-1: LemonAid's average variable costs, average fixed costs and average total costs.

Watching average fixed costs fall

Average fixed costs *(AFC)* are defined as fixed costs divided by quantity *(FC/q)*. The fixed costs of LemonAid are always the £100 the firm paid for the juicer machine, no matter what amount of output it produces. As a result, the more lemonade it produces, the lower its average fixed costs. That's why *AFC* falls (see the fourth column of Table 10-1) from a value of £2.00 per bottle when 50 bottles are produced using one worker down to only £0.21 per bottle when 470 bottles are produced using eight workers.

Average fixed costs always decline, because the same fixed cost gets divided up over a greater and greater number of units of output as output increases. When you plot out average fixed costs per bottle, as in Figure 10-1, you get a downward sloping *AFC* curve. Keep this fact in mind because it helps explain the shape of the average total costs *(ATC)* curve, as we explain in the next section.

Tracking the movement of average total costs

In the previous two sections, we show you that average fixed costs always decline as output increases, whereas average variable costs first fall (due to increasing returns) and then rise (due to diminishing returns). Because total costs are the sum of fixed costs and variable costs, *average total costs* obviously depend on how average fixed costs and average variable costs sum up.

Average total costs *(ATC)* are defined as total costs divided by quantity *(TC/q)*. Now, take a look back at equation (3) earlier in the chapter. If you divide every term in equation (3) by *q*, you get the following:

$$TC/q \ = \ FC/q \ + \ VC/q \qquad\qquad (4)$$

You can simplify equation (4) by realising that $ATC = TC/q$, $AFC = FC/q$, and $AVC = VC/q$. What you get is

$$ATC \ = \ AFC \ + \ AVC \qquad\qquad (5)$$

You can see clearly from equation (5) that average total costs depend on how average fixed costs and average variable costs interact. You need to understand two key points here:

- ✔ *ATC* must always be greater than *AVC*, because you have to add in *AFC*.
- ✔ *ATC* reaches its minimum value at a higher level of output than *AVC*.

To see that the first point is true, look at Figure 10-1, which shows that the *ATC* curve is above the *AVC* curve. The vertical distance between them at any particular level of output is equal to the *AFC* at that output level. As you move from lower output levels to higher output levels, the *ATC* and *AVC* curves converge because *AFC* becomes smaller and smaller. (In other words, the vertical distance between the *ATC* and *AVC* curves also gets smaller and smaller.)

To see that the second point is true, look at Table 10-1 again. You can see that average variable costs reach their minimum value of £1.09, when three workers are hired and 220 bottles are produced. Average total costs, however, reach their minimum of £1.43 when five workers are hired and 350 bottles are produced.

This happens because average fixed costs are always falling, meaning that in equation (5), the *AFC* part on the right-hand side of the equation is always getting smaller and smaller. This constant decline helps to offset temporarily the increases in average variable costs that happen when diminishing returns set in. Consequently, although average variable costs bottom out at three workers, average total costs don't bottom out and start increasing until the fifth worker.

Focusing on marginal costs

The manager of a firm wants to know what quantity, *q*, of output she needs to produce to maximise profits. To solve this problem, she needs one more cost concept: marginal cost.

Marginal cost is how much total costs increase when you produce one more unit of output. The marginal cost of one more unit of output depends on how much output has already been produced.

To see this, examine the total costs column of Table 10-1. Notice that total costs increase from £100 in the first row to £180 in the second row as output increases from 0 bottles to 50 bottles when the firm hires the first worker. In other words, costs go up £80 while output goes up 50 bottles. So each of these extra, *marginal* 50 bottles on average increases costs by £80/50 = £1.60 each. The marginal cost per bottle, *MC*, is defined as follows:

$$MC = (\text{Change in } TC) / (\text{Change in } q) \tag{6}$$

As you move down the marginal costs column of Table 10-1, you can see that marginal costs first fall and then rise: yet another reflection of the fact that LemonAid's production process exhibits increasing returns followed by diminishing returns. Because the second worker produces much more than the first worker but costs the same, the marginal cost falls when the second worker is added. For successive workers, costs keep increasing but marginal output keeps declining, which means marginal costs must rise.

Noticing where the MC curve crosses the AVC and ATC curves

Here's a fun fact that economists love: if you plot out marginal costs to create a marginal cost *(MC)* curve, that curve crosses both the average variable cost *(AVC)* curve and average total cost *(ATC)* curve at their minimum points – that is, at the bottom of their respective U shapes.

In Figure 10-2, we plot the *AVC*, *ATC* and *MC* curves that you get by plotting out the data in Table 10-1. The *MC* curve goes through the minimum points of both the *AVC* and *ATC* curves.

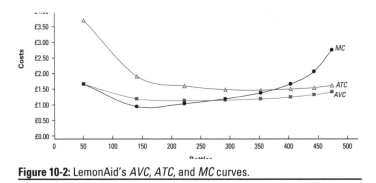

Figure 10-2: LemonAid's *AVC, ATC,* and *MC* curves.

This happens because the marginal cost at each unit determines whether the *AVC* and *ATC* curves are increasing or decreasing.

Think about a room with ten people in it. Suppose you determine that the average height of the people in the room is 156

centimetres. Now think about what happens to that average when another person walks into the room:

- ✔ If the 11th person is taller than the previous average, the average rises.

- ✔ If the 11th person is shorter than average, the average falls.

- ✔ If the 11th person is exactly 156 centimetres tall, the average stays the same.

The same sort of reasoning applies to marginal costs and average costs. After q units of output, you can figure out AVC and ATC, just like you can compute the average height after the first ten people enter the room. After that, AVC and ATC rise or fall depending on the MC of the next unit of output, just as the average height of the people in the room increases, decreases or stays the same, depending on the height of the next person entering the room. Here's what we mean:

- ✔ If the MC is less than the previous average costs, the averages fall.

- ✔ If the MC is greater than the previous average costs, the averages rise.

- ✔ If the MC is exactly the same as the previous average costs, the averages stay the same.

You can see these effects graphically by looking at various parts of Figure 10-2. First, look at the output level of 140 bottles (why not 150? We come to that in the next section). At that output level, the MC of producing one more bottle is less than both ATC and AVC, meaning that ATC and AVC decreases if output is increased by one more bottle. That's why the AVC curve and the ATC curve are downward sloping at that output level. The average curves are being pulled down by the low value of MC.

Next, look at the output level of 440 bottles. You can see that the MC at that output level is higher than the ATC and the AVC. Consequently, both AVC and ATC must be increasing, as reflected geometrically by the upward slopes of both the AVC curve and the ATC curve. The curves slope upwards because the high value for MC is pulling them up.

Now, to put some pieces together, notice that the *MC* curve causes both the *AVC* curve and the *ATC* curve to be U-shaped (albeit subtly). On the left side of Figure 10-2, the fact that *MC* is less than the average curves means that the average curves slope downward. On the right side of Figure 10-2, the fact that *MC* is greater than the average curves means that the average curves slope upward.

So we've come full circle to the fact that the *MC* curve has to cross the two average curves at their respective minimum points – at the bottoms of their respective U shapes. To the left of such a crossing point, the average must be falling because *MC* is less than the average. And to the right, the average must be rising because *MC* is larger than the average. But where the curves cross, the average curve is neither rising nor falling because the *MC* of that unit of output is equal to the current average.

Economists love to go on and on about this fact, but really it just reflects the effect that increasing and then decreasing returns have on cost curves. Costs first fall and then rise. And at some point in the middle, there's a magic level of output where increasing and decreasing returns are balanced, while transitioning from falling to rising. That point must be where marginal cost equals average cost, because only when *MC* equals average cost can average cost be stationary.

Marginal Revenues and Costs

In the previous section, we explain how marginal costs relate to average costs. With that info in mind, we're finally ready to explain how managers decide how much output to produce in order to maximise profits.

Here's a sad but true fact to keep in mind: firms can't always make a profit. In a perfectly competitive industry, a firm can't control the price for which its output sells, and sometimes that price is too low for the firm to make a profit, whatever quantity it produces. When that happens, the best the firm can do is minimise its losses and hope for the price to change. If the price drops low enough, the best thing to do may be to shut down production immediately, because that way the firm loses only its fixed costs.

Later in the chapter, we discuss this sad situation in more detail. But first, we focus on a happier situation – one in which the market price is high enough that a firm wants to produce a positive amount of output. As you're going to see, this may or may not mean that a firm is making a profit, but even if it isn't, the losses aren't great enough to halt production.

The magic formula: Finding where MR = MC

In the typical case where market prices are high enough that a firm wants to make a positive amount of output, a ridiculously simple formula is used to determine the optimal quantity of output, q, that the firm needs to produce. The firm wants to produce at the level of output where marginal revenue equals marginal cost *(MR = MC)*.

Producing where $MR = MC$ does two things:

- ✔ It minimises the firm's loss if it has to take a loss due to a low selling price for its output.

- ✔ It maximises the firm's profit if it can make a profit, because the selling price is high enough.

The idea behind $MR = MC$ is very simple and basically comes down to a cost versus benefit analysis. If producing and selling a bottle brings in more revenue than it costs to produce the bottle, produce it. If not, don't produce it. Easy, right?

Recall our example. Imagine that LemonAid can sell each bottle of lemonade that it produces for £2 each. Economists like to say that the *marginal revenue* of each bottle is £2, because each and every bottle when sold brings in an extra £2.

The firm's managers must decide how much to produce based on whether any given bottle costs more or less than the £2 marginal revenue that the firm would get by selling it.

Be very careful at this point. You have to remember that the relevant cost that the managers look at is an individual bottle's marginal cost, *MC*. That's because if they're deciding whether to produce that particular bottle, they need to isolate that bottle's production cost from the costs of all previously produced bottles in order to compare it to the revenue that the bottle brings if produced and sold. *MC* does just that by ignoring all previous bottles and focusing on what the next bottle is going to cost to make.

If the *MC* of that bottle is less than £2, obviously producing that bottle makes a gain, and so the managers choose to produce it. On the other hand, if the *MC* is bigger than £2, producing the bottle causes a loss, and the managers choose not to produce it.

By looking at the *MC* of each bottle (the 1st, the 5th, the 97th and so on) and comparing it with marginal revenue that the firm can get by selling it, the managers can determine exactly how many bottles to produce. These comparisons can be done by looking at a table of costs, such as Table 10-1, but making the comparisons graphically is even easier.

In Figure 10-3, we draw in the marginal cost *(MC)*, average variable cost *(AVC)* and average total cost *(ATC)* curves for LemonAid. We also draw in a horizontal line at £2, which is the marginal revenue for selling any and all bottles that the firm may choose to produce. We label the line *p* = *MR* = £2 to indicate the fact that the selling price of the bottle is £2, which is also the marginal revenue.

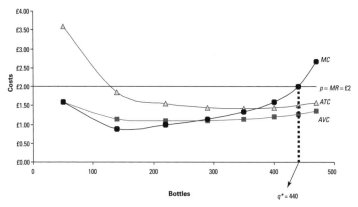

Figure 10-3: The firm's optimal output level, q^*, happens where *MC* and *MR* cross.

The quantity q^*, which corresponds to where the horizontal *p* = *MR* = £2 line crosses the *MC* curve, shows that q^* = 440 bottles. This quantity is the level of output that the firm chooses to produce in order to maximise profits.

To understand why adhering to $MR = MC$ maximises profits, look back at Table 10-1 and consider each unit of output, q, for which $q < 440$. For all these units, the marginal revenue is greater than the marginal cost $(MR > MC)$, meaning that producing and selling each of these bottles brings in more money than it costs to make them. For example, look at bottle number 140. It has a marginal cost of only £0.89 but can be sold for £2. The same is true for all the bottles for which $q < 440$; you need to produce them all because they all bring in a profit.

On the other hand, for all units above the q^* level of output ($q > 440$), the case is reversed: the marginal revenue is less than the marginal cost $(MR < MC)$. You lose money if you produce and sell those bottles. For example, at an output level of 470 bottles, the MC is £2.67 while the MR is only £2. Clearly, you don't want to do this.

By comparing the marginal revenues and marginal costs at all output levels, you can see that the managers of LemonAid want to produce exactly $q^* = 440$ units, the number of units where the MR and MC lines cross.

As we mention in the introduction to this section, producing where $MR = MC$ doesn't guarantee you a profit, but it does at least make sure that you only produce bottles that bring in more money than they cost to make. This formula by itself can't guarantee a profit because it doesn't take account of the fixed costs you have to pay no matter what level of output you're producing.

Visualising profits

Here's what we know from the previous section:

- ✔ Producing when $MR = MC$ allows a firm to determine its optimal (best possible) output level, q^*.

- ✔ Producing at q^* doesn't guarantee a profit – instead, it guarantees that you're making the biggest profit possible (if a profit is possible) or the smallest loss possible (if prices are so low that no way to make a profit exists given your cost structure).

We're now going to show you a quick and easy way to use the cost curves visually to determine whether the firm is making a profit or a loss. The trick is to realise that the two components of profits, total revenue *(TR)* and total costs *(TC)*, can each be represented by rectangles whose areas are equivalent to their respective sizes. As a result, you can tell if profits are positive or negative by determining whether the *TR* rectangle is larger or smaller than the *TC* rectangle. If the *TR* rectangle exceeds the size of the *TC* rectangle, profits are positive. And if the *TR* rectangle is smaller than the *TC* rectangle, profits are negative and the firm is running at a loss.

To see how this works, look at Figure 10-4, where we draw a generalised set of average total cost *(ATC)*, average variable cost *(AVC)* and marginal cost *(MC)* curves, in addition to a horizontal line labelled *p* = *MR* to indicate that price equals marginal revenue for this competitive firm. By *generalised*, we mean a typical-looking set of curves; we're no longer using the particular curves you get by plotting out LemonAid's costs.

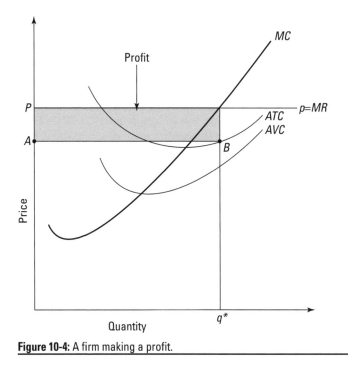

Figure 10-4: A firm making a profit.

The big trick behind expressing total revenue as a rectangular area is to remember that, when producing the profit-maximising output level, q^*, a firm's total revenue is simply price times that quantity, or $TR = P \times q^*$. Just as you can define the area of a rectangular room as length times width, you can define total revenue on a graph as a rectangle determined by price times quantity. In Figure 10-4, TR is a rectangle of height P and width q^*, with the four corners located at the origin, P, the point where the $p = MR$ line crosses the MC curve, and q^*.

You can also use a rectangle to represent the total costs that the firm incurs when producing q^* units of output. To see this rectangle, you have to convert the information that the average total cost (ATC) curve gives you into what you want to graph, total costs (TC).

First look at point B in Figure 10-4. B shows the average total cost (ATC) *per unit* when the firm is producing output level q^*. We see now that the rectangle whose width is q^* and whose height is given by the ATC at output level q^* is actually equal to the firm's total costs. That is, TC is equal to the area of the rectangle whose four corners are the origin, the point we label A, the point we label B, and q^*.

Now that you understand how the areas of rectangles that are derived from the firm's cost curves can represent a firm's TR and TC, you won't be surprised to discover that the firm's profits, which are by definition equal to $TR - TC$, can also be represented by the area of a specific rectangle. In fact, the profit is equal to the area of the shaded rectangle in Figure 10-4, because profits are simply the difference between TR and TC. Because the TR rectangle is larger than the TC rectangle in this case, the firm is making a profit whose size is equivalent to the area of the shaded rectangle that's defined by the area of the larger TR rectangle minus the area of the smaller TC rectangle.

An informative thing to do is to run a thought experiment using Figure 10-4. Imagine what happens if the price, P, increases. First, notice that the optimal output, q^*, increases, because the place where the horizontal $p = MR$ line crosses the MC curve moves up and to the right. Simultaneously, the total revenue rectangle increases in size, as does the total cost rectangle. But which one grows faster? Do profits rise or fall?

As the price rises, profits do in fact increase – that is, the shaded profit rectangle grows in size as the price increases. The next section explains how profits can go negative if the price falls far enough.

Visualising losses

Compare the situation in the previous section to the one illustrated in Figure 10-5, where the cost curves are the same as in Figure 10-4 but the price (and therefore the marginal revenue [*MR*]) of the product is much lower.

Following the *MR* = *MC* rule for selecting the optimal output level, the firm chooses to produce at the output level q^*_2 where the new lower *p* = *MR* line crosses the *MC* curve. But the low price at which the firm is forced to sell its output means it can't make a profit. (We label the optimal output level for the firm in Figure 10-5 q^*_2 to make clear that the optimal output level in this case, where the price is lower, is different from the optimal output level q^* in Figure 10-4 where the price was higher.)

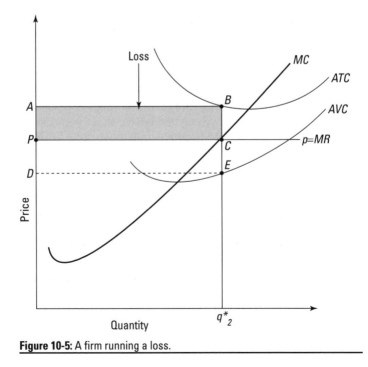

Figure 10-5: A firm running a loss.

You can see the size of the loss geometrically by comparing the TR and the TC rectangles that occur in this situation. Because $TR = P \times q^*_2$, total revenue is equal to the area of a rectangle of height P and width q^*_2. Consequently, the TR is equal to the area of the rectangle whose four corners lie at the origin, P, C and q^*_2. The TR is smaller than the TC rectangle defined by the origin, point A, point B and q^*_2. Because the area of the total cost rectangle exceeds the area of the total revenue rectangle, the firm is running a loss equivalent to the size of the shaded area in Figure 10-5.

Figure 10-5 shows that although a manager always wants to produce the level of output where $MR = MC$, doing so doesn't necessarily guarantee a profit. The problem is that fixed costs still exist. For example, suppose a firm has to pay £1,000 a month in rent. If the month has already started and the rent has already been paid, you produce all units for which $MR > MC$. That gets you to output level q^*_2 in Figure 10-5.

Suppose that $q^*_2 = 600$ and the price at which you can sell output is £1 each. That makes for £600 in total revenue. But with £1,000 in rent costs, you still sustain a loss for the month even though the marginal revenue exceeds the marginal cost for each of the 600 units. The tricky part is that although marginal costs don't take fixed costs into account, profits do.

We say it again: Producing at the output level where $MR = MC$ doesn't guarantee a profit. But it does guarantee that if you have to run a loss, that loss is as small as possible. Although you can't do anything immediate about your fixed costs, you can make sure to produce only those units for which the marginal revenue from selling them is larger than the marginal cost of producing them.

Pulling the Plug: When Producing Nothing Is Your Best Bet

You may wonder why a firm stays in business when running a loss rather than a profit. The usual answer is that it hopes things are going to turn around soon: the firm expects the price at which it can sell its products to rise, or it expects that it can somehow reduce its costs of production.

Even if these expectations are well founded, a firm may still be better off completely shutting down production rather than producing some positive amount of output. The determining factor is once again fixed costs.

The short-run shutdown condition: Variable costs exceed total revenues

Suppose you're in charge of a firm with a monthly rent of £1,000. If you produce nothing, you sustain a loss of £1,000. But that doesn't mean you *definitely* start producing stuff in order to try to make back some of that money. Instead, you want to produce only if by doing so you are better off than if you do nothing. That is, you choose to produce if doing so results in an outright profit or a loss of less than the £1,000 you stand to lose by doing nothing. As we're about to show you, sometimes the best thing to do is to produce nothing.

Consider Figure 10-6, where the price at which the firm can sell its output is so low that the marginal revenue *(p = MR)* line and the marginal cost *(MC)* curve intersect at a point *below* the average variable cost *(AVC)* curve. What does this mean? Put simply, the total revenues in this case are actually *less than* variable costs. (Total revenues are represented by the rectangle whose four corners are at the origin and points *P*, *B* and *Q**, where *Q** represents the optimal output level at this price. Variable costs are represented by the rectangle whose four corners are the origin and points *C*, *D* and *Q**.)

This situation means that by producing *Q** units, the firm doesn't even bring in enough total revenue to cover the variable costs associated with producing that many units. The firm is not only going to lose its fixed costs, but also even more money by not being able to cover the variable costs associated with producing *Q**.

The logical thing to do in such a situation is to produce nothing. By producing zero units, you lose only your fixed costs. By producing *Q**, you lose even more money because you can't even cover your variable costs.

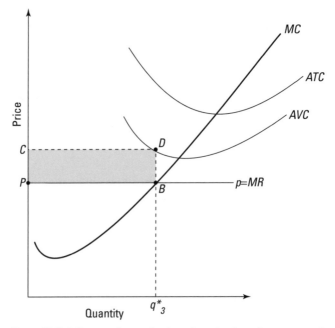

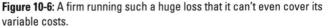

Figure 10-6: A firm running such a huge loss that it can't even cover its variable costs.

For example, suppose that fixed costs are £1,000 and that by producing Q^* units the firm makes total revenues of £400 and incurs variable costs of £500. Because total revenues cover only £400 of the £500 in variable costs, the firm loses £100 in variable costs by producing. Add to that the £1,000 of fixed costs it incurs no matter how much it produces, and the firm loses a total of £1,100 by producing Q^* units of output. In contrast, if the firm shuts down and produces nothing, it loses only the £1,000 in fixed costs. Clearly, in such a situation, the firm chooses to shut down.

Economists call this situation the *short-run shutdown condition*. If a firm's total revenues at Q^* are less than variable costs, better to shut down completely. Graphically, this happens any time the horizontal $p = MR$ line intersects the MC curve at a point below the U-shaped AVC curve.

The long-run shutdown condition: Total costs exceed total revenues

In contrast, look back at Figure 10-5. In this case, the firm is more than covering its variable costs because total revenues (represented by the box whose four corners are the origin, and points P, C and q^*_2) exceed variable costs (represented by the box whose four corners are the origin and points D, E and q^*_2). This firm is losing money, but it's better to produce q^*_2 rather than $q = 0$ because total revenues exceed variable costs. The firm can take the extra money left after paying variable costs and use it to pay some of its fixed costs.

Suppose that its fixed costs are £1,000 and that when producing q^*_2 the firm has a total revenue of £800 and variable costs of £700. The first £700 of the £800 in total revenues can go to paying off the variable costs, leaving £100 to pay off a portion of the £1,000 in fixed costs. The result is an overall loss of £900 rather than a £1,000 loss if it produces nothing.

A firm in the situation of Figure 10-5 continues to operate in the short run because by doing so it's better off than shutting down immediately. So although producing output in the short run is better, the firm eventually wants to stop losing money by closing down. As soon as its fixed cost contracts expire, it shuts down permanently.

At the mercy of the market price

Because competitive firms have to take the market price as given, the decision whether to continue operating is in some senses totally out of their hands. Only two possibilities exist:

- ✔ If the price is high enough, the firm makes a profit and stays in business in order to keep collecting the profit. Graphically, this happens whenever the horizontal $p = MR$ line crosses the MC curve at a point above the bottom of the U-shaped ATC curve, as in Figure 10-4.

- ✔ If the horizontal $p = MR$ line crosses the MC curve at a point below the bottom of the U-shaped ATC curve, the firm is taking a loss. What it does in such situations depends on how low the price is and, consequently, how big the loss is. Two possibilities (or conditions) exist, as we explain in the previous sections:

- The *short-run shutdown condition* occurs when a firm's total revenues are less than its variable costs. Graphically, this happens when the horizontal $p = MR$ line intersects the MC curve at a point below the low point of the U-shaped AVC curve, as in Figure 10-6.

  In such a situation, the firm is better off shutting down immediately and losing only its fixed costs.

- The *long-run shutdown condition* occurs when a firm's total revenues exceed its variable costs but are less than its total costs. Graphically, this happens in any situation where the horizontal $p = MR$ line intersects the MC curve at any point on the segment of the MC curve that lies above the bottom of the U-shaped AVC curve but below the bottom of the U-shaped ATC curve, as in Figure 10-5.

  In such a situation, the firm is guaranteed to lose money. But as long as the firm is stuck with its current set of fixed-cost commitments, producing rather than shutting down immediately is preferable.

As you can see, the perfectly competitive firm is in some sense totally at the mercy of the market price. If the price is high, it makes profits. If the price is low, it sustains losses. And even then, its decision about whether to shut down immediately or keep operating at a loss until it can get out of its fixed cost commitments depends entirely on the price.

Chapter 11

Why Economists Love Free Markets and Competition

· ·

In This Chapter

▶ Measuring the social benefits of different output levels

▶ Demonstrating that free markets maximise total surplus

▶ Reducing total surplus with taxes and price controls

▶ Producing at the lowest possible cost to society

▶ Adjusting to changes in supply and demand

· ·

*E*conomists love competitive free markets – markets in which numerous buyers freely interact with numerous competitive firms. Indeed, economists firmly believe that when they work properly, competitive free markets are the very best way to convert society's limited resources into the goods and services that people want to buy.

Why do economists place such great confidence in competitive free markets? Because the interaction of supply and demand leads to an outcome in which every produced unit of output satisfies two excellent conditions:

> ✔ Each unit is produced at the minimum cost possible, which means that no waste or inefficiency is involved.

> ✔ Each unit's benefits exceed its costs: only output that makes the world better off gets produced.

Economists also love competitive free markets because they provide a gold standard against which all other economic institutions can be judged. In fact, economists refer to many economic problems as *market failures* precisely because they are instances in which, if markets were able to function properly, the problems would quickly go away.

In this chapter, we show you that competitive free markets ensure that benefits exceed costs for all the output produced. We also show you that competitive free markets produce the *socially optimal quantity* of output – the level that maximises the benefits that society can get from its limited supply of resources. Finally, we show you how competitive industries adjust to changes in supply and demand to ensure that everything that's being produced is produced at the lowest possible cost to society.

The Beauty of Competitive Free Markets: Ensuring That Benefits Exceed Costs

Society has a limited amount of land, labour and capital out of which to make things. Consequently, society must carefully consider how to best convert its limited resources into the goods and services that people most greatly desire.

Economists love competitive free markets because, *if they are operating properly*, these markets make sure that resources are allocated *optimally*. In particular, such markets ensure that resources go towards producing only output for which the benefits exceed the costs.

This point can be easily demonstrated using nothing more complicated than a supply and demand graph. But before we show you how that's done, we need to explain the conditions under which competitive free markets can function properly and thereby deliver such good results.

Examining prerequisites for properly functioning markets

Free markets guarantee optimal outcomes only if the following conditions are met:

1. Buyers and sellers all have the same full and complete information about the good or service in question.

2. Property rights are set up so that the only way buyers can get the good or service in question is by paying sellers for it.

3. Supply curves capture all the production costs that firms incur in making the good or service in question.

4. Demand curves capture all the benefits that people derive from the good or service in question.

5. Numerous buyers and numerous sellers exist, so that nobody is big enough to affect the market price. This condition is often called the *price-taking assumption*, because everybody has to take prices as given.

6. The market price is free to adjust to equalise supply and demand for the good or service in question.

Basically, these six points accomplish two broad goals:

✔ They guarantee that people want to buy and sell in a market environment.

✔ They ensure that markets take into account all the costs and all the benefits of producing and then consuming a given amount of output.

We address each point separately in the next two sections.

Guaranteeing that people want to participate in markets

The requirement that both buyers and sellers have access to full and complete information guarantees that both are willing to negotiate without having to worry that the other person has secret information.

The requirement that property rights be set up in such a way that buyers *have* to pay sellers ensures that there are sellers willing to provide the product. As a counter example, consider trying to sell tickets to an outdoor fireworks display. Because everyone knows that they can see the display for free, nobody wants to pay for a ticket. But if sellers can't sell tickets, they have no incentive to put on a display.

Capturing all costs and benefits

The requirements that supply curves capture all costs and demand curves capture all benefits ensure that a proper cost-benefit calculation can be made. For example, if a steel factory can pollute for free, there's no way the price of steel can reflect correctly the damage that the factory's pollution does to the environment. On the other hand, if the government continuously forces the factory to pay for clean-up costs, these costs are going to be reflected in the market price, thereby allowing society to weigh the costs and benefits properly of the company's output.

If the first four requirements for free markets are met, market forces can still reach a social optimum only if they are free of interference. The fifth requirement eliminates problems like monopolies, in which individual buyers or sellers are so powerful that they can manipulate the market pricing in their own favour. The sixth requirement stipulates that supply and demand must be allowed to determine freely the market price and market quantity unimpeded by government-imposed price ceilings or floors.

If all six requirements are met, an amazing thing happens. Supply and demand automatically achieve the social optimum without the government or socially conscious activists having to do anything. This insight was the basis of Adam Smith's metaphor of an invisible hand that seems to guide markets to do the right thing despite nobody being in charge – and despite the fact that each individual in the market may well be looking out only for his or her own interests.

Analysing the efficiency of free markets

Economists use supply and demand curves to demonstrate that free markets produce socially optimal levels of output. But the simple insight behind this result is that a unit of output can be socially beneficial to produce and consume only if the benefits that people derive from consuming it exceed the costs of producing it.

This simple idea is, in fact, why demand curves and supply curves are so useful in analysing the social optimum. Demand curves quantify the benefits that people get from consumption by showing what they're willing to pay to consume each and every particular unit of output. Supply curves quantify the cost of producing each and every particular unit of output.

Using supply and demand to compare costs and benefits

By drawing the demand and supply curves for a good or service together on the same graph, you can easily compare the benefits and costs of producing each and every unit of output. To see how this is done, take a look at Figure 11-1, on which we draw a demand curve, *D*, and a supply curve, *S*.

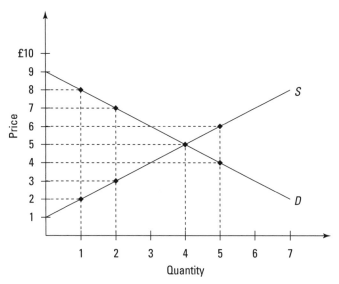

Figure 11-1: Comparing costs and benefits using supply and demand curves.

To start, take a look at one unit of output on the horizontal axis. At that output level, go vertically up to the demand curve and see that people are willing to pay £8 for one unit of output. At the same time, go vertically up to the supply curve to see that firms are willing to supply one unit at a cost of £2.

Putting these facts together, you can see that producing this first unit of output is socially beneficial because the value is worth more to buyers (£8) than it costs sellers to produce (£2).

Put slightly differently, although the resources to make this unit of output cost society £2, those resources bring £8 in benefits when converted into this particular good or service.

Now look at the second unit of output. Going vertically up to the demand curve tells us that people are willing to pay £7 for that unit, whereas going vertically up to the supply curve tells us that the second unit costs £3 to produce. Again, benefits exceed costs. Again, this unit of output should be produced.

In contrast, look at the fifth unit of output. By going up vertically, you can see that the costs as given by the supply curve for producing the fifth unit are £6, whereas the benefits as given by the demand curve are only £4. Because the costs of producing this unit exceed what anyone is willing to pay for it, this unit of output shouldn't be produced. Producing this unit destroys wealth.

Determining the socially optimal output level

The next thing to notice is that Figure 11-1 can tell you precisely what quantity (q) of output should be produced, because the supply and demand curves let you quickly compare costs and benefits for every possible output level.

Only three cost-benefit relationships exist:

✔ For every bit of output where $q < 4$, benefits exceed costs.

✔ At exactly $q = 4$ units, benefits equal costs.

✔ For every bit of output where $q > 4$, costs exceed benefits.

Economists look at these relationships and conclude that the socially optimal level of output to produce is $q = 4$ units, because for these units benefits exceed costs or are at least equal to costs. By producing the first four units of output, society gains or is at least not made any worse off.

The socially optimal output level is always devastatingly easy to identify on any supply and demand graph: just look to the quantity produced where the demand and supply curves cross.

Realising that free markets produce the socially optimal output level

Adam Smith's big insight was to realise that free markets produce exactly the socially optimal output level on their own without anyone having to direct them to do the right thing.

The proof of this fact is almost trivial. All you have to do is look at Figure 11-1 and realise that the market equilibrium quantity – which happens when the market price is free to adjust so that the quantity supplied by sellers equals the quantity demanded by buyers – is determined by where the supply and demand curves cross. The market equilibrium quantity is four units of output, which is exactly how many units you want to produce if you are using the demand and supply curves to compare benefits and costs.

Sensible business people are not in the habit of producing things when the cost of production is greater than the value received from sales. In this case, the calculation is simply that it costs £6 to produce and you'd make £4 from selling. Therefore you wouldn't do it.

This amazing result greatly simplifies life, because it eliminates the need to have a government official or any other sort of central planner constantly checking to see if exactly the right amount of output is being produced.

Using total surplus to measure gains

Economists use a concept called *total surplus* to total up the gains that come from producing the socially optimal output level. The gain, or surplus, comes from the fact that benefits exceed costs for the units of output that are produced.

The total surplus turns out to be divided between consumers and producers. The part of the total surplus that goes to consumers is (naturally) called *consumer surplus*, whereas the part that goes to producers is called *producer surplus*.

In the sections that follow, we tackle consumer surplus first and then move on to producer surplus. After we explain each separately, we add them together to explain total surplus.

Measuring the consumer surplus of a discrete good

Consumer surplus is the gain people receive when they can buy things for less than what they're willing to pay.

The easiest way to understand consumer surplus is to first look at a discrete good. A *discrete good* is a good that comes only in discrete units. For example, you can buy one car or 57 cars, but you can't buy 2.33 cars.

Look at Figure 11-2, which shows the demand for cows. Because cows come in discrete units, you don't get a smooth, downward-sloping curve. Instead, you get what mathematicians call a *step function*. This means, for example, that people are willing to pay £900 for the first cow, £800 for the second cow, £700 for the third cow and so on.

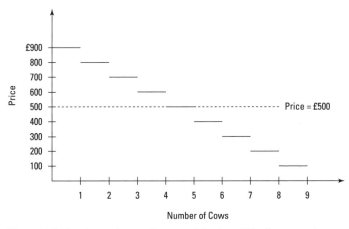

Figure 11-2: The demand curve for a good that is sold in discrete units looks like steps.

Now imagine that the market price of cows is £500, which is why we draw a horizontal dotted line at that price. Compare that price with what people are willing to pay for each cow.

For the first cow, people are willing to pay £900. Because the market price of cows is only £500, these buyers come out ahead because they're able to purchase a cow for £400 less than they're willing to pay. Or, as economists like to say, the *consumer surplus* on the first cow is £400.

Next, look at the second cow. People are willing to pay £800 for it, but because the market price is only £500, they receive a consumer surplus for that cow of £300.

Similarly, for the third cow, people get a consumer surplus of £200, because they're willing to pay £700 for it but have to pay only the market price of £500.

For the first four cows, a positive consumer surplus exists, whereas on the fifth cow people just break even because they're willing to pay £500 and the cow costs £500. This means that people want to buy only five cows.

To calculate consumer surplus for a discrete good such as cows, we need to total the surpluses that people get on each unit that they choose to buy. In this case, the total is £1,000 (£400 for the first cow, plus £300 for the second cow, plus £200 for the third cow, plus £100 for the fourth cow, plus £0 for the fifth cow).

To show this £1,000 of consumer surplus in the graph in Figure 11-3, we shade in the area below each step and above the horizontal price line at £500. The staircase-shaped area equals £1,000.

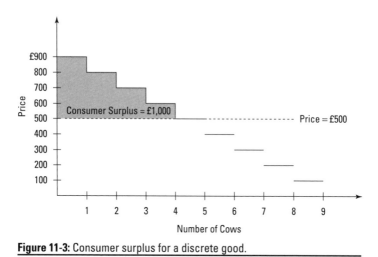

Figure 11-3: Consumer surplus for a discrete good.

Measuring the consumer surplus of a continuous good

Consumer surplus can also be computed for continuously measured goods and services – things like land, cooking oil or hours of music lessons, which aren't necessarily sold in discrete units. In other words, you can buy fractional amounts of continuously measured goods, such as 78.5 acres of land, 6.33 litres of cooking oil or 2.5 hours of music lessons.

The demand curves for continuously measured goods are much nicer than the step functions that you get for discretely measured goods. The demand curves for continuously measured goods are smooth, downward-sloping lines.

The smoothness of such demand curves means that when you graph consumer surplus for a continuously measured good, you get a triangular area that lies below the demand curve and above the market price. You can see this wedge illustrated in Figure 11-4, which depicts the cooking oil market.

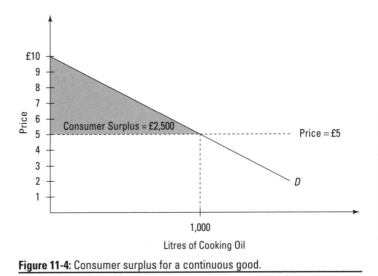

Figure 11-4: Consumer surplus for a continuous good.

In Figure 11-4, the price of cooking oil is £5 per litre. At that price, people want to buy 1,000 litres of cooking oil. The demand curve lies above the horizontal £5 price line, which means that buyers are made better off by buying these 1,000 litres because they are worth more to the buyers than the £5 per litre that it costs to buy them.

To calculate consumer surplus for a continuous good, you total up all the gains that people receive when buying for less money than they are willing to pay – just as for a discrete good. But because we're now dealing with a triangle, totalling up requires a bit of geometry. You simply use the formula for the area of a triangle ($\frac{1}{2}$ × base × height) to find the total surplus. In this case, you multiply $\frac{1}{2}$ × 1,000 × 5 = £2,500.

Measuring producer surplus

Producer surplus is the gain that firms receive when they can sell their output for more than the minimum price that they were willing to accept. In this section, we offer an example of calculating producer surplus for a continuous good.

To visualize producer surplus, take a look at Figure 11-5, which shows the supply curve, *S*, for cooking oil. This supply curve is crucial for determining producer surplus because each point on the supply curve tells you the minimum that you have to pay suppliers for them to supply you with the associated amount of output. By comparing each minimum value with the higher market price that they actually receive when they sell their output, you can compute producer surplus.

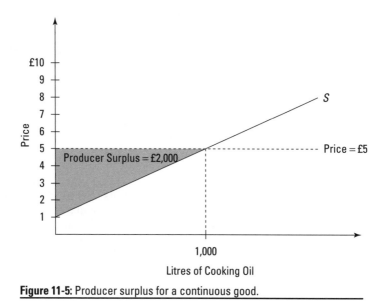

Figure 11-5: Producer surplus for a continuous good.

The price of cooking oil is still £5 per litre. And the way we draw the graph, producers are going to want to supply exactly 1,000 litres of cooking oil at that price. They want to supply this much because for each drop of oil up to and including the very last drop of the 1,000th litre, the production costs as given by the supply curve are less than the £5 per litre that producers get when they sell the oil.

Producers are willing to supply almost all that cooking oil for *less than* the £5 per litre market price. You can see that the supply curve lies below the horizontal price line up to the very last drop of the 1,000th litre. The fact that producers receive £5 per litre for all the oil, despite being willing to produce it for less, is the source of the producer surplus, which is represented by the area of the shaded triangle.

Using the formula for the area of a triangle ($\frac{1}{2}$ × base × height), you can compute that the producer surplus in this example is £2,000. Producers are £2,000 better off by selling the 1,000 litres of oil because the total cash they get from selling these 1,000 litres exceeds the minimum amount that they were willing to accept by £2,000.

Computing total surplus

The *total surplus* that society receives from producing the socially optimal level of output of a certain good or service is simply the sum of the consumer surplus and producer surplus generated by that output level.

Figure 11-6 illustrates total surplus for a market in which the equilibrium price and quantity are, respectively, p^* = £5 and q^* = 4. (If this graph looks familiar, that's because it resembles Figure 11-1.)

We draw the total surplus area so that you can clearly see that it consists of consumer surplus plus producer surplus. The horizontal line extending from the market equilibrium price (£5) separates the two parts. The consumer surplus triangle is filled with vertical lines, whereas the producer surplus triangle is filled with diagonal lines.

Again using the formula for the area of a triangle, we multiply $\frac{1}{2} \times 4 \times 8$ to figure out that for this graph the total surplus is £16. The total gain to society of producing at this output level is £16.

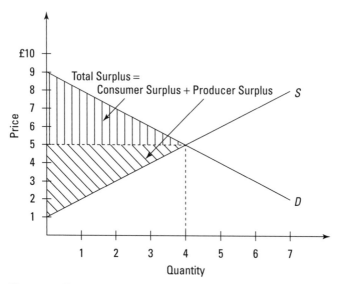

Figure 11-6: Total surplus is the sum of consumer surplus (vertically striped area) and producer surplus (diagonally striped area).

Contemplating total surplus

Total surplus is very important because it puts a number on the gains that come from production and trade. Firms make things to make a profit. People spend money on things because consuming those things makes them happy. And total surplus tells you just how much better off both consumers and producers are after interacting with each other.

By putting a number on the gains made by their interaction, total surplus also provides a benchmark by which economists can measure the harm that comes from government policies that interfere with the market. For example, saying that price subsidies hurt consumers is one thing, but being able to say by exactly how many pounds consumers are harmed is quite another. And that's the subject we cover next.

When Free Markets Lose Their Freedom

As we note earlier in the chapter, economists love free markets because free markets produce only those units for which benefits exceed costs. In other words, the market equilibrium ensures that total surplus is as large as possible.

Anything that interferes with the market's ability to reach the market equilibrium and produce the market quantity reduces total surplus. Economists use the colourful term *deadweight loss* to refer to the amount by which total surplus is reduced.

In the sections that follow, we give you detailed examples of deadweight losses caused by price ceilings and taxes. These types of market interference are both under the government's control, but don't think that *only* government policy causes deadweight losses. Anything that reduces output below the market quantity causes a deadweight loss. Monopolies and oligopolies can be to blame, as can asymmetric information, poorly allocated property rights and public goods problems – all things that we discuss in the next few chapters.

Dissecting the deadweight loss from a price ceiling

As an example of a deadweight loss, look at Figure 11-7 in which the government has imposed a price ceiling at p^C. As we discuss in Chapter 8, *price ceilings* are maximum prices at which sellers can legally sell their product. Generally, price ceilings are intended to help buyers obtain a low price, but, as we're about to show you, they can cause a lot of harm.

To see the damage that price ceilings can inflict, first notice that at a maximum price of p^C, suppliers are going to want to sell only q^L units of output (the L stands for *low*). In other words, at that price, only the first q^L units of output are profitable to produce. By contrast, if no price ceiling exists and the market is left to its own devices, suppliers choose to produce the market equilibrium quantity of output, q^*.

Consequently, if this were a free market, the total surplus would be represented graphically by the triangle defined by points A, B and C. But because only q^L units of output can be produced, the total surplus area is reduced down to the shaded area with corners at A, B, F and E.

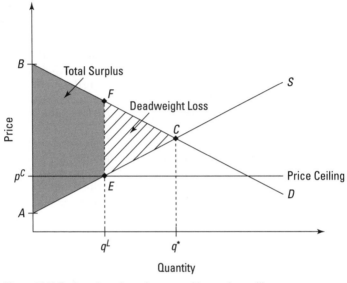

Figure 11-7: Reduced total surplus caused by a price ceiling.

The difference between the total surplus generated by producing q^* versus q^L units of output is the diagonally striped triangle defined by points E, F and C. The area of this triangle illustrates the deadweight loss that comes from reducing output below the socially optimal level, q^*.

By tallying up the gains that would come from producing and consuming the units between q^L and q^*, the deadweight loss triangle can precisely measure the harm that results from interfering with the market.

Analysing the deadweight loss of a tax

Taxes on goods and services also cause deadweight losses. This situation happens because such taxes raise the costs of producing and consuming output. When these costs are artificially raised by a tax, people respond by producing and consuming fewer units of output than they did before the tax was imposed. Because each unit consumed before the tax was imposed was a unit for which benefits exceeded costs, the reduction in output that results from the tax necessarily reduces total surplus and causes a deadweight loss.

Seeing how a tax shifts the supply curve

Before we discuss in more detail the deadweight loss that results from a tax, we have to show you that imposing a tax on the seller shifts supply curves vertically by the amount of the tax. Consider the supply of beef in a beef market in which the government is going to impose a tax of £1 per kilo.

Figure 11-8 shows two curves. The lower one, *S*, is the supply curve for beef. The higher one, labelled *S + tax*, is the supply curve after the tax is imposed. The important thing to realise is that the curve *S + tax* is simply the original supply curve shifted up vertically by the amount of the tax, which in this case is £1.

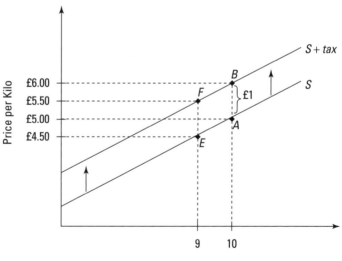

Figure 11-8: Imposing a £1 tax on beef shifts the supply curve vertically by £1, from *S* to *S + tax*.

The reason why the supply curve shifts up vertically by the amount of the tax is connected with the motivation of suppliers. In Chapter 8, we explain that each point on the supply curve tells you the minimum that you would have to pay suppliers to get them to supply the relevant quantity. For example, look at point A. Because point A is on the supply curve, you know that you have to pay £5 per kilo if you want suppliers to provide 10 million kilos of beef. Similarly, point E tells you that you have to pay suppliers £4.50 per kilo if you want them to supply only 9 million kilos of beef.

If the government imposes a tax of £1 per kilo, it affects how much you have to pay the suppliers to motivate them. If you still want 10 million kilos of beef, you have to pay the original amount required to motivate the suppliers to supply you with that much beef (£5 per kilo), as well as enough money to pay the taxes on that much beef (£1 per kilo).

Graphically, this means that point A on supply curve S shifts up by the £1 amount of the tax to become point B on the S + tax curve. Likewise, point E on the supply curve must shift up to point F on the S + tax curve. If you have to pay suppliers £4.50 per kilo to motivate them to supply you with 9 million kilos of beef in a world in which £1 per kilo must go to the government in taxes, you have to collect a total of £5.50 per kilo (point F).

Seeing how a tax causes deadweight losses

Figure 11-9 adds a demand curve, D, to Figure 11-8 so that you can see what happens to total surplus when the government imposes a £1 per kilo tax on the beef that's sold in the beef market.

Before the tax, the market equilibrium happens at point A, where supply curve S crosses demand curve D. At that point, producers supply 10 million kilos of beef at a price of £5 per kilo. The total surplus in this case is given by the triangle defined by points C, D and A.

After the tax is imposed, however, the equilibrium happens at point F, where the S + tax curve crosses the demand curve. At that point, the price of beef is £5.50 per kilo, and 9 million kilos are supplied.

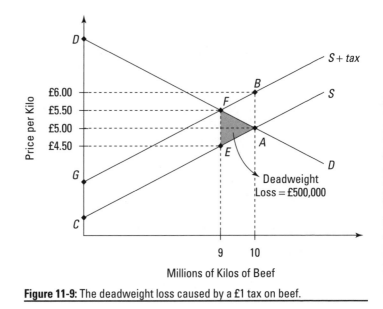

Figure 11-9: The deadweight loss caused by a £1 tax on beef.

Because of the tax, the amount of beef supplied falls from 10 million kilos to 9 million kilos. Furthermore, the total surplus is reduced to the triangle whose three corners are G, D and F.

You can immediately see that this new total surplus is much smaller than the old total surplus. But before we start ranting about the evils of government, we need to take account of the fact that taxes are being collected. Taxes (theoretically, at least) benefit society, so we need to include this amount when calculating the total surplus of this good sold at this price. At the new equilibrium, £9 million in taxes are collected because the 9 million kilos of beef sold are taxed at £1 each.

The £9 million in tax collections are represented graphically by the parallelogram whose corners are C, G, F and E. This area was previously contained in the old total surplus triangle whose corners were C, D and A. Consequently, the area that used to be part of the old total surplus hasn't been destroyed, but merely transferred to the government.

However, part of the old total surplus *has* been destroyed. This part is shown graphically by the shaded deadweight loss triangle (with corners at *E*, *F* and *A*). This area captures the fact that society is made worse off by the reduction in beef output from 10 million kilos to 9 million kilos.

Measuring the size of the deadweight loss as the area of a triangle (½ × base × height) tells us that the tax leads to a deadweight loss of £500,000. That's a big number representing a huge reduction in total surplus deriving from the fact that for each of the 1 million kilos of beef no longer being produced, benefits exceeded costs.

Deadweight losses are called deadweight losses because you can't say 'Your loss is my gain' in this situation. Benefit hasn't passed from consumers to producers, but instead the total level of benefit to society as a whole (in this case) is lower. Deadweight losses are losses in the sense of annihilation. The gains that would have resulted if those million kilos of beef had been produced simply vanish; they are a dead weight that we must bear in our efforts to maximise human happiness given our limited resources.

Hallmarks of Perfect Competition: Zero Profits and Lowest Possible Costs

Earlier in this chapter, we demonstrate that free markets produce only units of output for which benefits are at least as great as costs. Another wonderful thing about free markets and competition is that output is produced at the lowest possible cost.

This fact is extremely important because it means that free markets are as efficient as possible at converting resources into the goods and services that people want to buy.

In addition, markets save society a lot of money because they produce efficiently without requiring any human intervention.

Understanding the causes and consequences of perfect competition

To ensure that markets function efficiently, you need really strong competition between firms, a situation that economists refer to as *perfect competition*.

As we explain in Chapter 10, perfect competition exists when many firms within a given industry are all producing identical (or nearly identical) products. The following things are also true when perfect competition exists:

- ✔ Every firm is a *price taker* – that is, has to accept the market equilibrium price for what it produces – because its output is a very small fraction of the industry's total output (see Chapter 10).

- ✔ Every firm has identical production technology.

- ✔ Every firm is free to enter or leave the industry as it pleases.

When these requirements are met, perfect competition leads to two excellent outcomes:

- ✔ Every firm in the industry makes zero economic profits.

- ✔ Every firm produces output at the minimum possible cost.

The first outcome doesn't mean that businesses earn no money above the costs of doing business; otherwise, no one would go into business. Firms must earn enough money to keep entrepreneurs motivated to stay in business (and to attract other entrepreneurs to open new firms).

So what does the first outcome mean? Recall that the *economic profits* earned by a firm are any monies collected above and beyond what is required to keep an entrepreneur owner interested in continuing in business. So the fact that perfect competition leads to zero economic profits means that firms just barely want to stay in their industry.

It also means that nobody in the industry is getting filthy rich at anyone else's expense. Rather, they're doing just well enough to keep on supplying the output that society wants them to supply. This situation is great for society, because paying entrepreneurs more than necessary to get them to do what society wants is wasteful.

The second outcome of perfect competition – the fact that firms all end up producing output at the lowest cost possible, is also good for society because it means that the least possible amount of resources are consumed while making the output that society wants produced.

Peering into the process of perfect competition

The previous section gives you an idea of how perfect competitive markets emerge and how they benefit society. But how does perfect competition actually work? The following four steps explain:

1. The market price of the output sold by every firm in the industry is determined by the interaction of the industry's overall supply and demand curves.

2. Each of the firms takes the market price as given and produces whatever quantity of output maximises its own profit (or minimises its own loss if the price is so low that making a profit isn't possible).

3. Because each firm has an identical production technology, each chooses to produce the same quantity and consequently makes the same profit or loss as every other firm in the industry.

4. Depending on whether firms are making profits or losses, firms enter or leave the industry until the market price adjusts to the level where all remaining firms are making zero economic profit.

The fourth point in this process – firm entry and exit – is very important. To understand this point, break it into two cases, one where every firm is making a profit because the market price is high, and another where every firm is making a loss because the market price is low:

✔ **Attracting new firms by making profits:** If every firm is making a profit, new firms are attracted to enter the industry too, in hopes of sharing the profits. But when they enter, total industry output increases so much that the price begins to fall. As the price falls, profits fall, reducing the incentive for more firms to enter the industry.

The process of new firms entering the industry continues until the market price falls so low that profits drop to zero. When that happens, the incentive to enter the industry disappears, and no more firms enter.

✔ **Losing existing firms when making losses:** If every firm in an industry starts out making losses because the market price is low, existing firms that can't stand losing money exit the industry. When they do, total industry output falls. That reduction in total supply, in turn, causes the price to rise. And as the price rises, firms' losses decrease.

The process of firms leaving and prices rising continues until the remaining firms are no longer losing money.

As we explain in the preceding section, the fact that firms can freely enter or leave the industry means that after all adjustments are made, firms always make a zero economic profit. In other words, if perfect competition exists, you don't have to worry about firms exploiting anyone; they just barely make enough money to stay in business.

The other important result of perfect competition – that competitive firms produce at minimum cost – becomes apparent if we flesh out the four-step process of perfect competition by using the cost curves that we explain in Chapter 10.

Graphing how profits guide firm entry and exit

In this section, we use the firm cost curves that we introduce in Chapter 10 to demonstrate how market forces automatically cause firms to produce output at the lowest possible cost. To make this process clear, we present two cases. In the first, firms begin by making profits. In the second, firms begin by making losses. Either way, adjustments happen so that they end up making zero economic profits and producing at minimum costs.

Visualising firm entry when profits exist

To see how an industry adjusts when it starts off making profits, look at Figure 11-10, which consists of two graphs. The one on the left gives the market demand curve, D, and the initial market supply curve, S_o, for tennis balls. The one on the right gives the cost curves for one of the many identical firms that make tennis balls.

Because the firms in this industry are identical, they all have the same cost structures. In particular, they all have the same marginal cost curve *(MC)*. This point is important because, a competitive firm's marginal cost curve is its supply curve.

The firm in our example takes the market price, P_o, determined by supply and demand in the left graph, and uses it to work out its profit-maximising output level in the right graph.

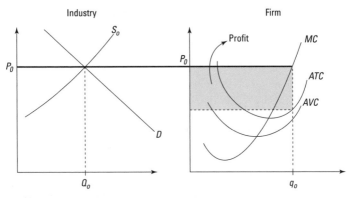

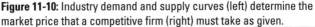

Figure 11-10: Industry demand and supply curves (left) determine the market price that a competitive firm (right) must take as given.

Each firm chooses to produce the output level at which the horizontal price line intersects the *MC* curve. In the right-hand graph, we label the output level q_o. In the left-hand graph, you can see that the industry's total supply is Q_o. The industry's total supply is simply each individual firm's output, q_o, times the total number of firms in the industry.

Next, focus on the fact that each firm runs a profit when the market price is P_o. The profit is shown by the shaded rectangle in the right graph.

This profit is important because it attracts entrepreneurs to enter the industry. They realise that they can set up yet more identical firms and make some nice profits. As economists like to say, profits attract entrants.

Seeing how new entry reduces profits

Figure 11-11 shows what happens when the new entrants to the industry arrive. Their new production increases overall production so that the total supply curve shifts from S_o to S_1 in the left-hand graph, lowering the market equilibrium price from P_o to P_1.

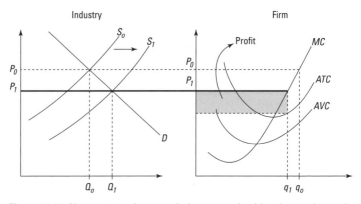

Figure 11-11: New entrants increase industry supply, drive down price and reduce profits.

Each of the price-taking firms reacts to the lower price by producing a lower output level, q_1, which you can see illustrated in the right-hand graph. More importantly, the firms' profits decrease, which you can see by comparing the shaded profit rectangles in Figures 11-10 and 11-11.

The new entry results in smaller profits. The smaller profits are less attractive to entrepreneurs. So although new entry continues – because some profits are still available – that new entry is less than when profits were larger.

Seeing how enough entry drives profits to zero

What ends up happening, in fact, is that entry continues until prices fall so far that all profits are driven away. This situation is illustrated in Figure 11-12, in which new entry increases supply still more, to S_2. The result is that the market price falls to P_2, which results in zero profits. Because profits fall to zero, entry ceases.

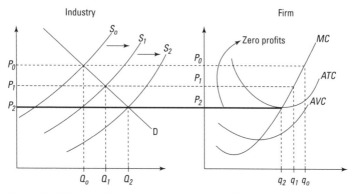

Figure 11-12: Eventually, new entry drives prices down so far that profits disappear.

Realising that zero profits also mean minimum cost production

When profits are driven to zero by the entry of new firms, the cost per unit at which output is produced is minimised. You can see this fact in the right-hand graph of Figure 11-12: notice that when faced with price P_2, firms choose to produce at the quantity that minimises per-unit production costs.

The output that firms choose to produce, q_2, lies exactly at the minimum point of the U-shaped average total cost curve *(ATC)*. When output is produced at that level, the average cost per unit is lower than at any other output level. This situation is wonderful because it means that each firm is being as efficient as possible, producing output at the lowest possible cost per unit.

Profits serve as a self-correcting feedback mechanism. High profits automatically attract new entrants who automatically increase supply and drive prices down. That process continues until no more profits and no more new entrants exist. But more importantly, it continues until each and every firm is producing output at the most efficient, least-cost output level. This is truly Adam Smith's invisible hand at work.

Visualising firm exit when losses exist

A similar feedback mechanism leads to zero profits and efficient production if the industry starts out making losses. To see this, take a look at Figure 11-13, where the initial supply curve, S_3, interacts with the demand curve, D, to produce a very low market price of P_3.

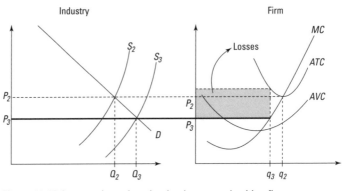

Figure 11-13: Low market prices lead to losses and exiting firms.

At this market price, you can see in the right-hand graph that each firm in the industry is making a loss, which is shown by the shaded rectangle.

This loss discourages all the firms in the industry, and those in the weakest financial condition begin to exit. As that happens, the industry supply curve in the left-hand graph shifts left (because supply decreases). That shift raises the market price and reduces the losses made by firms remaining in the industry. But as long as losses exist, firms continue to exit until the supply curve moves all the way back to S_2, at which point the market price is P_2, and firms are making zero profits as in Figure 11-12.

When the market price reaches P_2 and firms are making zero profits, the exit of firms stops and, more importantly, each firm is producing at the least-cost output level, q_2.

Understanding that entry and exit don't happen instantly

You've now seen that market pressures always push perfectly competitive firms to produce at the lowest possible per-unit

cost. Keep in mind that this nice result doesn't happen over-
night. Whether firms are making profits or sustaining losses,
it takes time for new firms to enter (if profits are available) or
for existing firms to leave (if losses exist).

The wonderful thing about perfect competition is that market
forces are always acting to drive firms to produce at the minimum possible cost. As we show you in the next few chapters,
this lovely result falls apart when monopolies, oligopolies,
public goods and other problems prevent or preclude perfect
competition.

Chapter 12

Monopolies: How Badly Would You Behave If You Had No Competition?

In This Chapter

▶ Producing less and charging more than competitive firms

▶ Maximising profit

▶ Benefiting society (in certain situations)

▶ Abiding by regulations

A firm that has no competitors in its industry is called a *monopoly*. Monopolies are much maligned because their profit incentive leads them to raise prices and lower output in order to squeeze more money out of consumers. As a result, governments typically act to break up monopolies or regulate them so that prices are lower and output is higher.

At the same time, however, governments also very intentionally create monopolies in other situations. For example, governments issue patents, which give monopoly rights to inventors to sell and market their inventions. Similarly, the BBC was originally a monopoly created by government.

In this chapter, we explain why society forbids monopolies in some situations and promotes them in others. First, we show you that profit-maximising monopolies compare unfavourably with competitive firms, because they set higher prices and produce less output than competitive firms. Then, we explain how these problems may, in certain cases, be outweighed by other factors.

Profit-Maximising Monopolies

Essentially, this chapter is one big exercise in cost-benefit analysis. Monopolies aren't all evil. Neither are they utterly good. A monopoly may in fact be preferred if the benefits outweigh the costs.

This section goes into detail about the costs associated with monopolies. When we finish our cost analysis, we move on to the benefits of monopolies. This chapter helps you understand why society ruthlessly forbids monopolies in some industries while enthusiastically endorsing them in others.

The problems that monopolies cause

In an industry with only one monopoly firm rather than lots of small competitive firms, three socially harmful things occur:

- The monopoly firm produces less output than firms in a competitive industry.
- The monopoly firm sells its output at a higher price than if the industry was competitive.
- The monopoly firm's output is produced less efficiently and at a higher cost than the output produced by firms in a competitive industry.

Although all these things are harmful to consumers, keep in mind that monopolies don't do these things for the sake of it. Instead, these outcomes are simply the result of monopolies acting to maximise their profits – which is, of course, the very same thing that competitive firms try to do.

Consequently, the difference in outcomes between a competitive industry and a monopoly results from the fact that monopolies are free from the pressures that lead competitive industries to produce the socially optimal output level. Without these pressures, monopoly firms can increase prices and restrict output to increase their profits – things that competitive firms would also love to do but can't.

The lack of competitive pressure also means that monopoly firms can get away with costly, inefficient production. You need to take this problem seriously when considering whether the benefits of a monopoly outweigh its costs.

The source of the problem: Decreasing marginal revenues

All the bad outcomes generated by a monopoly derive from the same source: unlike a competitive firm that faces a horizontal marginal revenue curve, the monopoly faces a downward-sloping marginal revenue curve. This simple fact causes monopolies to charge more, produce less and produce at higher costs than competitive firms.

How can one little curve cause such mayhem? A downward-sloping marginal revenue curve implies that each additional unit that the monopoly sells brings less revenue than the previous unit. For example, whereas the 10th unit sold may bring in £8, the 11th brings in only £3. Obviously, such a situation reduces the incentive to produce a lot of output.

This situation also stands in stark contrast to the marginal revenue situation facing competitive firms. Competitive firms face horizontal marginal revenue curves, meaning that whether they sell 11 units or 11,000, each unit brings in the same amount of money. Naturally, that's much more of an inducement to produce a lot of output.

Facing down demand

Why is there such a difference between the marginal revenue curves facing monopolies and competitive firms? A monopoly is free to choose the price it wants to charge along the demand curve it faces for its product. A competitive firm, on the other hand, has to take the market price as given.

A monopoly firm can choose its price because, being the only firm in its industry, it controls all the output in that industry. As a result, it can create a relatively high price by producing only a few units, or it can induce a relatively low price by flooding the market. In contrast, each firm in a competitive industry is such a small part of its industry that its choice of output makes too small a difference in total output to cause price changes.

The monopoly's ability to control the price by altering its output level means that it has to step back and consider what output level to produce. Obviously, because its goal is profit maximisation, it has to figure out what level of output is going to maximise its profits.

It turns out that a monopoly's profit-maximising output level is defined by the same condition as that of a competitive firm: produce at the output level where the marginal revenue curve crosses the marginal cost curve.

So the first step in working out how much a monopoly's going to produce is to figure out what its marginal revenue curve looks like. When you do, you can see where that curve crosses the monopoly's marginal cost curve to work out how much it's going to produce.

Deriving marginal revenue from the demand curve

A monopoly's marginal revenue curve has a precise relationship with the demand curve for the monopoly's output. The marginal revenue of each successive unit of output is less than the marginal revenue of the previous unit of output because demand curves slope downward. If the demand curve is a straight line, the slope of the marginal revenue curve is twice as steep as the slope of the demand curve, meaning that marginal revenue falls quite quickly as output increases.

To see how this works, take a look at Figure 12-1, in which we draw a demand curve and its associated marginal revenue (MR) curve.

We provide the data needed to draw these two curves in Table 12-1. The first column contains different output levels ranging from zero to ten units. The second column shows the price per unit that can be charged at each output level. The third column shows the total revenue that the monopoly would get for producing and selling each output level – the price per unit times the number of units. And the final column gives the marginal revenue – the change in total revenue – that happens as you increase output by one unit.

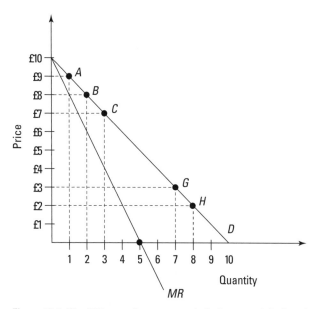

Figure 12-1: The *MR* curve for a monopoly facing a straight-line demand curve has a slope twice as steep as that of the demand curve.

To make it clear that marginal revenue represents the change in total revenue, the entries in the marginal revenue column are displayed between the two total revenue figures to which they correspond. For example, total revenue increases from £0 to £9 as you move from producing no output to one unit of output. That's why we place the marginal revenue of £9 at the top of the marginal revenue column, between the total revenue entries of £0 and £9.

As you can see in Figure 12-1, the marginal revenue *(MR)* curve starts at the same point as the demand curve, but it falls with twice the slope. It hits the horizontal axis at an output level of *q* = 5 rather than the *q* = 10 output level at which demand hits the horizontal axis.

Table 12-1	Price and *MR* for Various Output Levels on the Figure 12-1 Demand Curve		
Output	**Selling Price**	**Total Revenue**	**Marginal Revenue**
0	10	0	
			9
1	9	9	
			7
2	8	16	
			5
3	7	21	
			3
4	6	24	
			1
5	5	25	
			−1
6	4	24	
			−3
7	3	21	
			−5
8	2	16	
			−7
9	1	9	
			−9
10	0	0	

Relating marginal revenue to total revenue

You can see why the marginal revenue curve falls so quickly if you first examine total revenue, or *TR*. The total revenue that the monopoly can get is simply the output it produces times the price at which it can sell its output. That is, $TR = p \times q$.

The relationship between output produced and the price at which it can be sold depends on the demand curve. At point *A* on the demand curve in Figure 12-, one unit is being produced, and it can be sold for £9. Consequently, the total revenue at that point is £9. Next, look at point *B*, at which two units of output are being sold. At that output level, each unit can be sold for £8, and total revenue is £8 × 2 = £16. At point *C*, where three units can be sold for £7 each, total revenue is £21.

The important thing to notice is how total revenue changes as you move from *A* to *B* to *C* and output increases from one to two to three units. Total revenue goes from £9 to £16 to £21. Obviously, total revenue increases.

But look more deeply. Moving from *A* to *B*, *TR* increases by £7 (from £9 to £16). But moving from *B* to *C*, it increases by only £5 (from £16 to £21). Each successive increase in total revenue is smaller than the previous increase.

Increasing production, decreasing marginal revenue

Because marginal revenue is defined as the change in total revenue that happens as you increase production by one unit, the phenomenon we describe in the previous section is the same thing as saying that marginal revenue declines as the monopoly increases production.

If you look at Table 12-1, you can see that marginal revenue continues to fall for each successive unit. In fact, it becomes negative for all units after the fifth. You can see why by looking at points *G* and *H* in Figure 12-1 as examples. At point *G*, the monopoly can sell seven units of output for £3 each, making for a total revenue of £21. But if it increases output to eight units at point *H*, the monopoly can sell these units for only £2 each, implying a total revenue of £16. That's the same thing as saying that marginal revenue is *negative* £5 as you move from seven to eight units of output.

Sliding down the demand curve: Higher output, lower prices

Marginal revenue keeps declining and even becomes negative because the demand curve slopes downward, meaning that the only way to get people to buy more stuff is to offer them a lower price. You have to offer them a lower price not just on additional units, but on all previous units as well.

In other words, if the monopoly firm wants to sell only one unit (see point *A*), it can get £9 for that unit. But if the monopoly wants to sell two units (see point *B*), it has to lower the price down to £8 per unit for *both* the first unit *and* the second unit.

Because total revenue equals price times quantity *(TR = p × q)*, you can see that the monopoly faces a trade-off as it increases output and slides down the demand curve. As the firm produces more, *q* goes up, but *p* must fall. What happens to *TR* depends on whether the increases in *q* (output effects) are bigger than the decreases in *p* (price effects).

You can see from Table 12-1 that as the monopoly increases production through the first four units, total revenue keeps increasing, meaning that the gains from selling more units more than offset the declines from getting less money per unit. At an output of five units, the two effects cancel each other out. And for higher outputs, total revenue falls because the negative effect of less money per unit overwhelms the positive effect of selling more units.

Because marginal revenue tells you how total revenue changes as you increase output, the changes in *TR* caused by increasing output show up in *MR* as well. If you look at Figure 12-1, you can see that *MR* is always declining. That's because the negative price effect of getting less per unit keeps getting stronger and stronger relative to the positive quantity effect of selling more units.

Now that you've seen the marginal revenue situation facing a monopoly, you can combine it with the firm's marginal cost curve to figure out the profit-maximising output level. As we show you in the next section, this level is less than that chosen by a competitive firm – a behaviour that leads to social harm, which can be quantified using the method of deadweight losses that we explain in detail in Chapter 11.

Choosing an output level to maximise profits

A monopoly is no different to a competitive firm when it comes to the costs of producing output. Just like a competitive firm, a monopoly has fixed costs, variable costs and marginal costs.

More importantly, these costs all behave in the same way whether a firm is competitive or a monopoly. This means you can use costs to help analyse the decision-making process of a monopoly in the same way that you use them to analyse the decision-making of competitive firms.

The key difference is that the monopoly faces a downward-sloping marginal revenue curve. This factor causes a profit-maximising monopoly to produce less output than a profit-maximising competitive firm.

Setting MR = MC for a monopoly

The monopoly goes about maximising profits in much the same way as a competitive firm. To see this, take a look at Figure 12-2, in which we draw a monopoly's average total cost *(ATC)* and marginal cost *(MC)* curves on the same graph as the monopoly's demand curve and marginal revenue *(MR)* curve.

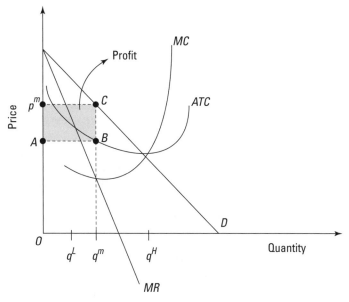

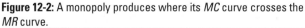

Figure 12-2: A monopoly produces where its *MC* curve crosses the *MR* curve.

As we explain in Chapter 10, for every output level, q, the *ATC* curve gives the average total cost per unit of producing q units of output. This curve is U-shaped because average total costs first fall due to increasing returns and then increase due to diminishing returns. The marginal cost curve gives the cost of producing one more unit of output; that is, it tells you how much total costs rise if you increase output by one unit.

As Figure 12-2 illustrates, the profit-maximising monopoly's optimal output level, q^m, is determined by where the *MR* and *MC* curves cross. As with a competitive firm, choosing to produce where marginal revenues equal marginal costs *(MR = MC)* maximises profits or minimises losses, depending on whether demand is strong enough for the firm to be able to make a profit (see Chapter 10).

The reason that q^m is optimal can be seen by looking at two different output levels, q^L and q^H, where L stands for low and H stands for high:

- ✓ **Low output:** At output level q^L, you can go up vertically to see that *MR* at that output exceeds *MC*, meaning that if you produce and sell that unit, it brings in more in revenue than it costs to produce. Clearly, this unit is a good one to produce. Because a similar relationship holds true for all output levels less than q^m, the monopoly should keep increasing output until it reaches q^m.

- ✓ **High output:** On the other hand, the monopoly doesn't want to increase output beyond q^m. To see why, examine output level q^H. At that output level, marginal costs are much bigger than marginal revenues, meaning that if you produce that unit of output, the cost of producing it exceeds the money you can get selling it. In other words, if you produce that unit, you lose money.

So, as you can see, the monopoly wants to produce exactly q^m units, because for all units up to q^m, marginal revenues exceed marginal costs.

Working out what price to charge

To figure out what the price of each unit of output needs to be, use the demand curve. Move up vertically from the monopoly's profit-maximising output level to the demand curve and then head sideways. In Figure 12-2, you can see that at output level q^m the monopoly can charge price p^m.

Eyeing the monopoly's profit

In Figure 12-2, the profit that the monopoly makes is shown by the shaded rectangle with corners at A, p^m, C and B.

For the monopoly that is maximising profits by producing q^m units and selling them for p^m pounds, total revenue is price times quantity $(TR = p^m \times q^m)$. Consequently, total revenue is the area of the rectangle whose length is equal to the price and whose width is equal to the quantity. That is, TR is the area of the rectangle that has corners O, p^m, C and q^m.

The total cost rectangle is a product of the average cost per unit times the number of units. If you go up vertically from point q^m until you hit the ATC curve, you get to point B. The vertical distance up to point B gives the average cost per unit of producing output q^m. So if you multiply that amount by the output q^m, you get total costs. Geometrically, therefore, total costs are given by the rectangle whose corners are O, A, B and q^m.

In Figure 12-2, the total revenue rectangle (O, p^m, C, q^m) is bigger than the total cost rectangle (O, A, B, q^m), meaning that the monopoly is earning a profit. That profit is given by the shaded rectangle whose points are A, p^m, C and B, which represents the difference in areas between the total revenue and total cost rectangles.

Understanding that monopoly doesn't guarantee profitability

Just because a firm has a monopoly doesn't mean that it's guaranteed a profit. If demand is too weak, prices are too low to make any money.

To see an example of this situation, look at Figure 12-3, where we draw a situation with weak demand. The new demand curve, D_I, leads to a lower marginal revenue curve, MR_I.

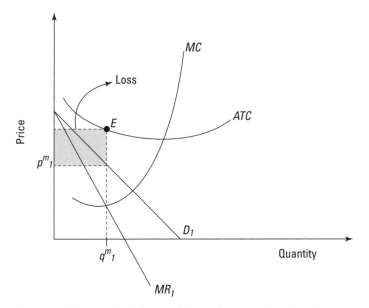

Figure 12-3: A monopoly facing weak demand can sustain a loss: being a monopoly does not guarantee a profit.

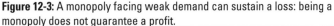

The monopoly again sets marginal revenue equal to marginal cost to find the optimal output level, q^m_1. But because of weaker demand, the monopoly operates at a loss represented by the area of the shaded rectangle.

To understand where the loss comes from in a different way, compare the monopoly's average total cost per unit with the price per unit it gets when producing and selling at output level q^m_1. At that output level, the price per unit, p^m_1, is found by starting on the horizontal axis at q^m_1 and then going up vertically to the demand curve. As you can see, you have to go up even farther to get to the ATC curve, meaning that the average total cost per unit to make q^m_1 units exceeds the price per unit you get from selling these units. This fact implies that the firm loses money producing at output level q^m_1.

As we show in Chapter 10, a firm in such a situation can't do any better. That is, any other output level besides q^m_1 produces an even bigger loss. If the monopoly can't work out a way to reduce costs or increase demand, it's quickly going bankrupt.

Comparing Monopolies with Competitive Firms

So far in this chapter, we've examined how a monopoly acts in order to maximise its profits. We now want to compare a profit-maximising monopoly with a profit-maximising competitive firm. This comparison comes off very badly for the monopoly because, competitive firms deliver socially optimal output levels. Because monopolies always end up producing less than competitive firms, their output levels are always less than socially optimal.

Looking at output and price levels

Monopolies produce less than competitive firms because they have different marginal revenue curves. As we show earlier in the chapter, monopolies face downward-sloping marginal revenue curves. By contrast, competitive firms face horizontal marginal revenue curves.

You can see the comparison in Figure 12-4, in which we draw both the downward-sloping marginal revenue curve of a monopoly, MR^m, and the horizontal marginal revenue curve of a competitive firm, MR^c. The graph also has an average total cost curve, ATC, as well as a marginal cost curve, MC.

Figure 12-4 assumes that the competitive firm and the monopoly have the same cost structure, which is why we show only one MC curve and one ATC curve. By assuming that both firms have the same cost structure, we can isolate the effect that the difference in marginal revenue curves has on each firm's output decisions.

Maximising profits for each firm

The marginal revenue curve for a competitive firm, MR^c, is a horizontal line set at the market price, p^c, because a competitive firm is such a small part of its industry that it can't affect the market price. As a result, it can sell as many or as few units as it wants at p^c, meaning that the marginal revenue it gets for every unit it chooses to produce is p^c. As we show in Figure 12-4, $MR^c = p^c$ for a competitive firm.

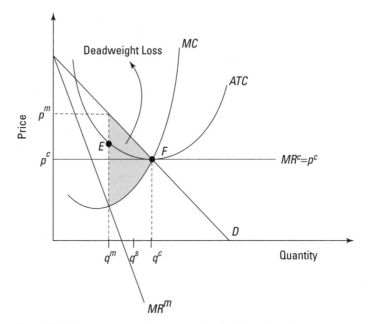

Figure 12-4: If a monopoly and a competitive firm have the same cost structure, the monopoly produces less, which causes a deadweight loss.

In addition, we show in Chapter 11 that market forces adjust supply and demand until the market price is equal to the minimum average total cost at which a firm can produce. Geometrically, this fact means that the horizontal $MR^c = p^c$ line just touches the bottom of the U-shaped ATC curve.

As we note earlier in the chapter, monopolies and competitive firms follow the same basic rule to maximise profits: they each produce where their marginal revenue curve intersects their marginal cost curve. But because they have different marginal revenue curves the competitive firm produces q^c, whereas the monopoly produces q^m.

Understanding why the monopoly produces less

The competitive firm produces more than the monopoly, because the competitive firm doesn't have to worry about reducing its revenue per unit if it increases output. No matter how much it produces, the competitive firm always receives $MR^c = p^c$ on every unit sold because its output is too small relative to total output to affect the market price.

In contrast, the monopoly faces the market demand curve, meaning that every additional unit it sells lowers the price per unit it receives on all units sold. Geometrically, this fact implies the downward-sloping MR^m, which leads the monopoly to restrict output because it knows that the more it produces, the less money per unit it gets.

Because the monopoly restricts output compared with the competitive firm, the monopoly price, p^m, is also higher than the competitive price, p^c. This fact hurts consumers, but the real harm comes from the reduction in output.

Deadweight losses: Quantifying the harm caused by monopolies

Monopolies cause harm because they reduce output below the socially optimal level produced by competitive firms. Take another look at Figure 12-4 and consider whether it would be good for society if all the units of output between the monopoly output level, q^m, and the competitive output level, q^c, were produced.

For example, look at unit q^s. At that level of output, the demand curve is above the marginal cost curve. This level implies that people are willing to pay more for that unit of output than it costs to make it. In other words, benefits exceed costs for that unit of output. Because this fact applies for all units between q^m and q^c, monopolies hurt society by failing to produce units of output for which benefits exceed costs.

If we go through the same exercise for each and every unit between q^m and q^c, we can total up the harm caused by the failure of the monopoly to produce those units. Graphically, the total harm measured in pounds is equal to the area of the shaded deadweight loss triangle in Figure 12-4.

This triangle of deadweight loss is the sum of all the vertical distances between the demand curve and marginal cost curve for all the units of output between q^m and q^c. The deadweight loss triangle sums up the pound losses that result when the monopoly restricts output.

Focusing on efficiency

Another problem with monopolies is that they aren't efficient producers. To see that this is true, look again at Figure 12-4.

Competitive firms produce at output level q^c the level of ouput that correspondsto point F, which happens to lie at the very bottom of the U-shaped ATC curve.

At the monopoly output level, q^m, if you go up vertically from that output level to the ATC curve, you get to point E. Because the vertical distance between the horizontal axis and E is longer than the vertical distance between the horizontal axis and point F, you know that total costs per unit when producing the monopoly output level, q^m, are higher than those when producing the competitive output level, q^c. Consequently, a monopoly firm produces output at a more costly output level than a competitive firm.

This bad result is yet another manifestation of the fact that monopolies face downward-sloping marginal revenue curves. A competitive firm has an incentive to increase output all the way to q^c because doing so lowers per-unit production costs and can thereby increase profits. The same incentive exists for a monopoly, but is more than offset by the reduction in revenue that happens if the monopoly firm increases its output. As a result, the monopoly's profits are maximised at q^m even though q^c is the lowest-cost output level.

Considering Examples of Good Monopolies

In this chapter we show you that compared to a competitive firm, a monopoly produces too little at too high a cost and turns around and sells it for too much money. Given these three bad things, you may want to get rid of monopolies altogether. But if you did, you'd be acting a bit too hastily. In some cases, the benefits of monopolies outweigh their costs. In other cases, the benefits outweigh costs in certain cases and in still other situations, society is still deciding whether the costs or benefits are the greater.

Encouraging innovation and investment with patents

The protection offered by patents is the most obvious case in which monopolies do society a lot of good. Patents give inventors the exclusive right to market their inventions for 20 years, after which time their inventions become public property. That is, patents given inventors the right to run a monopoly for 20 years.

Monopolies are vitally important in the context of innovation because without them inventors are unlikely to ever see any financial reward for their hard work: copycats are likely to steal their ideas and flood the market with rip-offs, thereby collapsing the price. Consequently, in a world without patents, far fewer people would bother to put in the time, effort and money required to come up with new inventions.

To remedy this situation, nations all over the world offer patent monopolies to inventors. The result is faster innovation, much more rapid economic growth and much faster increases in living standards.

However, those patents are limited so as to strike a balance between giving inventors incentives to invent and preventing people from holding permanent monopolies.

Reducing annoyingly redundant competitors

Societies have also stepped in to create monopolies in situations where competition means annoying redundancies. Consider the following examples:

- ✔ **Rubbish collection:** Bin lorries are loud and annoying. If one firm has a monopoly on collection, you have to endure a loud, annoying lorry only once per week. But if, say, seven different sets of bin men compete, you may have to endure a noisy lorry every day if you and six of your neighbours each choose to use a different firm that picks up on a different day of the week.

✔ **Cable television:** Only one cable TV provider exists for the whole of the UK. Think about the cost of laying wires to your home, and you can understand why. If ten different cable TV companies compete for your business, you'd need ten different sets of cable TV wires running underground – at much greater expense than running just one set of wires.

✔ **Natural gas:** Laying the pipes that deliver natural gas is expensive, and laying down multiple grids of gas pipe in one area would be wasteful.

As a result, most utilities and local services are supplied by a monopoly, whether state or private. Each company is given a monopoly and is then regulated to make sure that it doesn't exploit customers. For example, the supply of water in London (Thames Water) is a monopoly.

Keeping costs low with natural monopolies

Another area in which society may decide that a monopoly rather than competition is best is in the case of what economists call *natural monopoly industries*, or *natural monopolies*.

An industry is a natural monopoly if one large producer can produce output at a lower cost than many small producers. A good example is electricity distribution. The enormous fixed cost of setting up a national power grid means that there's no way of setting up a grid to serve a fraction of the market. In this case it has to be all or nothing.

Such an industry is called a *natural monopoly* because it naturally becomes dominated by a single low-cost producer. The perplexing problem here for policymakers is what to do with a natural monopoly.

On the one hand, everyone welcomes the fact that the grid serves the entire nation. But on the other hand, because there can be no economic competition, people now have to worry about the new monopoly charging high prices and producing less than the socially optimal output level.

These conflicting good and bad points typically mean that governments allow the natural monopoly to operate as the only firm in its industry, but at the same time they regulate it so that people don't have to worry about high prices or low output levels. Society gets the benefits that the most efficient production method generates without having to worry about the problems that may result if the monopoly was left unregulated.

Regulating Monopolies

Governments have to decide when to support and when to suppress monopolies. For example, patents support an inventor's monopoly right to produce and sell their invention for 20 years. After that, the production and sale of the invention is thrown open to competition.

In some monopolistic situations, various regulatory institutions have been developed to decide whether to destroy a monopoly by breaking it apart or let it continue to be the only firm in its industry and regulate it.

Subsidising a monopoly to increase output

We establish in the 'Comparing Monopolies with Competitive Firms' section, earlier in this chapter, that a profit-maximising monopoly produces an output level, q^m, less than the socially optimal level that would be produced by a competitive firm, q^c. One way to get the monopoly to produce more is to subsidise its production costs so that the marginal cost curve in effect shifts down vertically. Doing so causes the marginal cost and marginal revenue curves to meet at a higher level of output. And if the subsidy is big enough, the monopoly can be induced to increase output all the way to q^c.

Some governments use this type of subsidy to get gas, electricity and phone companies to serve more people, especially poor people. If the monopoly firms' costs of hooking up customers are subsidised, the firms are willing to hook up more customers than they would without the subsidy.

Some people object to subsidising a monopoly, so this sort of solution isn't necessarily the most popular politically; but it is effective in increasing output.

Imposing minimum output requirements

Another way to get a monopoly to produce more is simply to order it to produce more. For example, in some places telephone companies must provide basic telephone service to everyone – even to people who can't pay for it themselves. (The idea is to make sure that everyone is able to call for help in case of an emergency.) The same is often true of companies that provide heating in the winter; in some places, you can't turn off someone's heat for non-payment of bills.

Minimum output requirements can force a monopoly to produce the socially optimal output level. They are often politically popular because many people think of monopolies as evil and exploitative and don't mind seeing them ordered to produce more.

Regulators have to be careful, however, not to bankrupt a monopoly when regulating. Depending on a monopoly's cost curves, forcing a monopoly to produce at an output level where it loses money is quite possible. Because regulators don't want to bankrupt monopolies and thereby deny consumers access to the goods or services they produce, regulators are careful to take a monopoly's cost structure into account when considering minimum output requirements.

Regulating monopoly pricing

Perhaps the most common way to regulate a monopoly is to set the price at which it can sell each unit of output that it produces. This approach works because it changes the monopoly firm's marginal revenue curve from sloping downward to being horizontal, eliminating the monopoly's usual problem that the more it sells, the less it can charge per unit.

However, as with quantity requirements, regulators have to pay close attention to a monopoly's cost structure when choosing the regulated price so that they don't bankrupt the monopoly.

To see the problem facing the regulator, consider the monopoly whose cost curves are given in Figure 12-5. Left unregulated, the monopoly chooses to produce the profit-maximising output level q^m, defined by where MR crosses MC. From the demand curve, you can see that it's able to charge price p^m per unit for that amount of output.

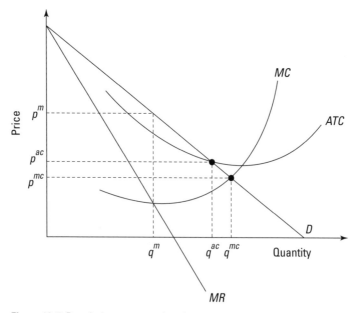

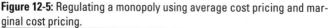

Figure 12-5: Regulating a monopoly using average cost pricing and marginal cost pricing.

Next, think about how a regulator may want to modify the monopoly's behaviour. For example, a well-intentioned regulator may want to get the monopoly to produce every single unit of output for which benefits exceed costs. Looking at Figure 12-5, you can see that the regulator wants to get the monopoly to produce output level q^{mc}, defined by where the downward-sloping demand curve intersects the MC curve.

As a result, the regulator sets the price at p^{mc}. At that price, the demand curve tells us that consumers want to purchase q^{mc} units of output. Because this is the output where price equals marginal cost, monopoly deadweight loss is eliminated. Better yet, the monopoly wants to supply that level of output because the marginal revenue from selling each unit exceeds the marginal cost of producing it.

However, a big problem exists with this policy given this particular monopoly's cost structure: the monopoly goes bankrupt, because at output level q^{mc}, the firm's total costs exceed its total revenues.

You can see this problem on a per-unit basis by noting that the average total cost per unit at output level q^{mc} (given by the vertical distance from the horizontal axis up to the ATC curve) is more than the regulator-imposed revenue of p^{mc} per unit. Because average total costs per unit exceed revenues per unit, the monopoly is going to be operating at a loss. If the regulator doesn't relent and allow a higher price, the monopoly eventually goes bankrupt, unless the government steps in to subsidise the firm by giving it a cash grant equal to the amount of its loss.

The method of regulation we just described is called *marginal cost pricing*, because the regulated price, p^{mc}, is set where the marginal cost curve crosses the demand curve. But because this method can cause a monopoly to lose money, a more common alternative is *average cost pricing*, which sets the regulated price where the average total cost curve *(ATC)* intersects the demand curve.

In Figure 12-5, a regulator using average cost pricing would set the price at p^{ac}. At that price, you can see from the demand curve that consumers demand q^{ac} units of output. The monopoly is happy to supply that output level because for every unit up to q^{ac}, marginal revenue (the regulated price per unit, p^{ac}) exceeds marginal cost – meaning that the monopoly gains financially by producing each of these units.

The main benefit of this system is that you don't have to worry about the monopoly going bankrupt (or where to get the money to subsidise a monopoly that would go bankrupt under marginal cost pricing). Average cost pricing guarantees that the monopoly is going to break even.

You can see this fact by comparing the average total costs per unit at output level q^{ac} with the revenue per unit at that output level. Because the average total costs per unit are equal to the regulated price per unit, the firm must be breaking even.

The downside to average cost pricing for this monopoly is that all the socially beneficial units between q^{ac} and q^{mc} don't get produced. On the other hand, the only way to keep this monopoly in business to produce those units if you imposed marginal cost pricing is to subsidise it.

Breaking up a monopoly into several competing firms

Another solution to the problem of a monopoly is to destroy it by breaking it up into many competing firms. (It's fair to say that this is regarded as something of a nuclear option in competition law, so it happens rarely; in general other penalties are preferred.) The most famous use of this solution was the division of American Telephone and Telegraph Corporation (AT&T) into a bunch of smaller competitors in 1984. (Economists often like to compare this treatment of AT&T with the more lenient handling of British Telecom by UK authorities.)

Before 1984, AT&T was a nationwide monopoly. If you wanted to make a telephone call anywhere in the United States, you had to use AT&T because it was the only telephone company in the country. It was highly regulated, with both quantity requirements to provide everyone a phone and price requirements that encouraged it to provide a high quantity of telecommunication services. But it was still a monopoly, and a judge ruled in 1984 that it should be broken up into numerous local firms in order to foster competition.

The policy change worked extremely well. A very competitive market for telephone services soon emerged between firms that had been part of AT&T. And more recently, the telephone service industry has become even more competitive due to the arrival of mobile phone companies, Internet telephony companies and even cable TV companies offering phone services. This robust competition eliminates the problems associated with monopolies and ensures that telecommunication services are provided at low cost and in large quantity.

Creating competition is also a handy way to deal with a monopoly because it eliminates the costs associated with having to continually monitor a regulated monopoly. As we explain in Chapter 11, competition gets you to the socially optimal output level without any sort of central control. That stands in stark contrast to regulated monopolies, which typically require expensive bureaucracies to develop and enforce laws and regulations.

Part IV
The Part of Tens

'He was a lousy economist but his charts caught the eye of a famous art critic & dealer.'

In this part . . .

The chapters in this part offer some fun, fast reading. Chapter 13 debunks ten very common but incorrect pieces of economic thinking – the kind of stuff you hear pundits and politicians refer to all the time. Chapter 14 features ten correct and truly great economic ideas that need to guide your thinking about public policy and how best to run an economy.

Chapter 13

Ten Seductive Economic Fallacies

In This Chapter

▶ Avoiding logical fallacies that catch intelligent people

▶ Steering clear of bad economic reasoning

*I*n this short chapter, we outline the most attractive and compelling incorrect ideas in economics. Some are logical fallacies. A few are myopic opinions that don't take into account the big picture. And others are poorly thought-out examples of economic reasoning.

The Lump of Labour Fallacy

The argument that a fixed amount of work exists, which you can divide up among as many people as you want, is often presented as a cure for unemployment. The idea goes that if you convert from a 40-hour work week to a 20-hour work week, firms have to hire twice as many workers. In 2000, for example, France reduced its work week to only 35 hours in the hope that firms would hire more workers and cure France's persistent unemployment problem.

The idea didn't work; such policies have never worked. One problem is that hiring workers involves many fixed costs, including training costs and health insurance. So two 20-hour-per-week workers cost more to employ than one 40-hour-per-week worker. What's more, two 20-hour-per-week workers don't produce any more output than one 40-hour-per-week worker.

So if laws were passed that forced firms to move from a 40-hour work week to a 20-hour work week, firms wouldn't double the size of their workforces. They'd hire fewer than twice as many workers because costs would go up, which is one reason why, in 2005, France relaxed its experiment with the 35-hour work week.

What you really want is a situation in which every worker who wants a full-time job is able to get one. Shortening the work week doesn't achieve this goal.

The World Is Facing an Overpopulation Problem

Various versions of the overpopulation myth have been floating around since the late 18th century when Thomas Malthus first asserted the idea. He argued that living standards can't permanently rise because higher living standards cause people to breed faster. He believed that population growth would outpace our ability to grow more food, so we would be doomed to return to subsistence levels of nutrition and living standards.

Even when Malthus first published this idea, lots of evidence indicated that it was bunk. For generations, living standards had been rising while birth rates had been falling. And because that trend has continued up to the present day, we're not going to breed our way to subsistence.

Indeed, many nations now face an *under*population problem. In most developed countries, birth rates have fallen below the replacement rate necessary to keep the population stable. As a result, their populations are soon going to start shrinking dramatically. And because birth rates are falling quickly all over the world, the United Nations expects the total human population to max out at around 9 billion people in 2070.

A related problem is that rapidly falling birth rates are wreaking havoc on government-sponsored retirement systems because too few young workers exist to pay all the taxes needed to fund retirees' pensions. In desperation, some countries are going so far as to pay cash bounties to mothers for each new child they give birth to.

Again, we cannot deny that the world faces many environmental problems over the coming century. However, as people become more educated and aware of their environmental impact, overpopulation is becoming less of a concern.

The Fallacy of Confusing Sequence with Causation

Post hoc ergo propter hoc is a Latin phrase that translates roughly as, 'Because you see one thing precede another, you think that it causes the other.' That is, if A happens before B, you assume that A causes B.

Such a deduction is false because A and B often don't have any relationship. For example, if it rains in the morning and you get a headache in the afternoon, that doesn't mean that the rain caused your headache.

Politicians try to pull this logical fallacy all the time when discussing the economy. For example, suppose that politician A gets elected, and a few months later a recession hits. The two may have nothing to do with each other, but you can be sure that during the next election, an opponent of politician A claims that the recession was the result of politician A's policies. The only proof offered is that one event happened before the other. In these cases, it's worth looking for good reasons to support the argument!

Protectionism Is the Best Solution to Foreign Competition

To be sure, you can find both good and bad arguments in favour of protectionism. The good arguments include the need for strategic security for certain goods. For example, most developed countries place a degree of protection on their defence industries. However, arguments in favour of trade barriers and taxes on imports, on the grounds that these policies benefit citizens and prevent jobs from being exported, tend not to be good arguments. The problem is that their arguments consider only the benefits of protectionism without also considering the costs.

Trade barriers and taxes on imports *do* protect the specific jobs that they're intended to protect. However, other jobs are often sacrificed in the process.

For example, raising tariffs on foreign coal protects the jobs of domestic miners. But such a policy results in higher energy costs all over the economy. Domestic manufacturers have to pay higher energy costs than if they had access to the cheaper foreign coal, and so they have to raise the prices of the goods they produce. As a result, demand for these goods decreases, and the manufacturers don't need as many employees.

Protecting an unproductive industry that faces foreign competition only allows it to keep using resources that would be better used by more vibrant industries. Workers who would otherwise move to jobs in innovative, highly productive new industries instead get stuck in an industry so unproductive that it can survive only by having the government rig the economy in its favour.

Granted, the move from a dying industry to an innovative new industry can be rough for an individual worker. But instead of protecting unproductive industries to avoid the need for change, the government can help domestic workers more efficiently by providing retraining programmes for employees.

The Fallacy of Composition

Assuming that what's good for one person to do is good for everyone to do all at once is another common fallacy. For example, if you're at a sold-out sporting event and want to get a better view, standing is a good idea – but only if you're the only one who stands up. If everyone else also stands up, everyone's view is just as bad as when everyone was sitting down (but now everyone's legs are getting tired). Consequently, what was good for you to do alone is actually bad for everyone to do at the same time.

The fallacy of composition is false because some things in life have to do with relative position. For example, if you start out as the lowest-paid employee at your firm but then get a 50 per cent rise while nobody else gets a rise, your relative position within the firm improves. However, if everyone gets a 50 per cent rise at the same time, you're still the lowest-paid person at the firm. If what matters to you is your relative standing within the firm, getting the same rise as everyone else doesn't make you any happier. On the other hand, if you are more interested in where you stand relative to people who work at other firms, getting a 50 per cent rise is good even if everyone else at your firm gets it too!

If It's Worth Doing, Do It 100 Per Cent

We all value safety. But was a famous US politician really being sensible when he said that we should spend whatever money may be necessary to make flying on commercial airlines 'as safe as possible'?

Economists would say, 'No!' The problem is that making commercial airline travel 'as safe as possible' would mean making it prohibitively expensive. Although safety is a good thing, achieving complete safety is not a worthy goal if doing so makes flying so expensive that only the extremely wealthy can afford it.

The politician failed to apply *marginalism* – the idea that the best way to approach a problem is to compare marginal benefits with marginal costs. Applying marginalism to airline safety, you realise that making flying 'as safe as possible' is wasteful.

The first few airline safety innovations (such as seatbelts and radar) are sensible to undertake because the extra, or marginal, benefit that each brings is greater than the extra, or marginal, cost required to pay for it. But after the first few safety innovations are implemented, successive innovations become more costly and less effective. At some point, additional innovations bring only small marginal increases in safety while running up high marginal costs.

We're not suggesting that investments in safety are not worthwhile. Although increased airport security does hurt airlines, it's something we can accept because the risks associated with someone getting through with bad intentions are so high that we are willing to pay the cost. However, even here there's a point where we'd draw the line and say no more. After all, if no one flies, terrorists cannot attack air flights, but the costs to the global economy would be enormous.

Free Markets Are Dangerously Unstable

Free markets are volatile because supply and demand often change very quickly, causing rapid changes in equilibrium prices and quantities (which we discuss in Chapter 8). Rapid change isn't a problem, however. The responsiveness of markets is actually one of their great benefits. Unlike a government bureaucracy that can never react quickly to anything, markets can adjust to huge changes in world events in only minutes.

The new equilibrium prices and quantities ensure that resources are allocated to their best uses and that society suffers from neither shortages nor gluts. So don't call markets unstable. Call them *responsive.*

Low Foreign Wages Mean that Rich Countries Can't Compete

You often hear that UK firms can't compete with firms based in developing countries because of vast differences in hourly wages. To see the problem with this thinking, compare a factory in Uttoxeter with a factory in Phnom Penh.

Say the UK factory pays its workers £20 per hour while the factory in Cambodia pays £4 per hour. People mistakenly jump to the conclusion that because the foreign factory's labour costs are so much lower, it can easily undersell the UK factory. But this argument fails to take into account two things:

- ✔ What actually matters is labour costs per *unit,* not labour costs per *hour.*
- ✔ Differences in productivity typically mean that labour costs per unit are often nearly identical despite huge differences in labour costs per hour.

To see what we mean, compare how productive the two factories are. Because the UK factory uses much more advanced technology, one worker in one hour can produce 20 units of output. The UK worker gets paid £20 per hour, so the labour cost *per unit of output* is £1. The factory in Cambodia is much less productive; a worker there produces only 4 units in one hour. Given the foreign wage of £4 per hour, the labour cost per unit of output in Cambodia is also £1.

Obviously, Cambodia's lower hourly wage rate *per hour* doesn't translate into lower labour costs *per unit* – meaning that Cambodia is unable to undersell its UK competitor.

People who focus exclusively on labour costs omit some of the most important parts of the analysis. The cost of production also depends on factors such as the availability of capital, machinery and resources, or the regulations imposed by the host government. Economists disagree on the exact impact of these factors, although they do agree that labour on its own is insufficient to account for differences in the cost of producing items in different countries.

Keep in mind that governments can seriously screw up what would otherwise be a near equality of labour costs per unit by fixing artificially low exchange rates. For example, if at an exchange rate of 8 Chinese yuan to 1 US dollar labour costs per unit are equal, the Chinese government can make labour costs per unit look artificially low to US consumers if it fixes its currency at, for example, 16 yuan to 1 dollar. In such situations, the inability of US workers to compete with Chinese workers is due to the currency manipulation, not to the lower wage rate per hour found in China. For this reason, among others, the US has been attempting to persuade China to revalue the yuan.

Tax Rates Don't Affect Work Effort

Some politicians argue for raising income taxes as though the only effect of doing so is to raise more money. But experience has demonstrated over and over again that beyond a certain point, people respond to higher taxes by working less. And that reduction in labour denies society all the benefits that would have come from the extra work. (Also, because people work less, the increased tax rate doesn't bring in nearly as much revenue as expected.)

So if you see a politician arguing for an increase in income taxes, look into the details to make sure that the disincentive effects of the tax hike don't cause more mischief than the benefits that are going to be derived from spending the money raised by the tax increase. A cost-benefit analysis on tax changes should be done to make sure that the result isn't unnecessary economic damage.

Forgetting that Policies Have Unintended Consequences Too

When evaluating a policy, people tend to concentrate on how the policy is going to fix some particular problem while ignoring or downplaying the possible other effects. Economists often refer to this situation as *The Law of Unintended Consequences*.

Suppose that you impose a tariff on imported steel in order to protect the jobs of domestic steelworkers. If you impose a high enough tariff, their jobs are indeed protected from competition by foreign steel companies. But an unintended consequence is that the jobs of some autoworkers are lost to foreign competition. Why? The tariff that protects steelworkers raises the price of the steel that domestic car makers need to build their cars. As a result, domestic car manufacturers have to raise the prices of their cars, making them relatively less attractive when compared to foreign cars. Raising prices tends to reduce domestic car sales, meaning that some domestic workers in the car factory lose their jobs.

Be aware of this whenever a politician tries to persuade you to see things his or her way. Chances are that the politician is mentioning only the good results of a certain policy; he or she may not even have thought about the not-so-good side effects.

Chapter 14

Ten Economic Ideas to Hold Dear

* *

In This Chapter

▶ Understanding basic economic principles

▶ Arming yourself against the economic follies of politicians

* *

*I*n this chapter, we list ten economic ideas that all informed people need to understand and be ready to use to evaluate the policy proposals made by politicians. Some of these ideas aren't necessarily true in all situations, but because they are usually correct, be wary if someone wants you to believe that they don't apply to a particular situation.

Society Is Better Off When People Pursue Their Own Interests

This concept is basically Adam Smith's famous invisible hand. If all economic interactions in a society are voluntary on the parts of all parties involved, the only transactions that are going to take place are those in which all parties feel they are being made better off.

If you trade your gold for another person's bread, you're likely to do so because you value his bread more than your gold. You trade because trading makes you better off. Meanwhile, you can be sure that the other person values your gold more than his bread. So trading makes him better off too.

This concept of what motivates people doesn't mean that charitable acts are bad for society. Instead, it means that even philanthropy is generated by self-interest. People give because they enjoy helping others. By doing so, both they and the people they help are made better off.

Free Markets Require Regulation

Economists firmly believe that voluntary transactions in free markets tend to work toward the common good. But they also believe that nearly every participant in the marketplace would love to rig the system in his or her own favour. Adam Smith, in particular, was quick to point this out and argue that for markets to work and serve the common good, the government has to fight monopolies, collusion and any other attempts to prevent a properly functioning market in which firms vigorously compete against each other to give consumers what they want at the lowest possible price.

Economic Growth Depends on Innovation

At any given moment, a fixed amount of wealth exists that can be divided equally among all people, like slicing a pie into equal pieces and giving each person one equal slice. But if living standards are to keep rising, you need a bigger pie to split up. In the short run, you can get a bigger pie by working harder or using up resources faster. But the only way to have sustained growth is to invent more efficient technologies that allow people to produce ever more from the limited supply of labour and physical resources.

Freedom and Democracy Make Us Richer

Very good moral and ethical reasons exist for favouring freedom and democracy. But a more bottom line reason is that, in general, because freedom and democracy promote the free development and exchange of ideas, free societies have more innovation and, consequently, faster economic growth.

Education Raises Living Standards

Educated people are not only productive workers – and hence get paid higher salaries – but also, more importantly, they produce innovative new technologies. Sustained economic growth and higher living standards are only possible if you educate your citizens well. Of course, other good reasons exist for getting an education, including the ability to appreciate high art and literature. But even if all you care about is living in a country that has rising living standards, you should work hard to promote education in the sciences and engineering, sectors where revolutionary technologies are created.

Protecting Intellectual Property Rights Promotes Innovation

People need incentives to encourage them to take risks. One of the biggest risks you can take is to leave a secure job in order to start a new business or work at developing a great new idea. Intellectual property rights, when deployed effectively, give you a bargaining chip to help ensure that the rewards are going to go to you and your associates rather than competitors. Without this assurance, fewer people would be willing to take the personal risks necessary to provide society with innovative new technologies and products.

Weak Property Rights Cause Many Environmental Problems

People always have to do some polluting. After all, even if you don't want gas-guzzling SUVs running around causing lots of pollution, you probably still want ambulances and fire engines to operate despite the fact that they too pollute the environment. The difference is that the overall benefit to society outweighs the cost of the pollution in the case of the emergency vehicles but not in the case of the SUVs.

Seen in this light, society's goal isn't to ban pollution completely, but to make sure that the benefit exceeds the cost for whatever pollution is generated. Strong property rights are key to ensuring that people weigh the complete costs and benefits of pollution. Property rights force people to take into account not only their personal costs of generating pollution, but also the costs that their actions impose on others.

Because nobody owns the atmosphere, you don't have to pay anyone for the right to pollute. Polluting the air is, in fact, free – which leads to much too much polluting.

If we want to throw rubbish on someone's land, we have to pay that person for permission or risk huge fines (or even prison) for dumping rubbish without permission. Also, because we have to pay rubbish collection fees to throw out our rubbish, we're discouraged from generating wasteful amounts of it.

All environmental problems tend to stem from poorly defined or non-existent property rights that allow polluters to ignore the costs that they impose on others. Therefore, economists favour the creation and enforcement of property rights systems that force people to take all costs into account.

International Trade Is a Good Thing

Opening your country to international trade means opening your country to new ideas and new innovations. Competition from foreign competitors causes local businesses to innovate to match the best offerings of companies from around the world.

Quite simply, throughout history, the richest and most dynamic societies have been the ones open to international trade. Countries that close themselves off from international trade grow stagnant and are quickly left behind. Of course, what economists have in mind when they think of the benefits of international trade is *free trade*, where companies compete across borders to provide people with the best goods and services at the lowest prices. Economists strongly condemn the many government subsidies and trade restrictions that impede free trade and that try to rig the game in one country's favour.

Free Enterprise Has a Hard Time Providing Public Goods

Private firms can provide goods and services only if they can at least break even doing so. To break even (or make a profit), whatever a firm is selling has to be *excludable*, by which we mean that only those paying for the good or service receive it.

Some goods and services are non-excludable. For example, a lighthouse provides warning services to all ships in the vicinity regardless of whether they pay the lighthouse keeper. Because every ship knows that it can get the service without having to pay for it, the private lighthouse quickly goes bankrupt because only a few ships are fair-minded enough to pay for the service.

Goods and services that are non-excludable are called *public goods* because they're essentially open to the public and can't be kept private.

Because private firms can't make a profit producing public goods, you typically need governments to provide them. Unlike private firms, governments can force people to pay for public goods. They do this by levying taxes and using the tax revenues to pay for public goods, such as the army, the police force, lighthouses, public fireworks displays, basic scientific research and so on.

Economists view the existence of public goods as one of the most important justifications for government intervention in the economy. Although private philanthropy can also provide some public goods, many public goods are so expensive that they can be provided only if the government uses its power of taxation to fund them. Consequently, public goods are typically publicly provided.

Preventing Inflation Is Easy (ish)

Governments can cause high rates of inflation by increasing the money supply too rapidly. A growing economy always has a growing demand for money because with more stuff to buy, you need more money with which to buy it. If you want to keep the overall level of prices constant, the correct response is to increase the money supply at the same rate that demand is increasing. If the supply of money increases faster than the demand for money, the value of money falls, creating inflation. (In other words, it takes more money to buy the same amount of stuff as before, meaning that prices go up.)

Index

• A •

A (autonomous expenditures), 114–116
accounting profits, 204–205
actual expenditures (Y), 112–114
actual investment (I), 114
AD. *See* aggregate demand (AD)
adjusting
  inventories instead of prices, 110–119
  to new market equilibriums, 172–175
  to shifts in aggregate demand, 99–101
advantage mechanism, 150
AFC (average fixed costs), 210–211
aggregate demand (AD)
  adjusting to shifts in, 99–101
  curve, 97–98, 104–105
  defined, 122
  in Keynesian Model, 112
aggregate supply/aggregate demand
  model, 91
allocative efficiency, 30
altruism, 19–20
analysing. *See also* cost structure,
  analysing
  cost-benefit analysis, 23–25
  deadweight loss of taxes, 241–245
  efficiency of free markets, 230–233
anticipating stimulus, 131–132
assets
  considerations, 67–68
  defined, 138
  tracking flow of, 54–55
ATC (average total costs), 211–215
AT&T (American Telephone and
  Telegraph Corporation), 277–278
autonomous expenditures (A), 114–116
AVC (average variable costs), 209–210,
  213–215
average cost pricing, 276
average costs
  compared to marginal costs (MC), 28
average fixed costs (AFC), 210–211
average total costs (ATC), 211–215
average variable costs (AVC), 209–210,
  213–215

• B •

balanced budget, 63
balancing money supply and demand,
  72–74
bartering, 72
base rate, 146
behaviour, human. *See* human
  behaviour
benefits, capturing, 230
bonds, 142–144
budget, balanced, 63
budget deficit, 63, 135–137
budget surplus, 63
business cycle, 92–95

• C •

C. *See* consumption (C)
calculating
  consumer surplus of continuous
    goods, 236–237
  consumer surplus of discrete goods,
    234–235
  consumption, 60–61, 114–116
  gains with total surplus, 233–239
  government purchases, 63–64
  happiness, 180
  inflation rate, 81–87
  investment expenditures, 61–63
  net exports, 64–65
  producer surplus, 237–238
  total costs, 206
  total surplus, 238–239
capital, as resource, 31
cardinal utility, 180
causation, relationship with
  sequence, 283
Choice Model, 25–28
circular flow, 53
classifying resources, 30–31
command economy, 45
commodity, 201
comparative advantage, 68–70

competition. *See also* perfect
  competition
  about, 200–201
  accounting profits and economic
    profits, 204–205
  compared with monopolies, 267–270
  foreign, 283–284
  price takers and quantity makers,
    202–204
  requirements for perfect, 201–202
competitive market, 41
composition fallacy, 284–285
constraints
  opportunity cost, 22–23
  resource, 21
  technology, 21–22
  time, 22
consumer choices, tracking
  about, 17
  Choice Model, 25–28
  human behaviour, 17–25
Consumer Price Index (CPI), 81–82
consumer surplus
  defined, 233
  measuring of continuous goods,
    236–237
  measuring of discrete good, 234–235
consumers
  about, 179
  behaviour, 17
  decision-making with limited budgets,
    184–192
  diminishing marginal utility,
    24, 181–184, 192–197
  measuring happiness, 180
  utility, 180
consumption (C)
  calculating, 60–61, 114–116
  defined, 59
  in Keynesian Model, 113
consumption function, 114–116
continuous goods, 236–237
conventions, explained, 3
copyrights, 48
Corn Laws, 68
cost structure, analysing
  about, 206
  average fixed costs, 210–211
  average variable costs, 209–210,
    213–215
  costs per unit of output, 206–209
  intersections of MC curve, AVC curve,
    and ATC curve, 213–215

marginal costs. *See* marginal costs (MC)
  tracking movement of average total
    costs, 211–212
cost-benefit analysis, 23–25
costs. *See also* marginal costs (MC);
    opportunity cost
  capturing, 230
  changes along supply curve, 165–166
  keeping low with natural monopolies,
    272–273
  sunk, 26–27
costs per unit of output, 206–209
counting output, 57–58
coupon payments, of bonds, 142
CPI (Consumer Price Index), 81–82
cross-price effects, 195–197

• *D* •

data, plotting to create demand curves,
    15–16
deadweight loss
  about, 240
  in monopolies, 269
  from price ceilings, 240–241
  of taxes, 241–245
decreasing marginal revenues, 257–262
decreasing returns, 208
deficits, 63, 135–137
demand. *See also* supply and demand
    model
  about, 154
  balancing with money supply, 72–74
  compared with quantity demanded, 154
  excess, 171–172
  for money, 72–74
  in monopolies, 257–258
  reacting to increases in, 173–174
  stimulating to end recessions,
    122–124
  terms, 154–156
demand curve
  about, 14–15
  deriving marginal revenue from,
    258–260
  from diminishing marginal utility,
    192–197
  forming, 194–197
  graphing, 156–159
  making predictions with, 16
  in monopolies, 261–262
  plotting data for, 15–16

demand elasticity, 160–162
democracy, 11, 290–291
depressions. *See* Great Depression
diminishing marginal utility, 24, 181–184, 192–197
diminishing returns, 30–33, 209
discrete goods, 234–235
downward price stickiness, 130
downward wage stickiness, 130

• *E* •

economic growth, dependence on innovation, 290
economic model, 14
economic profits, 204–205, 246
economic shocks
  about, 96
  adjusting to shifts in aggregate demand, 99–101
  defined, 91
  fixed prices in short run, 101–103
  price adjustments, 98–99
  short run compared with long run, 103–105
  terms, 96–98
economics. *See also specific topics*
  about, 2–3, 9
  future of, 11–12
  history of, 9–11
economy
  command, 45
  GDP for tracking, 52–58
  market, 45
  mixed, 45–47
  stimulating, 77–78, 124–133, 146–147
  traditional, 45
education, relationship with standard of living, 290–291
efficiency
  of free markets, 230–233
  in monopolies, 270
  types, 29–30
elasticity
  demand, 160–162
  perfectly elastic/inelastic supply, 167, 168
environmental problems, caused by property rights, 291–292
equalising marginal utility per pound, 190–192
equilibrium, 116–119, 169. *See also* market equilibrium

equilibrium interest rate, 142
equilibrium price level (P*), 97–98, 110, 169, 225–226
equilibrium quantity, 169
excess demand, 171–172
excess supply, 170–171
expenditure variables, of GDP, 59–65
expenditures. *See also* investment expenditures (I^P)
  actual, 112–114
  induced, 114–116
  planned, 112–114
expiration (bonds), 142
extreme supply cases, 166–168

• *F* •

face value payment, of bonds, 142
fallacies, 281–288
FC (fixed costs), 206
fiat system, 75, 138–140
financial markets, 55
firms, defined, 53. *See also* profit-maximising firms
fiscal policy. *See also* monetary policy
  about, 121, 133
  deficits, 63, 135–137
  increasing government spending, 133–135
  inflation, risk of too much, 124–133
  stimulating demand, 122–124
Fisher, Irving (economist), 88
Fisher equation, 88
fixed costs (FC), 206
fixed prices, 101–103
foreign competition, protectionism as solution to, 283–284
foreign wages fallacy, 286–287
free enterprise, providing public goods, 293–294
free markets
  about, 227–228
  analysing efficiency of, 230–233
  benefits of competitive, 228–239
  deadweight loss, 240–245
  fallacy, 286
  measuring gains with total surplus, 233–239
  perfect competition, 245–255
  prerequisites for, 228–230
  regulation of, 290
freedom, 290–291
frictional unemployment, 94

full-employment output (Y*)
  aiming for, 122–124
  increasing beyond, 125–127
  returning to after price adjustments, 95–96
  returning to without government intervention, 107–108
  striving for, 94–95
funds, tracing flow of, 55–56
future of economics, 11–12

● *G* ●

G. *See* government interventions (G)
GDP (gross domestic product)
  about, 58–59
  boosting in Keynesian Model, 119–120
  consumption, 59, 60–61, 113–116
  government purchases, 59, 63–64
  investment expenditures, 59, 61–63, 113
  levels of, 58
  net exports, 60, 64–65, 113
  tracking economy with, 52–58
The General Theory of Employment, Interest and Money (Keynes), 59
generosity, 19–20
gold standard, 75
government interventions (G)
  in Keynesian Model, 113
  pros and cons of, 40–45
  returning to Y* without, 107–108
government purchases/spending
  calculating, 63–64
  defined, 59
  increasing to help end recessions, 133–135
graphing
  about, 14–16
  demand curves, 156–159
  equilibrium, 116–119
  money supply increases, 148
  possibilities, 34–37
  profits, 248–255
  supply curves, 163–166
Great Depression, 108–120, 139–140
gross domestic product. *See* GDP (gross domestic product)

● *H* ●

happiness, 18–20, 180
higher living standards, institutions contributing to, 10–11

history of economics, 9–11
households, 53
human behaviour
  about, 17–18
  cost-benefit analysis, 23–25
  limitations, 20–23
  maximising happiness, 18–20
human capital, 31
hyperinflation, 71, 75–76

● *I* ●

I (actual investment), 114
icons, explained, 5
imperfect competition, 200
imports (IM), 64–65
income, tracking flow of, 54–55
increasing
  government spending to help end recessions, 133–135
  output by subsidising monopolies, 273–274
  production, decreasing marginal revenue, 261
increasing returns, 208
induced expenditures *(c[1-t]Y)*, 114–116
inferior goods, 155
inflation
  about, 71–72
  balancing money supply and demand, 72–74
  calculating rate, 81–87
  determining real standard of living, 85–86
  effects of, 78–80
  Fisher equation, 88
  generating, 124–133
  hyperinflation, 71, 75–76
  identifying price index problems, 86–87
  market basket, 82–83
  measuring, 81–87
  money, risks of too much, 72–80
  nominal interest rates, 87–90
  politics of, 76–77
  predictions, 89–90
  preventing, 294
  price indexes, 81–87
  real interest rates, 87–90
  temptation of, 74–78
inflation tax, 80
inflationary expectations, 149–150

innovation
  effect on economic growth, 290
  encouraging, 47–48, 271
  promoting, 291
An Inquiry into the Nature and Causes of the Wealth of Nations (Smith), 20
intellectual property rights, 291
interest rates
  base rate, 146
  changing money supply to change, 145–146
  effect of inflationary expectations on, 149–150
  link between bond prices and, 143–144
  lowering to stimulate economy, 146–147
international trade
  about, 65–66
  assets, 67–68
  benefits of, 292–293
  comparative advantage, 68–70
  trade deficits, 66–67
inventory
  adjusting instead of prices, 110–119
  investment, 114
inverse relationship, 15, 73, 97–98, 155
investment expenditures (I^P)
  actual, 114
  calculating, 61–63
  defined, 59
  in Keynesian Model, 113
irrationality, 26–28

• *K* •

Keynes, John Maynard (economist), 59, 108–120
Keynesian Model, 108–120
Keynesianism. *See* Keynesian Model

• *L* •

labour, as resource, 30
labour fallacy, 281–282
land, as resource, 30
Law of Demand, 15
legal monopoly, 145–146
limited budgets, relationship with utility, 184–192
limited liability corporation, leading to higher living standards, 11

literacy and education, leading to higher living standards, 11
long run
  compared with short run, 103–105
  defined, 96
  price adjustments in, 98–99
  shutdown condition, 225, 226
long-run aggregate supply curve (LRAS), 97–99
losses, visualising, 221–222
low-hanging fruit principle. *See* diminishing returns
LRAS (long-run aggregate supply curve), 97–99

• *M* •

macroeconomics. *See also specific topics*
  about, 4, 12, 51
  assets, 54–55, 67–68, 138
  comparative advantages, 68–70
  consumption, 59, 60–61
  counting output, 57–58
  GDP equation, 58–65
  goals of policy, 93
  government purchases, 59, 63–64, 133–135
  international trade, 65–70, 292–293
  investment expenditures, 59, 61–63, 113
  level of GDP, 58
  measuring GDP, 52–53
  model of, 96–98
  net exports, 59, 64–65, 113
  tracking flow of income and assets, 54–55
  tracking funds, 55–56
  tracking with GDP, 52–58
  trade deficits, 66–67
Malthus, Thomas (scholar), 282
marginal benefits, 28
marginal costs (MC)
  about, 212–213, 215–216
  compared to average costs, 28
  curve, 213–215
  equal to marginal revenues (MR), 216–218, 263–264
  pricing, 276
  visualising losses, 221–222
  visualising profits, 218–221
marginal propensity to consume (MPC), 61

marginal revenues (MR)
  about, 215–216
  decreasing with monopolies, 257–262
  equal to marginal costs (MC),
    216–218, 263–264
  visualising losses, 221–222
  visualising profits, 218–221
marginal utility (MU). *See also*
    diminishing marginal utility
  about, 23–25
  allocating money to maximise,
    187–190
  buying as much as possible, 185–187
  equalising per pound, 190–192
marginalism, 285–286
market basket
  creating, 82–83
  defined, 81
  outdated, 86–87
market demand curve, 202
market economy, 45
market equilibrium
  adjusting to new, 172–175
  finding, 168–170
  impediments to, 175–178
  stability of, 170–172
market price (P*), 97–98, 110, 169,
    225–226
market production, 41
market quantity (Q*), 169
market supply curve, 202
markets. *See also* free markets
  about, 153–154
  competitive, 41
  for factors of production, 55
  for goods and services, 55
  problems of, 42–43
maximum output, 94
MC. *See* marginal costs (MC)
measuring. *See* calculating
medium of exchange, money as, 79–80
metallic standard, 139
microeconomics, 5, 12–13. *See also*
    specific topics
minimum cost production, relationship
    with zero profits, 251
mixed economy, 45–47
models, 13–16. *See also specific models*
monetary policy. *See also* fiscal policy
  about, 138
  bonds, 142–143
  changing interest rates with money
    supply, 145–146
  defined, 77, 121
  fiat money, benefits of, 75, 138–140
  having too much money, 140–142

inflation, risk of too much, 124–133
  limiting with rational expectations,
    147–150
  link between bond prices and interest
    rates, 143–144
  stimulating demand, 122–124
  stimulating economy by lowering
    interest rates, 146–147
money
  allocating to maximise total utility,
    187–190
  balancing demand and supply of,
    72–74
  demand for, 72–74
  having too much, 140–142
  printing, 136–137
  risks of too much, 72–80
money supply
  about, 72–74
  changing to change interest rates,
    145–146
  graphing increases, 148
monopolistic competition, 200
monopoly
  about, 255
  choosing output levels, 262–266
  comparing with competitive firms,
    267–270
  deadweight loss, 269
  decreasing marginal revenues,
    257–262
  defined, 200
  examples of good, 270–273
  legal, 145–146
  problems with, 256–262
  profit-maximising, 256–266
  regulating, 273–278
MPC (marginal propensity to
    consume), 61
MR. *See* marginal revenues (MR)
MU. *See* marginal utility (MU)

• *N* •

National Accounts, 51
national debt, 135
National Income and Product Accounts
    (NIPA), 51
natural monopoly, 272–273
negative demand shock, 99–101
net exports (NX)
  calculating, 64–65
  defined, 60
  in Keynesian Model, 113

NIPA (National Income and Product Accounts), 51
Nixon, Richard (U.S. President), 75
nominal interest rates, 87–90
nominal prices, 85
nominal wages, 128
normal goods, 155
NX. *See* net exports (NX)

• *O* •

OECD (Organization for Economic Cooperation and Development), 82
oligopoly, 200
open-market operations, 146
opportunity cost
  as a constraint, 22–23
  defined, 20
  in Production Possibilities Frontier (PPF), 36–37
  taking account of, 204–205
optimal allocation, 33
ordinal utility, 180
organisation of this book, 4–5
Organization for Economic Cooperation and Development (OECD), 82
output
  choosing in monopolies, 262–266
  cost per unit of, 206–209
  counting, 57–58
  imposing minimum requirements, 274
  maximum, 94
  in monopolies, 267–269
  subsidising monopolies by increasing, 273–274
overpopulation fallacy, 282–283
own-price effects, 195–197

• *P* •

P* (equilibrium price level), 97–98, 110, 169
patent rights, 11, 271
perfect competition
  about, 245
  causes and consequences of, 246–247
  defined, 200
  graphing profits, 248–255
  process of, 247–248
  requirements for, 201–202
perfectly elastic/inelastic supply, 167, 168
planned expenditures (PE), 112–114

planned investment (I^P), 114
plotting data, to create demand curves, 15–16
policies, unintended consequences of, 288
politics of inflation, 76–77
positive demand shock, 100–101
possibilities, graphing, 34–37
PPF (Production Possibilities Frontier), 34–37
precommitment mechanism, 150
predictions, 16, 89–90
preventing inflation, 294
price adjustments
  along supply curve, 164–165
  on demand curve, 157
  effect on quantities demanded, 192–194
  in the long-run, 98–99
  in monopolies, 264–265
  returning to full-employment rate after, 95–96
  substitution effect of, 194
price ceilings, 176–177, 240–241
price elasticity of demand, 160–162
price floors, 177–178
price indexes
  about, 81–82
  calculating inflation rate, 83
  determining real standard of living with, 85–86
  identifying problems, 86–87
  market basket, 82–83
  setting up price index, 84–85
price level index. *See* price indexes
price systems, 42
price takers, 201, 202–204, 246
prices. *See also* sticky prices
  adjusting inventories instead of, 110–119
  average cost pricing, 276
  fixed, 101–103
  in monopolies, 267–269
  nominal, 85
  real, 85
  regulating for monopolies, 274–277
  upward/downward price stickiness, 130
printing money, 136–137
producer surplus, 233, 237–238
production
  about, 29–30
  allocating resources, 33
  classifying resources, 30–31
  cost of, 164
  determining what to produce, 39–47

production *(continued)*
  diminishing returns, 31–33
  encouraging technology and
      innovation, 47–48
  government interventions, 40–45
  graphing possibilities, 34–37
  mixed economy, 45–47
  technology, 37–39
Production Possibilities Curve, 34
Production Possibilities Frontier (PPF),
    34–37
productive efficiency, 30
profit-maximising firms
  about, 199–200
  competition, 200–205
  cost structure, 206–215
  goals of, 200
  marginal revenues and costs, 215–222
  shutdowns, 222–226
profit-maximising monopolies
  about, 256
  choosing output levels, 262–266
  decreasing marginal revenues,
      257–262
  problems with monopolies, 256–262
profits
  accounting, 204–205
  adding costs of wages and, 107
  economic, 204–205, 246
  equation, 203
  graphing, 248–255
  maximising, 267–268
  maximising in monopolies, 262–266
  visualising, 218–221
  zero, 250–251
promoting innovation, 291
property rights, 291–292
proportional, 74
protecting intellectual property
    rights, 291
protectionism, as solution to foreign
    competition, 283–284
public goods, provided by free
    enterprise, 293–294

• Q •

Q* (market quantity), 169
quantity (equilibrium), 169
quantity demanded, 154, 192–194
quantity makers, acting as, 202–204
quantity theory of money, 74

• R •

rate of return (bonds), 143
rational expectations, 132–133, 147–150
real interest rates, 87–90
real prices, 85
real wages, 127–129
recessions. *See also* fiscal policy;
    monetary policy
  about, 91–92
  business cycle, 92–93
  defined, 92
  full-employment output (Y), 94–96
  Keynesian Model, 108–120
  responding to economic shocks,
      96–105
  sticky prices, 105–120
recoveries, 92
regulating monopolies, 273–278
resources, 21, 30–31, 33
Retail Price Index (RPI-X), 81
revenues. *See* marginal revenues (MR)
Ricardo, David (economist), 68–70
risks
  of too much money, 72–80
  of too much stimulation, 124–133
RPI-X (Retail Price Index), 81
running a loss, 204
running a profit, 204

• S •

sales price, relationship with
    production cost, 164
scarcity, 13
self-interest, 20
sequence, relationship with
    causation, 283
shift in demand, 99–101, 157–159
shift in supply, 165–166
shocks. *See* economic shocks
short run
  compared with long run, 103–105
  defined, 96
  fixed prices in, 101–103
  shutdown condition, 223–224, 226
short-run aggregate supply curve
    (SRAS), 101–103, 104–105
shutdowns
  about, 222–223
  long-run condition, 225, 226
  relationship with market price,
      225–226
  short-run condition, 223–224, 226

Smith, Adam (economist), 20
socially optimal output level, 232–233
SRAS (short-run aggregate supply curve), 101–103, 104–105
stability of market equilibrium, 117, 142, 170–172
standard of deferred payment, 76–77, 79
standard of living, relationship with education, 290–291
sticky prices
  about, 92
  importance of, 130
  Keynesian Model, 108–120
  during recessions, 105–108
stimulating the economy, 77–78, 124–133, 146–147
stimulus expectations, 130–133
store of value, money as, 78–79
subsidising monopolies, 273–274
substitution effect of price changes, 194
sunk costs, 26–27
supply
  about, 162
  excess, 170–171
  graphing supply curve, 163–166
  of money, 72–74, 145–146, 148
  reacting to decreases in, 174–175
supply and demand model
  about, 153
  adjusting to new market equilibriums, 172–175
  comparing costs and benefits with, 231–232
  demand elasticity, 160–162
  demand terms, 154–156
  determining slope of demand curve, 159–160
  extreme supply cases, 166–168
  graphing demand curves, 156–159
  graphing supply curve, 163–166
  impediments to market equilibrium, 175–178
  market equilibrium, 168–172, 175–178
  markets, 153–154
  reacting to decreases in supply, 174–175
  reacting to increases in demand, 173–174
supply curves
  graphing, 163–166
  tax shifts of, 242–243
surplus
  budget, 63
  consumer, 233–237
  producer, 233, 237–238

• T •

target inventory levels, 111–112
tax
  deadweight loss from, 241–245
  inflation, 80
  rates fallacy, 287–288
tax revenues, 136
TC (total costs), 203, 206
technology
  constraints, 21–22
  defined, 164
  encouraging, 47–48
  improving production, 37–39
time constraints, 22
total costs (TC), 203, 206
total revenue (TR), 203, 260–261
total surplus, 233–239
total utility, maximising, 187–190
TR (total revenue), 203, 260–261
trade balance, 65
trade deficits, 66–67
trade surplus, 66–67
traditional economy, 45
transactions, pursuing own interests with, 289–290

• U •

unemployment rate, 94
uninformed decision-making, 25–26
unit of account, money as, 79
upward price stickiness, 130
upward wage stickiness, 130
utility. See also marginal utility (MU)
  about, 179–180
  decision-making with limited budgets, 184–192
  diminishing marginal utility, 24, 181–184, 192–197
  as measure of happiness, 19

• V •

variable costs (VC), 206
Vietnam War, escalating costs following, 75
violations of Choice Model, 25–28
visualising
  losses, 221–222
  profits, 218–221

• W •

wages
  adding costs of profits and, 107
  cutting, 106
  foreign, 286–287
  nominal, 128
  real, 127–129
  tracking movement of real, 127–129
  upward/downward wage
    stickiness, 130
workers, cutting, 106

• Y •

Y*. *See* full-employment output (Y*)
Y (actual expenditures), 112–114

• Z •

zero profits, 250–251
zero unemployment rate, compared
    with full-employment output, 94
zero-coupon bond, 143